THE ANCIENT EG

Beliefs and Pr

The Sussex Library of Religious Beliefs and Practices

This series is intended for students of religion, social sciences and history, and for the interested layperson. It is concerned with the beliefs and practices of religions in their social, cultural and historical setting. These books will be of particular interest to Religious Studies teachers and students at universities, colleges, and high schools. Inspection copies available upon request.

<u>Published</u>

The Ancient Egyptians   Rosalie David

Hinduism   Jeaneane Fowler

The Jews   Alan Unterman

Sikhism   W. Owen Cole and Piara Singh Sambhi

<u>In preparation</u>

Buddhism   Merv Fowler

Christian Theology   Nora Hill

The Diversity of Christianity Today   Diane Watkins

The Doctrine of the Trinity: God in Three Persons   Martin Downes

Gnosticism   John Glyndwr Harris

Humanism   Jeaneane Fowler

Islam: Faith and Practice   David Norcliffe

Zoroastrianism   Peter Clark

<u>Forthcoming</u>   *Bhagavad Gita (a student commentary)*
Confucianism   Jainism   Taoism   Zen

The Ancient Egyptians

Beliefs and Practices

Rosalie David

sussex
ACADEMIC
PRESS

2 4 6 8 10 9 7 5 3 1

*First published by Routledge; revised and expanded edition
published 1998 in Great Britain by*
SUSSEX ACADEMIC PRESS
Box 2950
Brighton BN2 5SP

and in the United States of America by
SUSSEX ACADEMIC PRESS
c/o International Specialized Book Services, Inc.
5804 N.E. Hassalo St.
Portland, Oregon 97213–3644

British Library Cataloguing in Publication Data
A CIP catalogue record for this book is available from the British Library.

Library of Congress Cataloging-in-Publication Data
David, A. Rosalie (Ann Rosalie)
The ancient Egyptians : beliefs and practices / A. Rosalie David.
— 2nd rev. ed.
Includes bibliographical references and index.
ISBN 1–898723–72–9 (pbk. : alk. paper)
1. Egypt—Religion.   2. Egypt —Religious life and customs.
I. Title.
BL2441.2.D32   1998
299' .31—dc21   97–39681
CIP

Printed by Biddles Ltd, Guildford and King's Lynn
This book is printed on acid-free paper

Contents

————

List of Maps, Figures and Plates   viii
Maps 1 and 2   xii–xiii
Preface   xiv
Acknowledgments   xvi
Abbreviations   xvii

PART I   A SURVEY OF THE HISTORICAL DEVELOPMENT
         OF RELIGION IN ANCIENT EGYPT

Introduction   3

1   **The Predynastic and Early Dynastic Communities**   10
    The Predynastic societies   10
    The Dynastic Race   11
    The political and social organisation of the Naqada II
        communities   14
    The Unification of Egypt   15
    The political organisation of the Early Dynastic period   17
    Religious beliefs and practices during the Predynastic
        and Early Dynastic Periods   19
    The contribution of the Archaic Period   40

2   **The Old Kingdom**   41
    Organisation of the society   42
    Religious organisation   44
    Cosmogonies   45
    The cult of Re'   48
    The Wisdom Literature   50
    The funerary beliefs and customs of the Old Kingdom   52
    The Pyramid Texts   70

The tombs of the nobility   74
Tomb art – the underlying principles   79
The decline of the Old Kingdom   87

3   **The First Intermediate Period and the
    Middle Kingdom**   **91**
    Collapse of the society   91
    Restoration of political order   93
    The Middle Kingdom   94
    Religious developments in Dynasties 11 and 12   97
    Royal funerary monuments of Dynasties 11 and 12   98
    The royal jewellery of the Middle Kingdom   100
    A pyramid workmen's village   104
    Osiris and the democratisation of funerary beliefs   105
    The tombs of the nobles during the First Intermediate
        Period and the Middle Kingdom   112
    Tomb equipment and furniture   113

4   **The New Kingdom**   **119**
    The period of Hyksos rule   119
    The role of Amen-Reʿ (Amun)   120
    The Egyptian temple   124
    The priesthood   134
    The role of religion in education   135
    The role of religion in the law   137
    The role of religion in medicine   139
    Household gods and personal piety   141
    The relationship between Egyptian and foreign
        cults and deities   143
    Funerary beliefs and practices in the New Kingdom   146
    The court of Amenophis III   153
    History of the Aten   157
    Aspects of Atenism   165
    The counter-revolution   169

5   **Some Contributions made by Egyptian Religion to
    other Religions**   **172**

**PART II PRIMARY SOURCES FOR THE STUDY OF
EGYPTIAN RELIGION**

Appendix A1   Primary sources: religious texts and
archaeological bibliography   182

Appendix A2   Selected passages from Egyptian religious
literature   196

Appendix B   A selective list of major religious sites in
Egypt   207

**PART III SECONDARY SOURCES FOR THE STUDY OF
EGYPTIAN RELIGION**

Appendix C   Secondary sources and additional
bibliography dealing with specific aspects and controversies   219

Appendix D   A chronological table of Egyptian history   253

Index   255

Maps, Figures and Plates

Maps

1   Map of Egypt from the Delta to the First Cataract.   xii

2   Map of Egypt from Aswan to Khartum.   xiii

3   Map of Tell el Amarna (Akhetaten)
    (after W. M. F. Petrie).   162

Figures

1   *Tomb scene showing harvesting.* In non-royal tombs of the
    Pharaonic Period, it became customary to decorate
    the walls with registers of scenes which included,
    amongst other activities, the processes of food produc-
    tion. This was intended to provide the tomb-owner
    with an eternal food supply. Here, workers cut the
    stalks with sickles and remove the sheafs in a basket.   5

2   *Symbol of Uniting the Two Lands.* This represented the
    unification of the northern and southern kingdoms in
    c. 3100 BC, tying together the lotus and papyrus
    plants which symbolised those two areas. As a potent
    visual image of the king's dominion over his whole
    country, it was frequently used to decorate the royal
    thrones.   16

3   Figures showing the development of the tomb and
    pyramid structures, consisting of pit-burial, mastaba
    tomb (after W. B. Emery, *Great Tombs of the First
    Dynasty*, vol. III, pl. 85), the Step Pyramid at Saqqara,
    section looking south (adapted from J.-P. Lauer, *La*

Pyramide à Degrés, vol. III, pl. II), and the Great
Pyramid at Gizeh, section looking west (adapted from
Col. H. Vyse, *Operations carried on at the Pyramids of
Gizeh*, vol. 1, plan facing p. 3).   54–6

4   Plan of the pyramid area at Gizeh.   61

5   Figure showing various stages in the preparation and
equipment of a mummy.   65

6   Reconstruction drawing of the pyramid complexes at
Abusir (adapted from L. Borchadt, *Das Grabdenkmal
des Konigs Ne-user-re'*, Leipzig, 1907, pl. 1).   69

7   *Tomb scenes showing food presentation.*Registers of wall
scenes in tombs of all periods showed the production
of food and its presentation to the tomb-owner. This
was intended to ensure his food supply even when
the duty of offering food at the tomb was neglected.
Here, bearers bring cakes, fowl, fruit, vegetables
and flowers.   81

8   *Tomb scenes showing preparation for a banquet.* Wall
scenes showed the upper classes attending banquets,
a favourite occupation enjoyed in life which they
hoped to continue in the next world. Here, servants
(left) prepare their mistresses for the banquet,
presenting them with floral wreaths.   85

9   Plan of a typical cultus temple, based on the Temple
of Horus at Edfu.   127

10   Section through a typical cultus temple.   128

11   Plan of the tomb of King Sethos.   147

12   Plan of a New Kingdom nobleman's tomb.   149

13   *Tomb scene showing anointing with perfume.* To prepare
women of the upper classes for banquets and entertainment, the servants (left) anointed them with
perfumed ointment. The noblewomen also wear
scented wax cones on their heads.   150

14   *Tomb scene showing noblewomen at a banquet.* These
women, wearing floral wreaths and perfumed wax
cones, represent the fashions and styles of the New
Kingdom (*c.*1400 BC). According to the traditions

of formal, religious art, they are represented in
profile.   152

15   *Mummy wrapped in bandages.* Flowers were regarded as
an important element in religious rituals associated
with both the living and the dead. Floral wreaths were
placed on mummies at the time of burial, since they
symbolised rebirth and renewal.   154

16   Scene showing King Akhenaten worshipping the
Aten.   156

17   Plan of the Central City of Tell el Amarna.
(Akhetaten) (after J. D. S. Pendlebury, *The City of
Akhenaten*, part III, p. 2).   160

Plates (between pages 142–3)

1   The Step Pyramid at Saqqara.

2   The pyramid of Chephren at Gizeh.

3   Statue of Ramesses II at Memphis.

4   A mummified baby in a reed cover.

5   A coffin for a mummified cat.

6   A mummy of the Graeco-Roman Period.

7   A pectoral from Riqqeh.

8   A mirror from the workmen's village at Kahun.

9   A lioness-headed snake goddess.

10   Scene of lassoing a bull in the temple of Sethos I at
Abydos.

11   Anthropoid coffins of the Two Brothers.

12   A model boat from the tomb of the Two Brothers.

13   A model boat from the tomb of the Two Brothers.

14   A canopic chest from the tomb of the Two Brothers.

15   A painted funerary stela.

16   A gilded cartonnage head-piece.

17   Ushabti figure from the tomb of Horudja.

18   An amulet representing the god Bes.

19   A bronze statuette of the god Osiris.

20   King Sethos I performs a temple rite.

21   Temple scenes showing the sequence of a ritual.

22   A bronze temple offering stand.

23   A terracotta figurine of the god Bes.

24   An ostracon showing a funerary scene.

25   A panel portrait of a woman, from the Ptolemaic Period.

26   A plaster head from the Roman Cemetery at Mellawi.

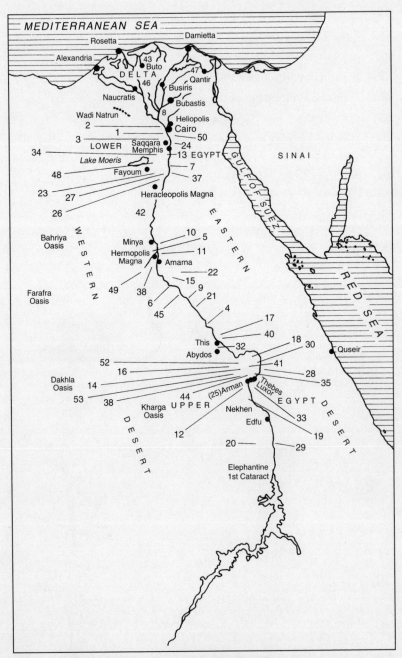

Map 1 Map of Egypt from the Delta to the First Cataract

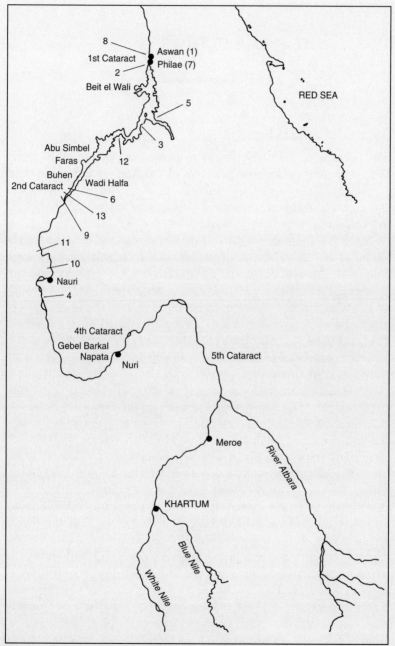

Map 2   Map of Egypt from Aswan to Khartum

Preface

The purpose of this book is to provide an introduction to the study of the religious beliefs and practices of the Ancient Egyptians. Part I gives an account of the historical development of the religion, tracing the great ideas and movements against the background of the internal and external policies of Egypt.

Since the Egyptians' conservatism ensured that concepts established in the early, formative periods of the country's history were frequently retained down to the Christian era, this study has concentrated on the religio-political developments of the three great periods of Egypt's growth, and has not attempted to trace the final stages of gradual decline. It is shown how, in the Old Kingdom, the religious concepts were almost completely interwoven with the political and social circumstances and how those beliefs and customs which were introduced in the earlier periods now became transformed into projects of significance for the whole country. The decline and disintegration of this highly-organised kingdom were replaced by decentralisation of power, with local rulers gaining virtual autonomy in their own areas; finally, during the Middle Kingdom, Egypt experienced a democratisation of all religious and funerary beliefs. By the New Kingdom, Egypt had acquired an empire and became an unequalled power in the Near East; not only did this enhance the prestige of the native gods, but it brought Egypt into direct contact with the religions and deities of other lands. Against this background, one king – Amenophis IV-Akhenaten – attempted to elevate one god, symbolised by the sun's disc and representing the sun's creative power, to a unique and unchallenged position as Egypt's 'sole god'. This 'heresy' was however doomed to failure, and traditional values and beliefs were restored. This study attempts to show not only the religious developments within the historical framework, but to demonstrate how the religion permeated nearly every aspect of the society, including the legal system, the medical service and the education of the young. Finally, the links are traced between some of the concepts formed during the creative periods of Egypt's history and the ideas and beliefs carried over into Christianity and into modern customs in Egypt and elsewhere.

In Parts II and III, a selection is given of the primary and secondary sources on which our knowledge and understanding of the subject are based. Much of the information is to be found in international journals devoted to Egyptology and related subjects and these sources are not known to the general reader. Therefore, although it would be impossible to provide here a comprehensive bibliography, an attempt has been made to highlight some of the major areas of research and, in order to present the reader with a readily accessible source of bibliographical reference, not hitherto available, it was thought worthwhile to devote a larger section to the bibliography than is customary in other books in the series.

Nevertheless, certain limits had to be set in compiling the references, and it was decided to include mainly English and some French publications, since this would meet the requirements of most readers. However, many excellent studies have appeared in other languages, especially in German, and the reader is advised to obtain reference to these through the major publications listed in this bibliography.

It is hoped that this introduction to the subject will stimulate further interest in an ancient religion which has had an undeniable if indirect effect upon some concepts and beliefs of the modern world.

Acknowledgements

I would like to express my gratitude to both Miss Helen Maclean and Mr A. Allen, whose detailed line drawings add significance to various points in the text. Where these drawings are adapted from other publications, due acknowledgment is made in the accompanying captions. I should also like to thank The Manchester Museum, University of Manchester for enabling me to illustrate the text from the Museum's collection, and I am particularly grateful to Mr G. Thompson for his skilful preparation of the photographs. My thanks are also due to Miss Kathryn Pickles for her help in compiling the revised bibliography for this second edition.

The literature of the ancient Egyptians directly illuminates our knowledge of their religious beliefs, and it is hoped that the extracts quoted from this literature will encourage and inspire the reader to explore further this rich heritage.

I would like to thank Routledge for granting the right to republish this second revised edition. With regard to the production of this edition, I am indebted to the editors at Sussex Academic Press for for their support, advice and co-operation.

Rosalie David,
The Manchester Museum
University of Manchester

Abbreviations

AJSL	*American Journal of Semitic Languages.*
ASAÉ	*Annales du Service des Antiquités de l'Égypte.*
BIFAO	*Bulletin de l'Institut français d'Archéologie Orientale.*
BJRL	*Bulletin of the John Rylands Library* (Manchester).
Brief Comms.	Brief Communications.
Bull.MMA	*Bulletin of the Metropolitan Museum of Art* (New York).
Chr.d'Ég.	*Chronique d'Égypte.*
Erman,	A. Erman, *The Ancient Egyptians: A Sourcebook of Their Writings* (translated by A. M. Blackman, with an introduction by W. K. Simpson) (New York 1966).
JARCE	*Journal of the American Research Center in Egypt.*
JEA	*Journal of Egyptian Archaeology.*
JMEOS	*Journal of the Manchester Egyptian and Oriental Society.*
JNES	*Journal of Near Eastern Studies.*
Porter and Moss	B. Porter and R. L. B. Moss, *A Topographical Bibliography of Ancient Egyptian Hieroglyphic Texts, Reliefs and Paintings*, 7 vols (Oxford 1927–51).
Rev.d'Ég.	*Revue de l'Égypte Ancienne.*
Wilson-ANET	J. A. Wilson, in J. B. Pritchard, *Ancient Near Eastern Texts Relating to the Old Testament* (Princeton 1950).
ZÄS	*Zeitschrift für ägyptische Sprache und Altertumskunde.*

Part I

A Survey of the Historical Development of Religion in Ancient Egypt

Introduction

Ancient Egypt produced one of the earliest and most magnificent civilisations the world has ever witnessed. Due largely to environmental and climatic conditions, many of its religious monuments, artifacts and literary sources have survived, and the historian has consequently usually found it necessary to approach any study of these people through an awareness of their religious beliefs and customs.

In any case, the relation of the Egyptian to his god and to the whole cosmic order was the cornerstone of society, and an understanding of the civilisation can only be gained through tracing the development of their religion. The internal political and religious changes were completely interwoven, and the many strands of the religion often appear confusing and even contradictory, but certain trends emerged at an early period and continued to dominate religious thought for 3,000 years. The conquest of the country by a number of different races had only a superficial effect upon native beliefs and practices, although contact with other lands sometimes led the Egyptians to expand their pantheon to incorporate deities of foreign origin whose powers were considered to be an asset.

The geography of Egypt

The religious beliefs were undoubtedly partly inspired by the nature of the land and its climate. Perhaps no other people were as dependent upon the regularity of natural phenomena, for Egypt has always been, in the famous words of a Classical writer, the 'gift of the Nile'. A map of Egypt clearly shows that a vast area of the country is desert, while only the Nile Valley, the Delta and the outlying oases in the Western Desert are fertile. The river follows a course of some 600 miles from Aswan in the south to the Delta where, through two main branches at Rosetta in the west and Damietta in the east, it finally flows into the Mediterranean. Only part of this fertile area can be cultivated, however, for much of the Delta is marshy or waterlogged, and it is possible to farm in the valley only to a maximum breadth of some thirteen miles. The weather varies considerably from one area to another, with Upper Egypt frequently experiencing high temperatures while the Delta enjoys a more moderate climate; however, throughout Egypt the rainfall is inadequate to support crops and animals, and without the annual inundation of the Nile, the land could not have been cultivated. Each year, the rains of tropical Africa increased the waters of the Blue Nile, and in late June, the effect of the inundation was seen at Aswan at the First Cataract. The flood finally reached Cairo in the north at the end of September, and the waters then gradually receded, with the river reaching its lowest level in the following April. A Nile which was too high would flood the land and bring devastation, and the ruination of the crops, whereas a low Nile brought famine, and the erratic nature of the inundation was a constant threat to the safety and prosperity of the people. The advent of modern technology has brought the building of dams at certain points on the river which now enables the volume of water to be held back and supplied for purposes of irrigation through a series of canals. However, in antiquity, a successful harvest was totally dependent upon Nature and to this end, the Nile god Hapy and Osiris, the god of vegetation and rebirth, were revered and petitioned for support.

The Egyptians named their country 'Kemet', meaning the 'Black Land'; this referred to the rich black mud which successive inundations deposited on the Nile banks. This mud fertilised the soil and made it productive, so that, with assiduous husbandry, the people could reap good crops. Surrounding the cultivation, and either stretching away to the horizon or rising rapidly and steeply into cliffs alongside the river, there was the desert, which the Egyptians feared as a place of death and terror. They called this desolate area by the name of 'Deshret', meaning the 'Red Land', which described the predominant colouring of the sand and the rocks.

The contrast between life and death, between the cultivation and the desert, was always expressed for the Egyptians in their environment, and this seems to have inspired some of their earliest and most enduring religious concepts. From the period of their earliest religous consciousness, it would seem that they believed in the

Figure 1 *Tomb scene showing harvesting*
In non-royal tombs of the Pharaonic Period, it became customary to decorate the walls with registers of scenes which included, amongst other activities, the processes of food production. This was intended to provide the tomb-owner with an external food supply. Here, workers cut the stalks with sickles and remove the sheafs in a basket.

continued existence of the individual after death; in order to facilitate his journey into the next world, funerary preparations, which
became increasingly sophisticated, were undertaken. Although the
place and state of this continued existence were envisaged in a
number of ways, the concept of eternity remained a constant feature
of the religion and influenced many religious customs. The life,
death and rebirth of an individual were regarded as cyclic processes
which reflected the natural cycles of the sun and the land. Their
observations told them that the sun died each night only to be reborn
on the horizon at dawn, and the annual destruction of the vegetation
due to the parching of the land was counteracted by the inundation
of the river which brought a resurgence of life. One of the most
important deities, Osiris, drew his strength from his symbolisation
of rebirth which he expressed both in his role as a vegetation god
and as king of the underworld where he offered the chance of resurrection to his worshippers.

The other great life-force of Egypt was the sun, and the cult of the
solar deity, Re', played an important role in religion, acknowledging
the power of the sun as a creative force and the sustainer of life.

The forms of many of the early deities were again drawn from the
familiar surroundings; they frequently possessed animal forms or
characteristics, and although some later underwent a process of
anthropomorphisation, many retained their non-human features.

The historical background

The history of ancient Egyptian civilisation covers a period from
*c.*3100 BC to the conquest of the country by Alexander the Great in
332 BC. The basis of our chronology of Egypt rests upon the work
of Manetho, a learned priest who lived during the reigns of the first
two Ptolemaic rulers of Egypt (323–245 BC). He prepared a chron-
icle of the Egyptian rulers, dividing his king list into dynasties, and
although his writings are preserved only imperfectly in the work of
the Jewish historian Josephus (AD 70) and of a Christian chronographer Sextus Julius Africanus (early 3rd century AD), and modern
research has shown that his observations are not always accurate, his
account is regarded as authentic and a valuable source. Indeed, he
almost certainly had access to source material including ancient
records and king lists, which were preserved in the temples and

would have been available only to a member of the priesthood.

After a period when Egypt was ruled by the gods and demigods, the kingdom was then passed on to human kings; Menes was the first king to rule a united Egypt in *c.*3100 BC, and from his reign until the conquest of Egypt in 332 BC, Manetho divides the rulers into thirty-one dynasties. It is impossible to offer a clear definition of an Egyptian dynasty, however, since, although it often comprised a number of rulers related to each other by family ties, and when there were no successors or another faction seized power the dynasty changed, this simple explanation will not suffice. Some family groups appear to span more than one dynasty and the change of dynasty was apparently carried out in peaceful and even amicable circumstances. Despite the inaccuracies in Manetho's system, it nevertheless provides a working structure for the study of Egypt's history.

Before the Dynastic Period (commencing *c.*3100 BC), the early communities in Egypt laid the foundations for the later great advances in technological, artistic and religious developments. This period is generally known as the Predynastic Period, and much of our present knowledge of this era was obtained as the result of the pioneering studies of Sir Flinders Petrie, often referred to as the 'Father of British Egyptology'. He excavated and published many of the early sites. At the other end of Egypt's history, after Alexander the Great had conquered the country in 332 BC, a line of Macedonian Greek rulers, descendants of Alexander's general Ptolemy, reigned in Egypt. The last of this line, Cleopatra, failed to prevent the absorption of Egypt into the Roman Empire in 30 BC, and subsequently the country was ruled by Rome as a province. This era, often referred to as the Graeco-Roman Period, saw the decline in the political and social status of the native Egyptians, but it is nevertheless of considerable interest in terms of Egyptian religion, for there was an exchange of beliefs and practices between the Egyptians and their conquerors, and also this period reflects the final stages in the development of the ancient religion before Egypt was converted first to Christianity and eventually to Islam. Nevertheless, it was during the earlier great periods of history that Egypt developed a unique set of religious beliefs and customs, and a study of these periods is essential to an understanding of their fundamental concepts.

The thirty-one dynasties given in Manetho can be further

subdivided into major periods which are characterised by distinctive political, social and religious features. Following the Archaic Period (Dynasties I and 2), the Old Kingdom (Dynasties 3 to 6) saw the first great flowering of Egyptian civilisation; the First Intermediate Period (Dynasties 7 to 11) was a time when the land was torn apart with internal dissension and decentralisation, but the Middle Kingdom (Dynasty 12) saw the restoration of peace under a strong ruler, and a consequent revival in architectural and artistic development. During the Second Intermediate Period (Dynasties 13 to 17), Egypt again suffered a decline, this time enabling foreigners to overtake the country, but these were eventually driven out and a strong line of kings established the New Kingdom (Dynasties 18 to 20), and inaugurated an empire in Western Asia as well as in Nubia. Egypt became the greatest and wealthiest kingdom in the Near East, but the Third Intermediate Period (Dynasties 21 to 25) saw the slow but inevitable decline of the country, and subsequently, in the Late Period (Dynasties 26 to 31), Egypt suffered conquest by the Persians and eventually by Alexander the Great.

To trace the development of the major religious ideas and movements, and to assess the interplay of internal and external politics and their effect upon the religion, it is necessary first to examine the Old Kingdom when the religious beliefs dominated the social and economic development of the country. However, the main trends present during this period had grown out of the beliefs and customs of the earliest communities and to understand their full significance to the Egyptians, it is essential to survey the beginnings of society in ancient Egypt.

Earliest relations with other countries

Compared with other ancient civilisations in the Near East, Egypt occupied an enviably secluded situation in Africa; protection was afforded by natural barriers and the people were able to develop distinctive art forms, architecture and religious beliefs during the earliest periods without foreign conquest and intervention. When they eventually came into direct contact with other influences, their own ideas were sufficiently formulated to enable them to absorb certain alien features without altering their own basic concepts.

To the north, Egypt was hemmed in by the Mediterranean which, although it provided a trading route between Egypt and the other lands which bordered it, nevertheless deterred invasion. The Red Sea to the east afforded protection, and to the west were the Libyan tribes; although they had always been in close contact with the early inhabitants of the Nile Valley and continued to trade with Egypt, they posed no real threat to Egypt's secure boundaries until the later periods. To the south lay Nubia (approximately the region of the modern Sudan), a land rich in gold and good building stone – commodities greatly desired by the Egyptians. From earliest times, the Egyptians had pursued a steady policy of colonisation of this area to ensure a continuing supply of these riches, and gradually the Nubians became 'Egyptianised', providing no military threat to Egypt until later times. The only comparatively easy route into Egypt which could be taken by determined marauders lay to the north-east, across the northern part of the Sinai Peninsula, and it was probably from this direction that the earliest bands of infiltrators came, lured to the Nile Valley by its lush vegetation and predictable climate which together ensured a comparatively stable lifestyle.

The Neolithic communities

The first evidence for religion in ancient Egypt is provided by the remains of the Neolithic communities who gathered into settlemeets and supported themselves by growing grain, domesticating animals and by increasingly infrequent hunting forays. They took advantage of the fact that the floor of the Nile Valley had become drier and they were able, once the inundation had receded, to move down into the valley and cultivate the rich soil. The previous inhabitants had lived above the valley on the desert spurs during the Palaeolithic Period, when the Nile Valley was virtually uninhabitable, either because for three months of every year it was under water or because it was otherwise covered with lush and almost impenetrable vegetation and teeming with wild animals. It can be concluded that these earliest men were hunters who pursued their game from the desert spurs, but they have left no evidence relating to any social or religious customs which they may have practised.

1

The Predynastic and Early Dynastic Communities

The Predynastic societies

The Neolithic communities which preceded the Unification of Egypt and the commencement of Dynasty 1 (*c.*3100 BC) comprise a stage in the development of the country's history which is referred to as the 'Predynastic Period'. These scattered groups had certain features in common, cultivating their land, organising themselves into communities with common social aims, producing pottery, other domestic articles, and tools and weapons, and developing religious customs which emphasised a marked reverence for the dead.

From his important excavations carried out at predynastic sites at the beginning of this century, Sir Flinders Petrie devised a method of relative dating for the excavated material, based upon a comparison of groups of pottery discovered in a series of graves; this system is known as Sequence Dating. He further divided the known cultures into three groups – Amratian, Gerzean and Semainian – which were names derived from the modern villages which lay in close proximity to his excavations. Although some of his work in this field has since been superseded, many of his conclusions have formed the basis of our understanding of this complicated period. Some scholars retain the use of the terms 'Amratian' and 'Gerzean' to refer to the two periods of predynastic culture which are continuous, exhibiting no well-defined break, but others use the terms 'Naqada I' and 'Naqada II' to refer to the two stages. These terms are based on the evidence of Petrie's discovery of both cultures at the one important site of Naqada. 'Semainian' is not now regarded as a Predynastic culture but as a term applicable to the earliest dynasties. The oldest known Predynastic culture has been named 'Badarian' after the village of el-Badari near Assiut in Middle Egypt, near which excavations were carried out by Brunton and Caton-Thompson.

Some of the problems posed by the evidence from this period have included the discussion as to whether these various settlements were part of an overall culture or whether there were distinct local variations, particularly between the communities situated in Upper or in Lower Egypt. Also, there has been argument concerning which culture – north or south – is earlier, and there have been suggestions that the communities in the north and south may have developed from separate racial origins. However, some degree of co-existence and lack of warlike behaviour must have been achieved in order to allow the seemingly peaceful development of the various settlements during the early period, and certain features marked the common pattern of these communities.

Little is known of the political or social organisation of the early societies, although from the Upper Egyptian evidence they were probably arranged as village settlements, each under the leadership of its own chieftain. Their dwellings were built of perishable materials and scanty evidence has survived. At Naqada, the inhabitants were probably organised as an urban community from an early period, for subsequently an important fortified town called Nubt (later Ombos) has been identified at this site, which seems to have played a central role in early gold-working and trading. Generally, these communities were supported by local mixed farming, but trading contacts had already been established with the south and ivory was imported, while copper was brought from the north, turquoise was acquired from Sinai, and shells came from the Red Sea or even the Persian Gulf.

The Dynastic Race

Some scholars today accept that at some time during the Predynastic Period (possibly *c.*3400 BC), a new group of people arrived in Egypt and that their advent resulted in profound changes in many aspects of the civilisation. It is thought that their fusion with the indigenous population, uniting their own originality and creativity with the artistic skills of those already settled in Egypt, ultimately produced the technological and other advances which steered Egypt towards greatness. The newcomers would have been gradually assimilated over a period of several hundred years, and from this grew the society which created dynastic Egypt.

These people are tentatively referred to as the 'Dynastic Race', and it is believed that the advent of the Naqada II period, with its distinctive features, was the direct result of these incursions. However, the evidence for the introduction of a new group of people at this period although substantial is not conclusive, and some scholars have maintained that the sudden artistic and technological advances can be explained in terms of a breakthrough springing directly out of the indigenous Neolithic communities, and that there is no need to envisage the introduction of inspiration and skills from elsewhere.

However, archaeological evidence does not at present support the indigenous theory; earlier stages in the development of writing, monumental brick architecture and certain distinctive art forms had not yet appeared within Egypt, although parallel developments elsewhere can be shown. The homeland of the proposed 'Dynastic Race' also remains conjectural, although elements in the writing, architecture and art forms which now begin to flourish in Egypt have led to the suggestion that the newcomers at least had contact with Mesopotamia. Cuneiform writing on mudbrick tablets in Mesopotamia predates the earliest examples of writing known from Egypt, although this could be due to chance of discovery or the fact that mudbrick would be more durable than the materials – paper or wood – which the Egyptians would probably have used for writing. Both cuneiform and Egyptian hieroglyphs are based on picture-writing, but if the concept of writing was borrowed by Egypt from Mesopotamia, it was only the underlying idea, for the form of the Egyptian script and the structure of the language was quite distinct. Another apparent innovation was the introduction of certain features in the burial practices of the leaders of the communities in Egypt. These included the use of recessed brick panelling to decorate the facade of the tomb, which perhaps echoed the external decoration of temples in Mesopotamia. Artistic devices which appear for the first time and do not seem to be of Egyptian origin include the representation of composite animals with entwined necks which occur on slate palettes. Although the palettes were made in Egypt, the designs are alien to Egyptian art but they exhibit a marked similarity to Mesopotamian types. Other articles which occur in both areas include stone maceheads and inscribed cylinder-seals.

The newcomers may have first made contact with the Nile Valley through trade. Apart from the possible link with Mesopotamia, other homelands suggested for them have included Syria, Iran or even an as yet undiscovered site which could have inspired both the Egyptian and the Mesopotamian forms. They may have come to Egypt via the Red Sea and then across the Eastern Desert to the upper part of the Nile Valley; the ivory handle of the famous Gebel el-Arak knife is carved with scenes showing a sea-battle in which ships of both the native Egyptian and the Mesopotamian types are represented. Alternatively, they may have taken the overland route, from Palestine via the Sinai Peninsula and into the Delta. The route through the Wadi Hammamat, across the Eastern Desert, would have involved practical problems of water supply, and it is difficult to imagine that a horde invasion came this way, although there is no conclusive evidence that these people penetrated Egypt in large numbers. They may have come by different routes, some using force and others perhaps infiltrating by peaceful means, but archaeological evidence and tradition both indicate that the main thrust of these people spread from the south to the north of Egypt. There is no suggestion that the infiltration continued after the beginning of Dynasty 1, when the 'foreign' features of the art and the architecture either disappear or become transformed into distinctively Egyptian styles. The writing also now becomes uniquely Egyptian, and from this time onwards, the newcomers and the indigenous population embarked on the slow but inevitable process of assimilation.

The newcomers settled first in Upper Egypt, and something of their lifestyle can be seen from the archaeological evidence discovered at the sites of Naqada (corresponding here to the Naqada II period), El-Hammamiya, El-Mahasna and Armant. At Naqada, the people now lived in rectangular houses, probably consisting of a roofed room and a forecourt. Considerable advances had apparently occurred in such specialised industries as metal-working, the production of painted pottery and of stone vessels, and prosperous trading contacts probably enabled them to import large numbers of silver objects.

The political and social organisation of the Naqada II communities

Little is known of the general political and social development of these communities, although there is evidence that, towards the end of this period, a Predynastic king named Scorpion was engaged in initiating an irrigation scheme. A scene on a macehead depicts him in the act of initiating the digging of a canal, although it is impossible to determine whether this represents the inauguration of an irrigation system for the country or whether it was already in use by this period. Although the Nile mud provided the Egyptians with fertile soil, it was nevertheless necessary to irrigate and prepare the land to take the crops, and to ensure that the water was spread to maximum advantage over as wide an area as possible. To achieve this, the farmer had to work patiently and diligently, and the methods used in antiquity can still be seen in Egypt today. The simple system included building up the river banks to prevent flooding and subsequent loss of water, and the cutting of canals to divert the water into barren areas which could then be brought under cultivation. However, its success was dependent upon constant supervision and the repair of the dykes, and the basic functions of irrigating the land and then tending the crops were the relentless occupations of most of the people in antiquity. The efficiency of the system was dependent upon the co-operation of all the communities along the river banks, and a common agricultural need had, at least as early as the end of the Naqada II period, united people who had different political and religious customs, and paved the way for their ultimate unification. Gradually, throughout this period, isolated village communities became loosely organised into larger units for protection and for the advancement of schemes of mutual benefit such as the irrigation process. Each unit was independent, with its own capital city and area of land to support the local inhabitants, who were ruled by a chieftain and worshipped their own deity, represented in the form of a fetish or ensign. Gradually, these units drew together into larger districts which eventually became the main geographical divisions of Egypt, and which are often referred to as 'nomes'. Finally, these districts developed into two separate and independent kingdoms, the northern one being based in the Delta and extending southwards perhaps as far as Atfih, while the southern realm was established from this area to as far south as Gebel el-

Silsileh. The centre of the northern kingdom was at the king's residence at Pe which lay near to the town of Dep (later known as Buto), where the cobra-goddess Edjo was worshipped. This kingdom was known as the 'Red Land' and its ruler wore the Red Crown. The capital of the southern kingdom, known as the 'White Land', was at Nekhen (later Hieraconpolis) near Edfu, and the protective deity was the vulture-goddess Nekhbet whose residence was Nekhen. This ruler wore the White Crown, and after the two kingdoms were finally united, the king of Egypt still wore these crowns, either separately on different occasions or in combination as the Double Crown, signifying his power over both these parts of his kingdom. Also, after Unification, these two ancient goddesses became the dual protectresses of the Egyptian kingship. Other symbols – namely the bee and the papyrus plant for Lower Egypt and the sedge for Upper Egypt – were also retained and incorporated in later tradition. The 'Two Lands', once a political reality, were never forgotten, and were retained as a fiction in art and literature throughout the historic period, long after Egypt had become one kingdom. Even today, there are distinct differences between Lower and Upper Egypt, for whereas the former supports the cities of Cairo and Alexandria and provides a cross-roads for ideas and influences from Europe, Asia and Africa, the upper areas of the Nile Valley are more markedly agricultural and traditional in their values.

The Unification of Egypt

In *c.*3100 BC, the two kingdoms were united under the powerful control of a southerner, Narmer. The events which preceded this subjugation of the north are not clear, but it is apparent that an earlier Upper Egyptian king, Scorpion, had already initiated this conquest. On a ceremonial limestone macehead discovered at Hieraconpolis in AD 1898, carved scenes show the king not only involved in an irrigation programme, but also undertaking military exploits, and the macehead may commemorate the inauguration of a policy of re-organisation throughout the country. However, it was his successor Narmer who completed the conquest of the north and who unified the two kingdoms, making himself the first king of Dynasty 1. He is almost certainly the same man as the king named Menes to whom tradition attributes the foundation of historic Egypt.

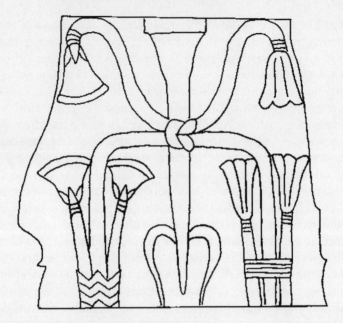

Figure 2   *Symbol of Uniting the Two Lands*
This represented the unification of the northern and southern kingdoms in
c.3100 BC, tying together the lotus and papyrus plants which symbolised
those two areas. As a potent visual image of the king's dominion over his
whole country, it was frequently used to decorate the royal thrones.

The Unification of Egypt is commemorated on a ceremonial slate
palette, discovered in AD 1898 in a great deposit of objects belonging
to the temple of the royal god Horus at Hieraconpolis; it may have
been placed there by the king as a thank-offering for his victory. The
palette, of great historical importance, shows on the obverse
Narmer, wearing the Upper Egyptian crown, in the act of smiting a
cowering captive northern chieftain with a macehead which he
clasps in his upraised hand; a hieroglyphic group above the captive's
head is believed to read 'Horus brings (to the king) captives of Lower
Egypt'. The sequel, shown on the reverse, depicts in the top register
the king, wearing the Lower Egyptian crown, inspecting slain northerners; this may have taken place either on the battlefield or at the
temple at Hieraconpolis where perhaps the sacrifice of a number of
captives formed part of a victory ceremony.

On another macehead, Narmer, wearing the Lower Egyptian
crown, is shown seated under a canopy over which hovers the

protective vulture of Upper Egypt; standard-bearers of the army, men and animals taken in war, and a seated figure also appear, and it has been suggested that the latter represents a northern princess and that the scene may represent a marriage between her and Narmer, for such a union would have helped to legitimatise his ruler-ship of the northern kingdom and to consolidate his claims for his heirs. Once Narmer, undoubtedly ably assisted by other local leaders sympathetic to his cause, had established his rulership over a united land, he moved his capital from the southern city of This to a new city in the north, later known as 'Memphis', but originally called 'White Wall' or 'White Walls', possibly with reference to a white gesso covering on its mudbrick buildings. Chosen for political and military motives, the site enabled its new ruler to curb any renewed upsurgence from the northerners. Herodotus, the Greek historian writing about Egypt in the 5th century BC, records that the priests of the god Ptah informed him that Menes founded both their temple and the city of Memphis, and coronation ceremonies performed at Memphis in the historic period included rituals which commemorated the unification of Egypt and the foundation of the city. Nevertheless, although Memphis became the new political centre, the early kings continued their old association with This in the south which was still regarded as the foremost religious centre.

The political organisation of the Early Dynastic period

At the main royal residence of Memphis, the king, his family and his retainers began to establish the political structure which was to survive for centuries and from which developed the elaborate and centralised bureaucracy of the Old Kingdom. Scanty evidence prevents any complete reconstruction of the political and social systems of this early period, but it is probable that some centralised departments already existed at Memphis, situated in the mudbrick palace which housed both the official and royal domestic quarters. Here, judicial and administrative matters, and Egypt's trading asso-ciation with other countries, were dealt with, while the collection and redistribution of the national revenue were centred at the treasuries of the Two Lands, namely the White House and the Red House. Some kind of system, however rudimentary, doubtless already existed to link the capital city with the provinces, but the political and economic developments which occurred during the early dynasties would have been part of a gradual process, for the settled, urbanised and closely organised communities of the Delta region would have had different administrative requirements from the loosely associated groups of people who lived along the Nile in Upper Egypt and pursued a more nomadic lifestyle.

Already, however, the king was an absolute monarch, identified with the royal hawk-deity Horus; regarded as the earthly embodiment of the god, the king bore the title of Horus in his lifetime, handing it on to his royal successor at death. Some duties must now have been delegated to trusted followers, and offices and titles found later in the Old Kingdom were already established in the Archaic Period.

It is also evident that the queens were of considerable significance; the king's mother is specifically mentioned, suggesting that the later order of succession through the king's principal wife was already established. In subsequent periods, the fiction was maintained that every king was the child of the divine union between the chief state god and the ruling king's principal queen, his Great Royal Wife. Divine conception and birth to a human mother was thus believed to endow the king of Egypt with a unique nature, enabling him to act on behalf of both gods and men. The role of the Great Royal Wife was therefore of utmost importance to the succession, and the woman chosen for this exalted position was usually the Great Royal Daughter, the eldest daughter of the ruling king and queen. As the future divine consort and mother of the next heir apparent, she endowed her human husband with the strongest claim to rule Egypt and to defeat any rival claimants. Indeed, in order to substantiate his claim to the throne and to ensure the acceptance of his son as the next heir, the male heir to the throne theoretically had no choice but to marry the Great Royal Daughter. Frequently this was necessarily his own full-sister or half-sister, although in some periods it was not unknown for 'upstart' claimants who had only secondary or tenuous links with the main royal line to legitimatise and consolidate their rulership by marrying the Great Royal Daughter.

The basis on which the Egyptians would organise their country for the next 3000 years was already established, and the political and social evolution was mirrored by developments in religion.

Religious beliefs and practices during the Predynastic and Early Dynastic Periods

A lack of available written evidence inevitably limits our perception of the religious ideas and practices of the inhabitants of Egypt down to the end of the Archaic Period. Apart from certain passages which occur in the later Pyramid Texts and which may refer to earlier customs prevailing during the Early Dynastic Period, excavations have so far failed to produce religious texts of a contemporary date. Most available evidence is provided by material excavated from tomb sites.

It has already been remarked that information regarding the earliest people who lived in the Delta and the Nile Valley during the Palaeolithic Period is such that it is impossible to conclude whether or not they possessed a religious awareness. However, in the Neolithic communities of the Predynastic Period, there is sufficient surviving material to indicate that in both the north and the south, they had developed a specific belief in the continuation of life after death and that this afterlife was envisaged as similar to existence before death. Great consideration was given to the burial of the dead, and the Predynastic cemeteries are greater sources of information for contemporary religion than the corresponding settlements of the living. The deceased were provided with the requisites for continued existence – implements, personal adornments and the provision of food – and these provide the basis of knowledge for early religious beliefs and customs. The reasoning behind their consideration for the dead will never be known, but it is possible that either they feared the dead and their revenge from beyond the grave and so sought to propitiate them with elaborate funerary equipment, or that they regarded the dead as having a continuing association with the living as well as a new and special relationship with the gods whose favour they could now seek on behalf of the living.

FUNERARY PRACTICES IN THE PREDYNASTIC PERIOD

The cemeteries of the earliest Neolithic communities which comprised the Badarian civilisation were situated away from the dwellings of the living. Most of the graves were oval in shape, although some of the larger ones were rectangular with rounded corners, and these appear to have been used for women at first although their use was later extended to male burials. Most graves contained single burials, although some have been discovered which accommodated two bodies.

The body was placed a few feet deep in the sand, in a contracted position on its left side, with the head towards the south, facing west; it was often covered with coarse matting or placed inside a hamper woven of twigs, or an animal skin. The grave was probably marked by placing a small pile of sand or stones on top of the burial. There is no evidence to suggest either that the body was dismembered or that any artificial methods were used in an attempt to preserve the bodies. Any preservation of the skin and hair which did occur was the direct result of natural dehydration which was brought about by the heat and dryness of the surrounding sand. However, the body was clothed in linen and some wore turbans, while jewellery and beaded belts were added for adornment.

The burials of the Naqada I period which followed the Badarian imply a continuous development; the shape of the grave was retained, although some of the Naqada I graves accommodated multiple burials with as many as seven bodies interred in the same grave.

With the presumed arrival of the Dynastic Race, ushering in the Naqada II period, many new ideas flourished, and this is reflected in the burial customs. Previously, the chieftain of a community had apparently been regarded as an ordinary member of that society, although he may have been attributed by his contemporaries with special magical powers which he could use for their benefit. However, although his grave may have been larger than those of his people, it differed from theirs in no other way. In the burials of the Naqada II period and the subsequent cemeteries of the dynastic period, there is a marked distinction made between the burials of the ruling class and those of the subservient masses, and it has been argued that this represents a racial difference, with the members of the Dynastic Race and their immediate descendants practising burial customs which differ from those of the indigenes. Some even consider that it is possible to determine the continuation of a separate racial type amongst the bodies of the nobility in the early historic period and would argue that the newcomers possessed larger bodies and wider skulls than the indigenous inhabitants and that these features are present in the bodies interred in later cemeteries. Although existing evidence is insufficient and inconclusive, it has been suggested that the 'separateness' of the ruling class in the early historic period was the result of this early racial distinction, and that the lower social levels of the society, descended from the subjugated indigenous population, continued to be buried in the shallow round or oval graves, whereas the newcomers and their descendants, who formed the new royal and noble class of the early dynastic period, constructed more elaborate tombs for themselves.

These tombs, whatever their origin, contained all the basic features which established the pattern for tomb architecture for the well-to-do in the dynastic period. The substructure below ground accommodated the burial, while a superstructure, consisting of a complex of rooms above ground level, was used to store the grave goods. The most sophisticated examples of the Naqada II tombs were rectangular in shape, and their walls were lined with matting or strengthened with wooden planks, a feature which developed into the later wooden coffins or the wood-panelled central chambers found in the royal tombs of Dynasty 1. The use of the wooden 'coffin', placed in a recess hollowed out of the side and floor of the burial pit, eventually replaced the custom of wrapping the body in matting. As in the later period, grave goods were stored in the super-structure of the tomb.

It is not possible to determine whether the newcomers introduced such advances in burial customs from outside Egypt, or whether they adopted the customs from the indigenous population and adapted and improved them for their own use. However, these two distinct types of burial custom eventually merged, and this fusion is particularly noticeable in those areas where the amalgamation of the two 'races' was probably well-advanced by the end of Dynasty 2. Nevertheless, a distinction between different forms of burial continued throughout the course of Egypt's history, although it came to be an indication of a man's social status and wealth rather than of any remnant of different origin.

GRAVE GOODS AND ASSOCIATED RELIGIOUS BELIEFS IN THE PREDYNASTIC PERIOD

It is possible to draw some tentative conclusions regarding religious beliefs and practices from the contents of the graves in this period. In the Badarian cemeteries, grave goods included jewellery, deco-rative combs, small ivory cosmetic vases, cosmetics and slate palettes. The most important cosmetic seems to have been green malachite which was ground on the palette and then mixed with oil or fat for application to the skin. Flint tools and an abundance of 'black-top' pottery was also included, probably intended for domestic use in the afterlife.

Similar goods were discovered in the graves of the Naqada I period, and some of the pottery for domestic use now suggests contact with areas of the Near East, while the presence of imported commodities such as lapis lazuli and turquoise indicates a flourishing foreign trade.

The grave goods of the Naqada II period continue the earlier trends, but a distinctive pottery known as 'Decorated Ware' is now included with these burials. Also, a new ceremony may have been introduced to mark the interment of members of the ruling class, since some evidence suggests that the grave goods and food supplies of the deceased were now burnt before being placed with the body in the grave. The grave goods of the predynastic period in general formed the basis of the type of equipment provided for the mass of ordinary people throughout the historic period.

However, the Predynastic grave goods afford some evidence of specific early religious beliefs. From the Badarian period onwards, amulets were included in human graves. It was probably intended that these pieces (the modern name of 'amulet' is derived from the Arabic 'hamulet', meaning a thing borne or carried) should impart something of their supposed power to the wearer and should imbue him with certain qualities, such as prowess in hunting, which would enable him to obtain a continuing food supply even after death. Amulets occur in the form of many different animals, including the gazelle, hippopotamus, cow, pig, bull's head, crocodile, fly, fish, serpent, lion, the Seth-animal, and, from the end of Naqada II, the royal falcon.

Magical protection and power were also afforded to the deceased by the presence of other grave goods. Figurines of women were found with the burials of both sexes during the Badarian period, although male statuettes, crudely modelled from ivory, were discovered only in later burials. The female figurines were dedicated to the mother-goddess, although their exact function remains uncertain. Various explanations of their purpose have been made: that they were concubine figures or servants bearing offerings; that they were votive offerings to the mother-goddess in request for children; or, since they occurred in the graves of both men and women, that they represented an attempt on behalf of the deceased to beg the assistance of the mother-goddess in bringing about the re-birth of the deceased in the next world. The name of this mother-goddess is not known, although her cult, in which she appeared as a cow, was undoubtedly influential and widespread during this period. Indeed, her considerable importance in these Predynastic communities may be reflected in the apparently significant role which some women played in these societies. Some of their graves were relatively large and their grave goods indicate that they may have been regarded as the possessors of special religious and magical powers.

The decorated pottery provides further indications of the characteristics of the goddess and events in her mythology. Scenes painted on to the pottery of the Naqada II period depict boats carrying standards which bear the ensign of the goddess; she appears in the form of a cow-goddess with a human head and cow's horns and has acquired a young consort, her son and lover, who is known in a later period as the 'Bull-of-his-mother'. It has been suggested that by the historic period he had developed into the fertility god Min. One Predynastic vase scene shows their sacred marriage, while other scenes depict ritual dances, probably part of some ancient fertility rite. Both the goddess and her consort were probably regarded as deities who had close associations with the fertility of the land, its crops and its inhabitants, and through the cycle of life, death and re-birth they may also have been attributed with powers over life in the next world.

Amulets, painted vases and human figurines may all have heen placed in the grave with the intention of obtaining specific benefits after death; figurines of the hippopotamus found in women's graves may also have been associated with fecundity, while groups of cattle figurines on trays were perhaps included either as food supplies for the deceased, or to ensure the fertility of the herds. The green eye-paint may have had important magical associations at this period; certainly at a later date green was the colour which symbolised life and re-birth.

In addition to these magical aids found in the graves of the community, in some of the larger graves of the Naqada period, implements have been discovered which may indicate that the leaders were already regarded as magicians with special powers over the fertility of men, animals and the soil. Later, the divine kings of

Egypt were regarded as absolute rulers who had total control of the
land and its people; they ensured good harvests by their magical
powers, and in the earliest period, there is some reason to believe
that they may have been required to sacrifice their lives on certain
occasions to rectify poor harvests and to revitalise the prosperity of
the country.

Figurines of men and women and slates found in these important
graves were possibly used in divination rites, and small receptacles
may have contained 'medicine', while in the grave of one woman, a
pair of ivory tusks of which one was hollow and the other was solid
was discovered. The exact purpose and use of such objects is uncertain but possibly they were regarded as ritual objects which the
leader could use to approach the great goddess of fertility, and thus
obtain benefits for his people. The grave may already have been
envisaged as a gateway into the underworld where the dead could
meet with the gods and where the deceased chieftain could use his
extensive magical powers to persuade the gods to renew the vigour
and fertility of the living.

ANIMAL CULTS

The importance which the Egyptians later attached to animal cults
is already apparent in these early communities. In Badarian villages,
the bodies of dogs or jackals, sheep and cows were carefully
wrapped in linen and matting and interred amongst the human
burials, although the animals were not supplied with grave goods.
There may be a connection between these early jackal and cow
burials and the later status of the jackal as the god of embalming and
of the cow as the most important Predynastic deity, and it is possible that even at this early period, these animals were regarded as
especially sacred and worshipped as supreme goddess and god of
the dead.

The amulets placed with human burials were of animal form, and
although they were probably included to provide a magical food
supply, their presence may supply evidence of the importance of
animal cults. By the Naqada I period some of the slate palettes occur
in the shape of animals and others are decorated with the horns and
ears of the cow, while animal statuettes were also placed in the
graves. The painted pottery of the Naqada II period, representing
animal deities as the gods of the various nomes or districts, indicates

that some animals and inanimate objects were already regarded as the abode of divinity.

RELIGIOUS ORGANISATON OF THE LIVING DURING THE PREDYNASTIC PERIOD

Our knowledge of the religious rites and customs of the living is very limited. No chapels or sacred centres have been found in the settlements of the living, but the Decorated Ware found in the Naqada II graves provides some evidence. Scenes painted on the pottery are mainly religious in content; boats are depicted which carry gods' shrines, and deities, represented by animate and inanimate objects, are shown. Some of the deities occur on pottery discovered at sites in both Upper and Lower Egypt, perhaps suggesting that they were of more than local significance. Most common were the ensigns of the great goddess and her son.

Before the Unification there appear to have been many localised and unconnected cults. Each community had its own deity which was the object of tribal worship and only gradually did certain deities achieve a wider recognition. As political development occurred and villages joined together to form clans and eventually districts (nomes), so the gods were transformed from tribal deities into gods of nomes with far-reaching powers. At each stage of this amalgamation, the process known as syncretism occurred, as the deities of the conquered or subordinated areas were assimilated. The victor's god would embrace and adopt any of the desirable features and characteristics of the deity of the subordinated tribe, or the conquered god would become an assistant or follower in the mythology of the omnipotent god, or in some cases, the subordinate god would die out completely. The chief god of a nome afforded protection to the chieftain and was represented by the ensign of the nome.

The expanded pantheon became increasingly confusing; whereas worshippers had originally honoured only their local god, the amalgamation of cults which had taken place by the historic period gave the erroneous impression that the Egyptians worshipped many deities. This probably gave a distorted view of the situation and the individual would still have directed his devotion towards the one local god or group of gods. Nevertheless, by the Old Kingdom, syncretism had resulted in such an apparently confusing situation that the priesthood attempted to organise the multitude of gods in the pantheon either into family groups or into ogdoads or enneads which were associated with specific cult centres. Some of the deities were also then linked together in their mythologies or cosmogonies.

Most of the deities were originally represented in animal or fetish forms; it may have been thought that the divine power could manifest itself in these. It is not clear why the Egyptians deified animals on such a wide scale and why these cults continued to hold sway throughout the historic period. Various explanations have been suggested – it is possible that animals were worshipped because they assisted mankind, as in the case of the cat who rid the houses of vermin, or because they were feared and it was hoped the acts of worship might propitiate them. This may explain why the jackal – an indiscriminate destroyer of tombs and their contents – was deified as the god of the necropolis and of embalming.

Throughout the early dynastic period and possibly earlier, a gradual anthropomorphisation of the deities occurred. Some appeared at first with a degree of humanisation and are shown with bird or animal heads on human bodies, but by Dynasty 2 there are examples of 'animal' gods with full human forms. A very few deities, such as Ptah the creator-god of Memphis, were always shown with a full human form. The effect which the advent of the Dynastic Race had upon the deities of Egypt remains uncertain. Any foreign influences which they may have introduced seem to have had little impact on the indigenes, for many of the early tribal deities apparently continued to exist. Political considerations may have prompted the newcomers to tolerate the older gods, and perhaps as the religious elements of the two peoples gradually fused, the old and new deities merged into one pantheon. Even if the indigenous gods lost some of their earliest characteristics, they retained many of their identifying features which enabled at least some of them to be recognisable in the historic period.

COSMIC AND TRIBAL DEITIES

In addition to the tribal gods, it seems that there was a distinct group of deities which are referred to as 'cosmic deities' by Egyptologists. It has been suggested that these had a different origin and were perhaps brought into Egypt from elsewhere, possibly by the Dynastic Race. Fusion with the established gods of the local people would ultimately have enabled them to adopt some of the characteristics of the older deities. Some of the cosmic gods did not require cult centres, while others seem to have taken over the earthly centres as well as the physical form and attributes of those deities they absorbed. Fusion of the two races, reflected in the religion, appears to have been completed in the Archaic Period, by which time the cosmic deities had acquired distinctive forms and attributes, and by the historic period they are shown with human forms and identifying symbols on their heads.

However, another explanation of the origin of the cosmic deities has been suggested. This claims that they were not introduced by the new race but that they were worshipped by the indigenous population who had however never personalised them or given them forms. The remoteness of the sun, moon, stars and elements from the affairs of men may have prompted their worshippers to regard them as inaccessible and only the later fusion between local and cosmic deities enabled the cosmic forces to acquire names and attributes. Both cosmic and local gods were worshipped throughout Egypt's history, and had a significant effect upon modes of worship and concepts of existence after death.

SOME OF THE EARLY DEITIES

Some deities known from the later periods were already in existence but the extent of their influence is uncertain and we do not know if they already displayed the features which distinguished them later. Some gods occurred on the early maceheads and palettes as the allies of Scorpion and Narmer in their conquest of the north; these included Min, the ithyphallic fertility god with centres at Koptos and Akhmim; Wepwawet, the 'Opener-of-the-Ways' who was the wolf-god of Assiut, and who, although originally a god of war, later became a god of the dead; Anubis, the jackal-god of the dead and protector of the necropolis; and Thoth, the moon-god who was patron of writing and the exact sciences.

Ptah, master of destiny and creator of the world, was worshipped at Memphis during the early dynastic period. Always represented as a mummiform man, he also manifested himself as the Apis-bull who was a fertility god and, through his association with Soker, as a funerary god. Various important goddesses who occurred in the Archaic Period included Edjo and Nekhbet, the protectresses of

Lower and Upper Egypt; Neith, the goddess of hunting and warfare; and Seshat, the goddess of writing.

It is also possible that the cult of Re', the sun-god, was established in Egypt as early as the Later Predynastic Period. A foreign origin has been suggested for Re', but although Arabia, Crete, Western Asia or elsewhere may have been his homeland, it is also possible that a native sun cult existed which might have facilitated the reception of Re' and his followers if they did enter Egypt from elsewhere. Re' appears to have taken over 'Iwnw (later Heliopolis) as his cult centre from its original deity, Atum, and by Dynasty 2, the king, associated at this period with the royal god Horus, reflected the growth of the cult of Re' by adopting the title "son of Re'". The symbol of the sun – a circle with a central spot – occurs in the late Predynastic Period, and the Old Kingdom royal burials may owe something to the customs of the early dynastic period, when evidence suggesting that boat burials were associated with large tombs at Saqqara, Helwan and Abu Roash has been found. This may indicate that, in addition to a belief in a continued existence in the tomb, there was already provision to enable the deceased to join the gods in his solar barque, encircling the heavens.

THE MYTH OF HORUS AND SETH

One of the great myths of Egyptian literature may reflect some of the political events of this early period. Later sources give the main outline of the myth, and tell of a human king, Osiris, who brought civilisation and knowledge of agriculture to Egypt. Osiris was murdered by his brother Seth, and his body was dismembered and scattered throughout Egypt, but Isis, his sister and devoted wife, collected the pieces and restored them by magic. She then conceived his child Horus whom she reared in the Delta marshes, hidden from the wrath of Seth. When he was fully grown, Horus wished to avenge his father's death and he fought Seth; the dispute was finally brought before a tribunal of gods who decided in favour of Osiris and Horus. Osiris was restored to life, but was reinstated not as king of the living but as king and judge of the underworld, while Horus became identified with the living king of Egypt. Seth, however, was condemned as the personification of evil and became a reviled outcast.

The origin of the various personalities in this myth remains obscure. The worship of Osiris and Isis probably existed in Egypt at least as early as Dynasty 1; it has been suggested that Osiris represented a human king who had once lived as a Predynastic ruler, and who led Asiatic tribes into the Delta from somewhere in Asia Minor, possibly Syria, and finally settled at Busiris, a Delta site which may have been the god's first cult centre in Egypt. Other possible homelands for Osiris include other parts of Asia Minor, or of Africa, or Libya; an indigenous origin also cannot be ruled out, and he may have been a local fertility god of Lower Egypt.

Seth's cult appears to have been centred at the Predynastic town of Nubt (Ombos) in Upper Egypt, which was probably the capital city during the Naqada I period. He may have been the chief god of the indigenous population and at this stage had none of his later evil characteristics, which may have been attributed to him by the victorious newcomers who subdued his worshippers. Seth is later represented by a strange animal, identifed variously as a pig, ass, a species of dog now extinct, or an imaginary animal. The earliest known representation of an animal with these features (although not specifically identified here with Seth) occurs as a carving on an ivory haircomb from El-Mahasna, which dates to the Naqada I period.

Horus may have been the supreme god of the newcomers. He was regarded later as the patron and protector of the first kings of Egypt who may have descended from the newcomers, and he came to be closely associated with royal ritual and ceremonial, ultimately being absorbed into the theologies of the two other great royal gods, Re' and Osiris. His homeland is again unknown, although Punt, Arabia or Mesopotamia have been suggested as possibilities; again, however, the newcomers may have brought a sky-deity and then adopted an indigenous falcon-god as his symbol. Predynastic examples of a falcon deity include representations of the bird on a crescent surmounting a standard painted on the decorated pottery of the Naqada II period. Here again, however, these falcon symbols cannot be decisively identified with the god Horus, and may represent another deity.

Some scholars argue that this important myth reflects political events which actually occurred during an early period, although the exact time at which such a struggle developed remains conjectural. It has been suggested that the myth reflects the Predynastic conflict between the indigenous population, worshippers of Seth, and the immigrants, who followed Horus; alternatively, it could be interpreted in terms of the religio-political conflicts which occurred later in Dynasty 2. Any reconstruction of events which is based on this myth is inconclusive, and each theory has its adherents and critics. However, the main arguments may be summarised as follows.

The theory supporting the predynastic interpretation argues that Seth (representing the indigenes) routed a group of newcomers who entered Egypt via the Delta and put their human king, Osiris, to death. Another group of immigrants (perhaps associated with the first) may then have invaded Lower Egypt and under their god, Horus, begun to consolidate their conquest before moving south into Upper Egypt (the centre of Seth's worship and following) where they proceeded to conquer the indigenous population and to bring all the land under the rulership of Horus. If this interpretation of the myth is accepted, then further controversy surrounds the problem of whether the cult of Horus was established first in Upper or in Lower Egypt, and thus whether the newcomers entered Egypt from the north or from the south. The archaeological evidence does not provide a conclusive answer, and Horus and his followers may have settled first in Upper Egypt before his cult was brought northwards when Scorpion and Narmer led their southern forces against Lower Egypt.

However, the myth, if it is to be regarded as an accurate reflection of the political events, states that the original home of Horus was the Delta in Lower Egypt. Some scholars have therefore supported the theory that the immigrants gained power first in the north, and then progressed southwards to Upper Egypt, thus establishing a "predynastic union", the capital of which may have been situated at the northern site later known by the name of 'Heliopolis'. The south may then have broken away and re-established an independent kingdom from which Scorpion and Narmer finally led their conquering campaigns northwards and achieved the unification of the 'Two Lands'.

The evidence suggests that, in the period immediately prior to the Unification of Egypt, the people of both Upper and Lower Egypt were worshipping Horus, and the later Turin Papyrus indicates that the kings of Upper and Lower Egypt before Narmer were referred to as the 'Followers of Horus' and had the supreme falcon-god as their patron.

The myth may well preserve the outline of the conflict in Predynastic times between the indigenous worshippers of Seth and the incoming followers of Horus, who made their god supreme.

With the rise of Horus, the cult of Seth became defamed, and of all the deities, his cult alone seems to have been irreconcilable with that of Horus; his supporters and their descendants gradually accepted the other gods of the pantheon and eventually Seth became the embodiment of all evil, ostracised by the Egyptians.

However, the conflict of Horus and Seth does not appear to have been finally resolved before Dynasty 2, when further rivalry broke out between the followers of the two gods, and some scholars affirm that the myth could equally well reflect this later conflict. There is evidence from the royal names that not all the early dynastic kings supported the persecution of Seth, and a religious and political upheaval and confrontation seems to have resulted between the followers of the two gods. A large proportion of the population may still have supported Seth.

After a period of strife, perhaps described in the myth in terms of the fight between Horus and Seth, a strong ruler named Khasekhemwy once again united the country and ushered in a period of peace in which the political and religious foundations were laid for the great developments of the Old Kingdom. The reconciliation of north and south was further emphasised by his marriage to a northern princess and the conflict between the supporters of the rival gods was finally resolved with the supremacy of Horus assured and the disgrace of Seth achieved.

RELIGIOUS ORGANISATION OF THE LIVING DURING THE EARLY DYNASTIC PERIOD

The rituals which were performed as acts of worship before the gods are not preserved to us, but it would not be unreasonable to suppose that the priest of the community carried out rites which did not differ greatly from those used in later periods, when offerings of food, drink and clothing were made to the deity. In the later periods, it was the king or his delegate, the high-priest, who performed the rituals in the temples of the gods, but before and during the Archaic Period, the tribal leaders enacted the rites for the local deities. The cult statue rested in a local sanctuary, but little is known of the structure of such places. Traces of these constructions have been discovered at Abydos and Hieraconpolis, and at Saqqara, within the enclosure of a mastaba-tomb dating to the reign of King Qaa, a mortuary temple has been excavated. This is similar to a Dynasty 3 mortuary temple of King Zoser. However, the materials – a matting of woven reeds attached to a wooden framework – have invariably perished, leaving few remains of these structures. Other evidence is also scanty, but early shrines occur as stylised ideograms in the hieroglyphic texts of the later periods, and cylinder seals and ebony and ivory tablets of the Archaic Period sometimes show representations of these shrines. One ebony tablet dating to the reign of King Horaha of Dynasty 1 shows a temple or shrine dedicated to the goddess Neith, and already the basic plan and some of the architectural features are present which can be seen in the great stone temples built hundreds of years later.

The shrine was probably a light structure, perhaps made of wood or wickerwork, and it had a hooped roof beyond which the corner posts projected. It stood at the rear of an open courtyard which was enclosed by a fence; two poles with banners marked the entrance to the enclosure, and these are later used in hieroglyphs to represent the word *ntr* which meant 'god' or 'divine'. The emblem of Neith is displayed on another pole in the centre of the open courtyard, in front of the shrine which contained the cult statue. By the Archaic Period, these 'temples' may have incorporated more permanent features such as brickwork, roofs made of wooden beams, and solid wooden doors. Essentially, however, these hut-shrines were simply larger versions of the domestic dwellings of the village communities which surrounded them.

The ritual offerings were probably presented to the deity thrice daily, as in later times, but the fact that frequent festivals are recorded on the Palermo Stone (an early inscribed record of major events) would suggest that there were already important religious occasions celebrated when the god's statue or cult symbol may have been paraded before the worshippers.

Other religious customs are only hinted at in the later sources, but an element of barbarism can probably be detected in at least the early part of the Archaic Period. There is conclusive evidence that, in some of the royal and noble burials of Dynasty I, women and servants were buried with their lord to accompany and serve him in the next world. This was gradually replaced during the Archaic Period by the custom of placing statuettes and models in the tomb to carry out the necessary duties for the deceased. The slaughter of the king's enemies, vividly depicted on the Narmer palette, was later simulated in a less barbarous manner by placing scenes on temple walls which showed the ceremonial slayings and were intended to achieve the destruction of the king's enemies by means of sympathetic magic.

Other evidence suggests that cannibalism may have existed at an early period. In the Pyramid Texts, compiled and written down in the Old Kingdom, there are passages, probably embodying concepts from earlier periods, which may reflect older customs of this kind. One example is found in the Pyramid Texts, Utterance 273-4:

> He [i.e. the king] it is that eateth their magic and swalloweth their lord-liness.
> Their great ones are for his morning meal, the middle-sized ones for his evening meal, and their little ones for his night meal.
> Their old men and their old women are assigned for his fumigation.
> The Great Ones who are in the north of the sky, they place for him the fire to the kettles, that which is under them being the thighs of their eldest ones.

FUNERARY PRACTICES IN THE EARLY DYNASTIC PERIOD

There is an absence of archaeological evidence from the dwellings of the period, and therefore much information has to be derived from the excavation of the tombs and their equipment.

There continued to be two main types of burial, perhaps based upon the customs practised by the indigenes and by the newcomers. On the one hand, the lower orders placed their dead in pit-graves, continuing the tradition of the Predynastic burials, although some variation existed in the size and interior construction of the grave and in the use of oval, circular or rectangular shapes for the stone or gravel mounds built above the graves. On the other hand, the new burial customs were gradually adopted by at least some of the indigenous population, probably as the result of fusion between the races, especially in the urban areas.

The most notable feature of the new burial customs was the introduction, perhaps by the newcomers, of a type of tomb which was used for the burial of the ruling classes. It was designed to resemble a house for the deceased and may have been regarded as the residence where the dead person continued his existence. It was similar in shape and concept both to the domestic dwellings of the living and to the temple, the residence of the god. Egyptologists have applied the term 'mastaba-tomb' to this type of structure, as the superstructure resembles the shape of a bench for which the Arabic word is 'mastaba'. Its use continued, with some variations, throughout the later periods.

In his book dealing with the Archaic Period, Emery has indicated that six stages of development can be discerned in the architectural design of the tomb during Dynasties 1 and 2. The six stages are further subdivided according to the social status of the occupant – whether he was royal, a member of the great nobility or of the lesser nobility, of the aristocracy or of minor officialdom, of the artisan class or of the peasantry.

At the beginning of Dynasty 1, the royal tombs and those of the great nobles consisted of a substructure cut into the desert rock and divided by a series of cross-walls into a number of brick-built chambers. The largest of these formed the burial chamber, and the other 'cells' contained some of the funerary equipment. The substructure was roofed with a ceiling of planks supported by wooden beams, and the internal rock-cut walls were covered in mud-plaster and decorated with woven reed-mats. At ground level, a brick superstructure was erected in the shape of an oblong rectangular platform; it extended beyond the limits of the substructure and imitated the palaces or houses of the period. The outer surfaces were covered with recessed brick panelling as a decorative feature and this reflected the contemporary design of the palace. A series of compartments, also used for subsidiary funerary equipment, occupied the lower part of the hollow interior of the superstructure. The tomb was surrounded by an enclosure wall; in some burials, on the north side beyond the enclosure, a brick-lined boat-pit was included to accommodate a wooden boat which was perhaps intended for the celestial journeys of the deceased.

In some complexes, subsidiary burials occur outside the enclosure wall of the main tomb; rows of graves were built parallel to the sides of the mastaba and these contained the bodies of women and members of the lord's household, buried to serve him in the next life. There is little doubt that these subordinates were buried at the time of the owner's death, for in some examples at Abydos, the superstructure was erected over both the main tomb and the subsidiary graves. Some of these burials represent the artisan class, and they were interred in single oblong pits which were roofed with timber and surmounted by a low rectangular superstructure with a rounded top. The contracted body, wrapped in linen, lay inside a small wooden coffin. Food and toilet equipment were placed with him, together with the tools of the trade which he had followed in life, so that he could use them in the next world for the benefit of his master.

These servants may have taken poison or simply have allowed themselves to be buried alive at the time of their master's death. The extent and development of human sacrifice in this period is uncertain. Some complexes incorporate subsidiary burials which were not placed under the main superstructure and probably therefore indicate that the subjects here met natural deaths and were interred close to their lord only when they had completed their normal lifespan. The custom of human sacrifice may have reached its peak in the reign of King Zer, whose tomb complexes at Abydos contain more than 500 subsidiary burials. The sacrifice of retainers had probably ceased in the north by the end of Dynasty 1, but survived in the south; the evidence indicates that any continuation of the custom in Dynasty 2 was greatly reduced in scale, and it had ceased completely by the end of the Archaic Period.

The general trend in tomb architecture during Dynasty 1 was to deepen and enlarge the substructure, in an attempt to protect the increasingly elaborate funerary equipment from the tomb robbers. Changes were introduced which centred on the increased size of the tomb and the inclusion of a stairway, built on the east side of the superstructure which led directly to the burial chamber. It provided an easier means of access for the more extensive funerary equipment and it was possible to block it with stone slabs as an additional deterrent to the tomb robbers. Two important tombs date to this period. One, probably attributable to Enezib, was discovered at Saqqara, and the other dates to the time of Queen Her-neith. They incorporate features which may represent preliminary stages which ultimately resulted in the building of the first stepped pyramid at Saqqara at the beginning of Dynasty 3.

Fundamental changes in the structure of the tomb had been introduced by the end of Dynasty 1. The enlarging and deepening of the substructure continued, but the storerooms which had once been incorporated in the superstructure were now discontinued. Instead, the funerary furniture was placed inside the burial chamber, although food and drink were still stored in subsidiary rooms. Apart from the royal tombs, where standards were maintained, the quantity of funerary goods was reduced, but greater attention was paid to constructing an elaborate tomb structure. With one exception, the 'palace facade' decoration of the mastaba also disappears, and the recesses in the panelled facade came to be regarded as niches and were perhaps seen as 'false doors' on the outside of the superstructure which gave access to the storage cells within. Once these storage rooms were discontinued, the recesses were reduced to two, situated at the east end of the mastaba; one now represented a false entrance to the tomb where funerary offerings could be placed and through which the owner's Ka or spirit could emerge from the burial chamber to partake of the offerings. The other was a subsidiary entrance. Another feature which was now introduced was a mudbrick temple, built on the north side of the mastaba but within the inner enclosure wall.

The tombs of the lesser nobles followed the pattern of the great burials but were reduced in scale. The cemeteries of the peasants suggest that the customs which had prevailed for all classes during the Predynastic Period were now retained for these poorest groups. The body, placed in the contracted position and wrapped in a reed mat or length of linen, was put in an oval or oblong pit cut into the ground. After burial, the pit-grave was covered with a low mound. Pottery, stone vessels, copper and flint tools, and toilet equipment were placed with the body. However, by the middle of Dynasty 1, the customs of the higher classes were starting to exert an influence throughout society, and some of the peasants began to adopt new customs. They continued to use pit-graves, but the body was now sometimes interred in a wooden coffin, and by the end of the Dynasty, the use of brick linings within the burial pits is more widespread.

The burial customs continued to develop throughout Dynasty 2. In the great tombs, the structure becomes more elaborate, the burial chamber is now situated on the west side of a complex of rooms which represent apartments found in the domestic dwellings of the wealthy; some even include areas for servants' quarters, bathrooms and lavatories, and are surrounded by gardens.

By the end of Dynasty 2, the type of tomb used for royalty or the nobility had become standardised. Although the owner's wealth dictated the size and number of chambers, the subterranean 'house' usually included a reception hall flanked by guest rooms; the innermost chamber – the burial chamber – which represented the master bedroom; a living room and harem, or women's quarters where, in life, many domestic chores were completed; and a bathroom and lavatory to which both the harem and the master's bedroom had access. Storage magazines now opened off the stairway entrance.

The burials of the peasants again reflect the general pattern of expansion set by their superiors, and the tomb structure is made more extensive at the expense of the tomb equipment. Some small shaft tombs, built for the peasantry, occur at Saqqara towards the end of Dynasty 2, and these contain two pottery vessels for food and drink, representing the owner's possessions.

Two customs which continued throughout Egypt's history and which were established during this early period were the practise of equipping the tomb and of preserving the body. A basic religious belief which apparently dated back to the predynastic period and was held regardless of the status of the deceased was the concept that life continued after death. The form which this hereafter was thought to take varied according to the social position of the deceased, but for all classes there were two essential requirements. First, the deceased had to be provided with the necessary equipment for a continued existence after death. This ranged in quality and quantity from the simple possessions placed with the peasant to the elaborate funerary goods put into the tombs of royalty and the nobility. Apart from items of everyday use, much attention was paid to providing a continuing food supply for the deceased; in some tombs, a complete meal of cereal, fish, meat, sweets, fruit and wine was set on alabaster and pottery dishes outside the coffin but near to the body. Reserve food supplies were placed in the storage magazines of the tomb and additional offerings were brought by relatives of the deceased and laid outside the 'false doors' or niches let into the outer wall of the tomb. A supplementary, magical food supply was provided by putting inscribed stelae, listing various items, in the tombs.

The Egyptians believed that the vital force of the deceased continued after death to be tied in some way to this world, and although it could pass eternity in another form of existence elsewhere it still needed to return to the tomb periodically to obtain sustenance from the food supplies placed there. It was considered that, for the spirit to partake of the food and drink, it was necessary to preserve the body of the deceased in as perfect and lifelike a condition as possible. This was the second essential requirement of funerary preparation. Mummification (a chemical method of preserving the body) was not practised in the earliest periods, but the hot, rainless climate and the dryness of the sand produced a rapid and natural process of dessication on the bodies buried in the pit-graves. Bodily fluids were absorbed by the surrounding porous sand and this rapid drying process prevented decomposition of the body so that skin tissue and hair often remained in a remarkable state of preservation. However, increasingly sophisticated building techniques introduced the brick-lined mastaba-tomb and the custom of lining even the pit-graves of the peasantry with wood or mudbrick. The result was that the body, now no longer surrounded by absorbent sand, decomposed before dessication could occur.

The Egyptians therefore had to find other methods of preserving the lifelike appearance of the body. The first experiments in this field almost certainly took place in the Archaic Period, and although there is as yet no evidence that any attempt was made to remove the viscera to prevent decomposition, there is one example to indicate that natron (later used as a dehydrating agent in mummification) may have been applied as a coating on the skin underneath the bandages. However, another less sophisticated technique was generally employed in the Archaic Period to reconstruct a lifelike resemblance of the deceased. The shape and contours of the living body were moulded on to the corpse; replacing the linen cloth which had been wrapped around the body in the earlier periods, by Dynasty 2 the body was enclosed in layers of linen pads and bandages which had been soaked in a resinous substance, and these were carefully moulded over the body to imitate the face, torso and limbs. This stiffened wrapping continued to retain the contours of the body although the body inside the bandages rapidly decomposed and became skeletal. Particular attention was paid to the preparation of the arms, legs and fingers which were separated and individually wrapped, and to the details which were painted on to the moulded face, genitalia and breasts.

The procedure was obviously time-consuming and was carried out only for members of the royal family and the great nobles. The body was finally placed, still in the contracted position, in the burial chamber of the mastaba-tomb, either on a bed or in a house-shaped wooden coffin. Some, probably only royalty, took a further precaution by providing an almost lifesize wooden figure in the tomb which was perhaps intended to act as a substitute for the body if it should be damaged or perish in some way.

THE ROYAL TOMBS OF THE EARLY DYNASTIC PERIOD

The location of the royal tombs of this period has been the subject of speculation. In AD 1895, the archaeologist Amélineau began excavating at Abydos and discovered brick pit-tombs at Umm el-Ka'ab. The site was re-investigated by Petrie in AD 1899, and inscribed objects discovered there gave the names of one queen and all the kings of Dynasty I and of two kings of Dynasty 2. The ancient writer Manetho connects these early dynasties with This at Abydos, and it seemed a reasonable and acceptable assumption that these were the tombs of these rulers, situated near to their religious capital. No human remains were found in the tombs, but this was explained in terms of plunder or desecration by marauding animals.

However, some years later in AD 1938, excavations were carried out at Saqqara in the north and, in the Early Dynastic cemetery at the north-east corner of the necropolis, a large brick mastaba-tomb was discovered which contained sealings bearing the name of King Hor-aha. Finally, twelve large mudbrick mastabas and their subsidiary burials were found here by Emery, who maintained that they had belonged to the kings and two of the queens of Dynasty 1. There are therefore two sets of funerary structures; each has some claim to be regarded as the site where the rulers of the earliest dynasties were buried, but the evidence is not conclusive in either case. The ownership of the Abydos 'tombs' cannot be disputed, for mud-sealings and other inscribed objects identify the buildings with their royal owners and a pair of stelae, inscribed with the name of the royal owner, were found outside eight of the 'tombs'. Also, more than 1300 subsidiary burials have been discovered here which include royal servants, domestic animals and high-ranking members of the royal harem. However, since no human remains have been found in these royal 'tombs', they may never have been occupied by the kings and queens with whom they are obviously associated.

At Saqqara, the principal mastabas were better preserved than the 'tombs' at Abydos, and they were obviously used as burial places since they were found to contain human remains. They were also surrounded by subsidiary burials, but these had been plundered and were less numerous than those at Abydos. The problem at Saqqara is to determine the ownership of these tombs, for although inscribed material found here connected them with particular reigns, it is impossible to identify each tomb with a particular ruler. Also, unlike

Abydos, there were no stelae to indicate ownership.

Various theories have been proposed to explain the existence of these two sites: the Abydos buildings may have been the royal tombs while those at Saqqara were built for the great nobles of the period, but the Saqqara tombs are much larger than the southern ones and it is therefore difficult to envisage the funerary monuments of subordinates surpassing those of the royal family. More acceptable is the idea that both Abydos and Saqqara were royal sites, but that the Saqqara buildings actually housed the human remains of the kings and queens, whereas the empty southern set at Abydos were intended as cenotaphs. In later periods, some kings possessed more than one funerary monument, and in this instance, the sites at Abydos and Saqqara may have reflected the king's role as ruler of Upper and Lower Egypt. Also, Saqqara may have been selected as the burial site because of its proximity to the Royal Residence at Memphis, while the kings may have also wished to preserve their strong religious associations with Abydos by erecting funerary monuments there.

The contribution of the Archaic Period

During this period, the foundations of Egyptian civilisation were already being established, amidst a ferment of political and social change. Religion was an essential and integral part of both government and society and many fundamental aspects were already apparent in the earliest dynasties. These included a tolerance of many deities, the characteristics and roles of some important deities, the form of divine worship, the special relationship which existed between the king and the gods, and the funerary beliefs and customs. Indeed, funerary practices inspired experimentation and development in many fields including architecture, art, pottery, carpentry, and metal-working, and the effect of this was soon apparent throughout other areas of society.

In general, these years saw the foundations laid for the great advances which were to symbolise the magnificent achievements of the Old Kingdom.

2

The Old Kingdom

———

The foundations of society had been established during the Archaic or Early Dynastic Period, and Egypt was now ready to develop from a loose and essentially tribal system into a highly organised and centralised theocracy. During Dynasties 3 to 6, the country achieved great technological advances which are perhaps best appreciated in the construction of the famous Great Pyramid which was built at Gizeh in Dynasty 4. The absolute power of the king enabled him to use a large proportion of the country's resources and manpower to construct a monumental royal burial site, but the economic pressures which this induced finally led to the decline of the Old Kingdom and of the kingship. Neverthelesss, most of the basic concepts were established in this period, and some would argue that the levels achieved in art, architecture and technology were never again equalled. Also, many advances in a variety of fields, pursued at first to enhance the king's funerary preparations, eventually affected and improved conditions in the general quality of life throughout the society.

Organisation of the society

The society revolved around and was dependent upon the concept of kingship. The king was regarded as a part-divine being, who was the god's son born to a human, royal mother; this unique status not only separated him from the rest of his subjects, but enabled him to mediate effectively between gods and men. In theory, he owned all the land, its resources and its people and they were at his mercy and disposal. However, he too was subject to Ma'at, the goddess who represented the principles of order and balance in the universe and law and justice on earth. Even he was bound by precedent, and he certainly consulted and was advised by his courtiers. His extensive role had developed out of that of tribal chieftain, and theoretically, he still exercised the many duties – religious, legal, political, military and social – which such men had once performed on behalf of their communities. However, it was now necessary to delegate some of his authority to royal officials who were usually members of his own family. Because of the custom of polygamy or bigamy in the royal family, there were usually subsidiary branches of the family, descended from secondary or minor wives of previous kings, and inter-family strife over the succession to the throne was not uncommon in the Old Kingdom. Therefore, it was shrewd political sense on the part of the king to attempt to secure the absolute loyalty of his closest relatives by establishing their dependence upon him for their positions, their wealth, and ultimately their tombs and expectations for eternity. He supervised the education and upbringing of his courtiers and their children, and made them gifts of royal land and of possessions; eventually, he provided them with their tombs, close to his own pyramid, and he endowed them with funerary goods and estates with which to maintain their tombs. Through the king's bounty, these men were believed to attain a degree of eternity.

At first, all appointments were made by the king; loyal men held their positions during their lifetimes but their posts were not hereditary and they were made fully aware that their continuing power rested solely on the king's goodwill. Although the royal family retained most of these influential positions, at least until the end of Dynasty 4, lowly birth was not a complete deterrent to a man's ambition, for the king could and did promote and advance able and loyal subjects.

The most important position after the king was the vizier who usually had close family ties with the king. He had considerable powers of organisation and administration, for he was head of the judiciary, the chief royal architect, keeper of the state archives, and some were even attributed with the ability to heal or to impart great wisdom. They were obviously men of wide-ranging ability, perhaps the best example being Imhotep, the vizier of King Zoser, who was not only accredited with being the architect of the first pyramid at Saqqara, but was also deified later as a great healer and was worshipped by the Greeks as the god of medicine.

As a long, narrow country, Egypt must have caused many administrative problems for the early rulers. Local governors were appointed to the various nomes; at first, when they wrere temporarily appointed subject to the king's wishes, their loyalty could be assured, but when royal influence waned and these positions became hereditary, the governors, often isolated and far from Memphis, became increasingly rebellious, regarding themselves as independent princelings ruling their own territories. Indeed, the creation of such governorships was to provide future generations of rulers with a continuing and difficult problem.

Supporting the top level of administration, there was an extensive bureaucracy, comprised of a hierarchy of officials who were responsible for the efficient daily organisation and running of the system. They manned the treasuries which dealt with the revenue and expenditure, the armoury, the granaries and the department of public works. These departments continued to be housed at Memphis and were still grouped together in one complex which also accommodated the living quarters of the royal family. This complex was known as the 'Great House', rendered in Egyptian as 'Per Wer', and this term was eventually applied to the person of the king of Egypt, who became known as 'Pharaoh'. It was also from Memphis that the priesthoods of the great temples were probably administered, as well as the king's burial complex with its pyramid, mortuary temple and residence city. Other areas of administration may have been organised on a local basis in the various districts into which the land was divided.

Memphis, however, was the centre of all major activity, and it was here that the craftsmen and artisans came to take up residence, where there would be a great demand for the wide variety of goods and equipment which they could produce for the royal and noble tombs. At this period, the arts and crafts reached a level of excellence which was copied and imitated by many later generations, and the artisans created a style which can be recognised as the 'Memphite school'. Advances in technology were constantly being sought to improve not only the funerary buildings themselves, but also to enhance the beauty of the equipment placed in the tombs, and once discoveries were made, they were soon employed for more general purposes such as producing furniture, jewellery, toiletries, pottery and other items for the living.

This society, with its obsessive desire to perpetuate the afterlife of the god-king, was nevertheless dependent for its food, resources and manpower upon the mass of serfs whose lives were spent in never-ending toil. Not literally slaves, these peasants nevertheless had no choice but to involve themselves in some arduous labour for their royal lord in order to obtain food for their families. For most of the year, they were occupied with irrigating the soil and cultivating the crops not only to feed the living but to provide eternal food supplies for the tombs and pyramid complexes. However, for three months of the year, the inundation put much of the land under water and it has been suggested that during this annual period of enforced unemployment, the peasants may have been paid in kind to work on the king's pyramid. Not only would this have averted starvation, but they would then have had little time or inclination to foment rebellion against the state. However, it is not altogether clear how such a programme would have been organised, and the labour for building the pyramids may have been raised more simply by corvée-duty. Other duties which were forced upon the peasantry probably included stone quarrying and military service. The army was as yet a non-professional organisation, but when military forays were required to obtain hard stone or gold from Nubia, royal courtiers were sent at the head of a party of conscripted men.

Religious organisation

This increasingly complex, stratified society had developed from the tribal communities, but the genius of the Old Kingdom kings and their advisers enabled them to draw together many diverse elements and to create a centralised, powerful state. These trends are visible not only in the political sphere, but also in the religious developments. The earliest communities had worshipped local tribal gods who were gradually amalgamated into a confusing pantheon which seemed to absorb all the major deities except Seth who was perhaps too closely associated with the conquered indigenes to survive unscathed. It became the custom that when a family of rulers came to power, they elevated to the status of supreme royal god the deity they had previously worshipped at a local level.

Nevertheless, despite the apparent multiplicity of deities and the confusion of the pantheon, there was a marked attempt during the Old Kingdom to centralise and rationalise the cults and to create some order out of the existing situation. This was undertaken by the priesthoods of the various gods. Certain cities had now become great religious centres associated with particular gods or groups or deities, and at these centres the deities were now grouped into families, ogdoads (groups of eight deities) or enneads (groups of nine deities). The most important priesthoods associated with the foremost centres developed individual theologies, each one aimed at advancing the claims of their own god and establishing his primary role in the creation of the universe, the other deities, and mankind.

Cosmogonies

At 'Iwnw (later Heliopolis), which lay near to the site where Egypt's modern capital of Cairo was founded thousands of years later, the god Re' had taken over the cult of an earlier god, Atum. He had assimilated some of his features and characteristics and, as Re'-Atum, was now worshipped as the creator of the world according to the Heliopolitan theology, and his priests sought to distinguish his various characteristics. He was identified with Khepri and shown associated with or depicted as a beetle, pushing the sun; the Egyptians had come to regard the beetle as the symbol of self-regeneration, for their observation of dung-beetles showed that the beetles pushed dung-balls in front of them through the sand. These balls were in fact a food supply, but the Egyptians mistakenly regarded them as a conglomeration of eggs from which the new generation emerged. As the symbol of renewal, Khepri was identified with the sun-god as he appeared in the early morning; Re' also, on other occasions, took the forms of Atum and of Re'-Harakhte.

Many myths came to be associated with the sun and its relation to the earth and the sky. It was believed that the earth was flat and was formed by the back of the god Geb who lay in the centre of a circular ocean, the lower half of which flowed through the underworld while the upper half formed the sky above the earth. The sun-god was thought to follow a daily course, travelling in a day barque, across the sky, and then at nightfall, to transfer into his night barque, in order to pass below the horizon into the underworld. The god then emerged at dawn on the earth's surface, and brought the return of daylight. The mythology associated with the sun-god's journey was closely interwoven with the afterlife of the king in the Old Kingdom.

However, it was through the Heliopolitan cosmogony – the most famous and influential of the creation myths – that Re''s unique and powerful role was emphasised. Here, his association with both cosmic and other gods is clearly underlined; the nature-deities – sky, earth, wind, sun, moon and stars – play important roles in this myth while the non-cosmic deities have only minor parts. The main source for the myth is the Pyramid Texts.

The myth concerns two groups of nine gods: the Great Ennead, consisting of Re'-Atum, Shu, Tefnut, Geb, Nut, Osiris, Isis, Nephthys and Seth; and the Little Ennead, made up of lesser deities under the direction of Horus. It tells how Atum, the first god of Heliopolis (now completely identified with Re'), emerged from the great primaeval ocean, Nun, after he had brought himself into existence by self-generation, or alternatively had been born as the child of Nun. The god created a mound on which to stand (the Heliopolitan priests claimed that their temple was built on this very mound), and then dispelled the gloom and chaos by introducing light. Taking the form of the mythical Bennu bird, Atum then alighted on the Benben, which was a pillar associated with the sun-god. A fetish in the form of a pillar had probably existed in the temple at Heliopolis since earliest times, and by this period, the conically shaped stone, probably derived from the fetish and now known as the Benben, had become the sacred symbol of the sun at Heliopolis. Here, it was regarded as the god's cult-object and as the place of creation where the gods had alighted.

Re'-Atum, who was believed to possess bi-sexual powers, then masturbated to beget Shu, the god of the air whom he spat forth, and Tefnut, goddess of moisture whom he vomited out. In turn, they produced Geb, the earth-god, and Nut, the sky-goddess, and thus completed the family of cosmic deities. The children of Geb and Nut – Osiris, Isis, Nephthys and Seth – were not cosmic and appear elsewhere in other myths.

Other Old Kingdom cosmogonies show that other priesthoods were attempting to rival Re''s supremacy. These also incorporated nature deities who had little popular appeal but were essential elements of the state cults, and some non-cosmic deities whom they perhaps wished to subordinate to the main god. In the same way as the Heliopolitan myth, these describe creation in terms of the appearance of a primordial island arising from the ocean on which life came into being. Each priesthood claimed that this mound was the site of their god's temple, and a place of great spiritual potency. After this occasion of creation, development was envisaged as progressing slowly until a golden age arrived when the gods ruled on earth and when law, ethics and religion were established. This passed, and the king, as direct heir and successor of the gods, took over the rulership of Egypt, upholding the precepts of Ma'at so that the ideal conditions of the divine age could be preserved for eternity.

The greatest threat to Heliopolitan supremacy came from the theological centre of Memphis, where Ptah, the creator-god, was worshipped. Here, the college of priests, anxious to prove that Ptah preceded Re'-Atum, identified Ptah as Nun who begot a daughter Naunet by whom he fathered a son, Atum, the principal Heliopolitan deity. According to Memphite theology, Ptah was supreme creator of the universe, and acted through thought (expressed by the heart) and will (expressed through the tongue). Atum was only the agent of Ptah and in some versions, was replaced altogether by Horus and Thoth. Ptah created not only the world but also all the gods, their cult centres, shrines and images; he made the cities, food, drink and all the physical requirements of life. He was also 'Lord of Truth', who created divine utterance and established ethics. However, he had limited appeal, with his intellectual ability and unexciting mythology, and only through his later identification with Osiris and other funerary deities did he achieve a more wide-spread popularity. Despite his many admirable qualities, however, he failed to attain a position of unrivalled supremacy and was never adopted by any of the kings as a special royal patron.

A third great centre developed at Hermopolis; here, the myths took various forms which were not contradictory but sought to establish the supremacy of the centre and its major deities. The mythology centred around the Ogdoad which included four male gods – Nun (the primaeval waters), Huh (eternity), Kuk (darkness), and Amun (air or "that which is hidden") – and their female consorts – Naunet, Hauhet, Kauket and Amaunet. The males were represented with frog's heads while the females were serpent-headed. Together, these eight deities created and ruled the world in the period following the 'First Occasion' when creation had occurred. They died and went to live in the underworld where they ensured that life could continue on earth by making the Nile flow and the sun rise. In another version of the myth, a Cosmic Egg replaced the concept of the primordial ocean as the source of life; this had been laid on the island by a bird which was either a goose called the 'Great Cackler' or an ibis which represented Thoth, the great god of Hermopolis. The egg contained either air (necessary to the creation of life) or Re' in the form of a bird who proceeded to create the world. In yet another version, the Ogdoad created a lotus flower which arose from the 'Sea of Knives' (claimed to be the sacred lake of the temple at Hermopolis) and opened its petals to reveal either the child Re' who created the world, or a scarab-beetle. This changed into a boy whose tears became men and women.

Apart from the three main cosmogonies, there were other lesser myths associated with other deities, as well as the Theban cosmogony of the New Kingdom. However, it was the Heliopolitan, Memphite and Hermopolitan versions which greatly affected religious belief in the Old Kingdom.

The cult of Re'

Until the end of the Old Kingdom, no cult rivalled that of Re' in power and importance. From Dynasty 2, when the kings had adopted the title 'son of Re'', the power of the cult and its priesthood increased throughout Dynasties 3 and 4 until, under royal patronage, it reached its zenith in Dynasty 5. It became the royal cult and the kings incorporated the solar epithet in their royal titularies, perhaps thus indicating that the king's status was demoted and that, instead of being regarded as one of the gods as in earlier times, he was now designated as the sun-god's son. Other evidence also suggests that the kingship was subordinated to Re' and his priesthood in Dynasty 5.

There is much to support the idea that the pyramid form was a symbol which was closely associated with the sun-cult and that the development of the pyramid throughout Dynasties 3 and 4 indicates the advancing status of the cult. If this suggestion is accepted, then it may also be true that Shepseskaf, one of the kings who ruled towards the end of Dynasty 4, attempted to break the power of these priests who now posed a threat to the king's own position. Such a stand may be reflected in the fact that he claimed no association with Re' in his name or titles, and also, instead of constructing a pyramid as his funerary monument after the style of his predecessors, he returned to an earlier practice and built a variant of the mastaba-tomb.

Even if such a power struggle did occur, it was doomed to failure, for in Dynasty 5 the solar priests increased their influence while the role of the king declined. His relatives no longer filled the senior administrative posts and the bureaucracy became an independent establishment made up of men who no longer owed their positions or their allegiance to the king. Gradually, the provincial governorships became independent and hereditary posts, and the king's authority was further decreased.

Whether willingly or under pressure, the kings of Dynasty 5 raised Re' to a pre-eminent position. It is, however, possible that the kings of this dynasty owed their accession to the throne to the intervention and active support of the priests of Re', and were then expected to show their gratitude to the deity. Elements of historical fact may be preserved in a legend which occurs in a literary source, the Westcar Papyrus. The papyrus itself is almost certainly later than the time in which the story is set, and may date to the Second Intermediate Period, but the tale, known as 'King Kheops and the Magicians', was undoubtedly a folk-story which was passed down by generations of public story-tellers. It relates events which are supposed to have occurred immediately before the start of Dynasty 5. The main events of the story are given in the translation in Appendix A2; briefly, some magicians are called to the palace to entertain King Cheops, the builder of the Great Pyramid at Gizeh. One, who can forsee the future, unwillingly tells Cheops that the end of his line will come and will be brought about by the birth of three children. The prophecy states: 'Thy son, his son, and then one of them', thus assuring the king that his own son, Chephren, and his son, Mycerinus, will succeed him before the throne is usurped. The historical facts claim that two other kings ruled between the death of Mycerinus and the start of Dynasty 5, but it is quite probable that only the three great rulers of Dynasty 4 were remembered by later generations. The aim of the story is to establish the divine origin of Dynasty 5 and the omnipotence of the sun-god.

The wife of a priest of Re' gives birth to triplets; these children were fathered by Re' and survive all attempts by Cheops to destroy them. They live to become the first three kings of Dynasty 5, namely Userkaf, Sahure and Neferirkare (Kakai). Again, there is insufficient information about the origin of these rulers to ascertain whether or not they were born to a priest's wife, but historically, these kings were not brothers, Sahure and Neferirkare being the sons of Userkaf. Nevertheless, the story succeeds in conveying the impression that these rulers were good men and legitimate kings who were chosen by Re' as his earthly representatives, and who built temples for the god and replenished his altars. The tale also shows that the cult could expect the support and patronage of the new dynasty.

Historical facts bear out the conclusion that these kings, whatever their origin or methods of gaining power, patronised the solar cult on an unprecedented scale. The first three kings of the dynasty and another three rulers built special solar temples to Re' during this period; inscriptional evidence states their existence although only those of Userkaf and Niuserre have actually been discovered and excavated at Abu Gurob. They were built on the pattern of the main solar cult-temple at Heliopolis, and from the excavations at Abu Gurob, it is possible to determine that the temples, situated on the edge of the desert, probably incorporated a series of enclosures which led to a wide, paved, open-air court. Here, a rectangular limestone podium was placed, which was probably intended to represent the primaeval hill; a squat obelisk was mounted on this and may have imitated the Benben stone in the original sun temple at Heliopolis. A low altar stood in front of the podium on which animals were sacrificed, their blood draining away along specially cut channels. Other elements in the complex included magazines for the storage of offerings, and a brick-lined pit beyond the enclosure which probably contained a wooden boat for the sun's celestial journeys. In the temple of Niuserre, the walls were carved with figures which represented the seasons and which were shown bringing offerings to the sun-god. The personifications of the nomes and other minor deities were also depicted and, together with other temple reliefs of this dynasty, provide valuable information relating to the pantheon of the Old Kingdom. Other scenes here included events in the king's jubilee festival, and representations of the flora and fauna of Egypt which the sun's powerful creativity brought into existence. The kings devoted time and expense to the construction of these solar temples and, consequently, their own funerary monuments suffered a decline. Nowhere is the diminution in royal prestige more apparent than in the inferior pyramids of Dynasty 5 and of the subsequent period.

The Wisdom Literature

A general survey of the religious beliefs and practices of the Old Kingdom gives the impression that religion was organised for the sole benefit of the king and the state, and that any benefit society might derive was of secondary importance. However, a relationship with some of the gods, expressed through individual prayers and worship, existed at all levels of society. During this period, the first literary evidence is available to show that the Egyptians had already developed an ethical code which they believed to have been divinely authorised. Rules for conducting personal relationships and the established standards of behaviour were taught to young people as an acceptable pattern for life. The idea was already beginning to emerge that a man's deeds in this life had a direct bearing upon his attainment of immortality after death.

The body of writings which preserve these concepts are referred to as the 'Instructions' or 'Wisdom Literature' and were a major contribution to Egyptian literature. They usually take the form of a wise man (either a vizier or the king) addressing his son, and handing on to him the advice necessary to advance his position in society. The content of many of the 'Instructions' undoubtedly dates back to the Old Kingdom, but the papyri on which these texts occur date to the later periods, and especially to the New Kingdom. It seems that the 'Instructions' were regarded as excellent models which successive generations of schoolboys were required to copy, not only to instruct them in good manners and conduct but also to set standards for style and literary mode of expression. In these schoolboy copies, the wise dictates of the Old Kingdom have been preserved to us.

Three main 'Instructions' can probably be attributed to the Old Kingdom, and a selection from these texts is given in Appendix A2. The 'Instruction of Ptah-hotep' was apparently composed by a vizier of King Isesi of Dynasty 5, named Ptah-hotep; such a man is known to have lived and acted as vizier to this king and a tomb belonging to a noble of this name has been discovered at Saqqara. The vizier gives counsel of a practical nature to ensure his pupil's advancement in life, advising caution in speech and prudence in friendship, good manners in another's house, and correct behaviour towards superiors, peers and inferiors. The true qualities of good leadership – treating kindly with inferiors who seek help – are indicated; the young man is also urged to marry young and to care for his wife and treat his son with solicitude. Warnings are also issued against covetousness, regarded as the most evil emotion, and against unseemly friendships with women in other households.

In another 'Instruction', this time addressed to Kagemni, the son of King Huni of Dynasty 3, Huni's vizier is commanded by his royal master to advise his young charge; again, he counsels wisdom and discretion in speech, modesty, restraint over greediness and delicacy in table manners.

The third text has a rather different context. It is known variously as the 'Instruction of Duauf', the 'Instruction of Khety' or the 'Satire on Trades'. The composition of this text is attributed to a man named Duauf, the son of Khety, and unlike the other 'Instructions', the author here is a man of humble origin who nevertheless sets out to give good advice to his son, Pepy. Unlike his father, Pepy has the good fortune to be placed in the 'School of Books' among the children of the magistrates, and Duauf is anxious that he should devote himself to his tasks and his books and become a man of letters, so that he can escape from the toil associated with various trades which might otherwise be his lot. To emphasise his point, Duauf describes the different trades which are all subject to supervision and bring woes and hardships; he extols the excellence of the scribe's profession (a 'learned man' in Egyptian society) and urges Pepy to follow this career. These texts, and similar ones which date to the Middle Kingdom, give sound practical advice; the underlying principle is that personal attainment brings contentment. Ethical values, stressing kindness to petitioners, moderation in all dealings, and the exercising of wisdom and good judgment, suggest that the Old Kingdom established a high standard of behaviour for the official. The society, stable and hierarchical, expected those who held power to exercise it with clemency and righteousness. Although the 'Instructions' provide a picture of a stereotyped 'ideal', they nevertheless provide a rare opportunity to gain an insight into the personal attributes which the Egyptians considered desirable.

The funerary beliefs and customs of the Old Kingdom

Although the gradual development of self-awareness characterised the Old Kingdom for later generations, it was the funerary monuments, culminating in the pyramid form, which became the symbols of this period of history.

During the Old Kingdom, Egypt was able to develop her political and religious systems with little outside interference. Trade with other areas was intensified, especially with parts of the Near East, and Egypt expanded her sphere of influence in Nubia where it was essential to maintain access to valuable commodities, particularly gold and the hard stone required for building projects at home. However, during these years, the country suffered no invasion or major infiltration and was therefore free to devote all efforts to the most important concept – the preparation of a royal burial place which would protect and preserve the king's body after death and which would enable him to pass safely from this life into eternity.

By the beginning of the Old Kingdom, the belief was firmly established that only the king could hope to achieve an eternal existence which he could spend traversing the heavens. His family and favoured members of the nobility, by virtue of his beneficence in providing them with tombs, funerary possessions and funerarv endowments, could hope to enjoy the delights of immortality only vicariously through their royal lord. The craftsmen, who by their skills created the tombs and their contents, might hope to participate in the royal hereafter through their contribution to the royal burial. The peasants who laboured on the king's pyramid might also hope in this way to partake of a vicarious eternity, and it was perhaps this religious incentive as much as their regular food supplies which spurred on the workforce.

By centralising the spiritual and material hopes of all his subjects upon the king's continuing well-being after death, the rulers succeeded in creating a state which, in political, social and religious terms, was united with one aim. Thus a country which was composed of diverse elements and was geographically difficult to coordinate became willing to accept centralised rule. It is impossible to determine whether or not the kings were prompted by such political considerations when they first began to build pyramids, but the results were far-reaching.

Not only was the production of food directed towards the support of the vast mortuary complexes which surrounded the pyramids and towards the more mundane purpose of feeding the priests who serviced these, but the development of arts and crafts and of building and technology was aimed at providing the king with a more elaborate and safer burial place.

It has been shown that the tomb had two main functions – to house the body and to accommodate the funerary equipment for use in the next world. From earliest times, the site of the grave was marked

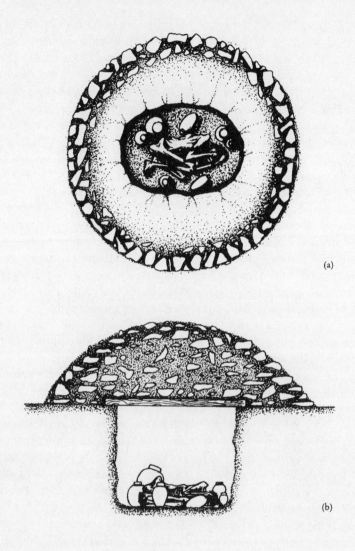

Figure 3 Figures showing the development of the tomb and pyramid structures, consisting of (a) pit-burial, (b) mastaba tomb, (c) the Step Pyramid at Saqqara, section looking south, and (d) the Great Pyramid at Gizeh, section looking west.

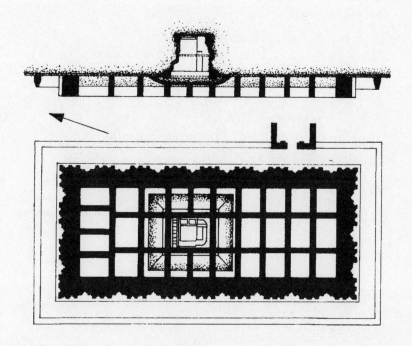

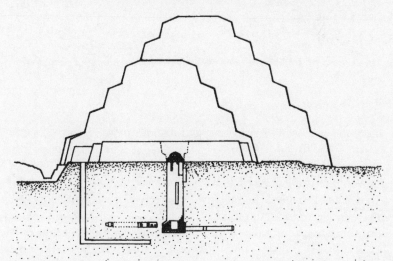

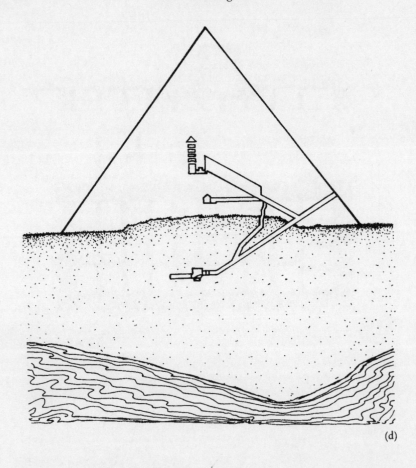

(d)

with a mound of sand or stones, and this mound may have become associated with the mythological 'Island of Creation' where the cosmogonies claimed that the first god had alighted and life had come into existence. As such, the mound would have been regarded as a centre of magical potency for the renewal of life from which the deceased could draw strength. It is clear that this mound was of considerable importance to the tomb, for it was later incorporated in the superstructure of the brick mastaba-tomb. In the early dynasties there are some examples of mastaba-tombs which had already developed a stepped, layered brick superstructure, and it has been argued that this trend was continued to produce the first stone Step Pyramid at Saqqara, in which the superstructure, or pyramid, consisted of a series of superimposed mastaba-tombs of decreasing size. From the step pyramids, there developed the true pyramid of the later dynasties, and the pyramid could therefore be regarded as the culmination of the mound, symbolising the Island of Creation.

On the other hand, the pyramid form may simply have been a more elaborate architect's design for the royal burial place, or perhaps it was hoped that its very size would deter tomb-robbers from entering and that the great sloping sides would protect the burial and would make it possible to conceal the entrance within one of these slopes.

However, if the pyramid is considered within the context of the religious trends of the Old Kingdom, it is difficult to ignore the evidence that it was associated directly with the solar cult. The king passed his eternity in the realm of the sun-god, and therefore at death he needed to ascend to the sky where, in the east, he was greeted by the gods; here, he continued his royal duties, sat in judgement, and accompanied Re' in the celestial barque as he made his daily journey across the heavens.

These great funerary monuments are called 'pyramids', a word which is derived from the name 'pyramis' which the Greeks gave them. In their own language, 'pyramis' meant 'wheaten cake' and to the Greek visitors to Egypt these monuments, seen from a distance, had the appearance of such cakes, in both shape and colour. However, the ancient Egyptian word for a pyramid was 'Mer'; this has tentatively been translated as 'Place of Ascension' and some scholars suggest that the pyramid was regarded as a means of access for the king to climb to heaven where he joined his father the sun-god. In the religious texts which were inscribed in the later pyramids and which are known today as the 'Pyramid Texts', spells occur which refer to a 'staircase . . . provided for the king's ascent to heaven' and this may be a description of the purpose and supposed function of the pyramid. The Egyptians believed that models or representations of objects or people could take on the substance and properties of the original, and it has been suggested that the pyramid in its complete form, covered in shining white limestone, may have been intended to represent a shaft of sunlight or sun's ray descending to earth. Along this the king could ascend to heaven and could also return to his earthly burial place to obtain sustenance from the food offerings placed daily in his mortuary temple attached to the pyramid.

The stone which capped the Benben, the cult-symbol of Re' at Heliopolis, was also represented as a pyramidion or small pyramid, and the similarity between this and the pyramid is a further indication that the pyramid form was closely associated with the sun-cult and may have been regarded as a variant of the Benben.

However, the true pyramid which occurs at Gizeh in its full impact and magnificence was only the final stage in a series of experiments. The first pyramid, also the oldest existing stone building in the world, was built at Saqqara at the beginning of Dynasty 3 by Imhotep for King Zoser. The Step Pyramid still retains much of its original grandeur today, towering over the ancient necropolis of Saqqara; its isolation on the edge of the desert provides the visitor with an impression of a great mortuary complex and much of the original form is preserved, although the outer limestone casing has long since been removed for building material.

Apparently originally designed as a mastaba-tomb, for some reason this was later extended into six superimposed mastaba-type superstructures which produced the first stepped pyramid. Below ground level, the substructure included a deep shaft which gave access to a series of subterranean corridors and rooms; some of these were adorned with reliefs and blue faience tiles which were intended to represent the matting rolls suspended over the doorways of palaces and houses. In this substructure, Zoser and members of his family were buried; thus, this pyramid retained the main divisions of the mastaba-tomb – superstructure and substructure containing the burial.

It has been suggested that the step pyramids, unlike the later true pyramids, were associated not with the solar cult but with an earlier star-cult; their purpose would probably still have been to provide access to the sky for the king. Various features suggest that there may have been a transition in religious beliefs in this period and that the solar cult may have absorbed an earlier star-cult. Some spells which occur in the Pyramid Texts seem to relate to a star-cult and it is thought they may have had a different origin from those associated with the sun-cult; again, the mortuary temple in the pyramid complex changes position from the north side in the step pyramid complexes, to the east side (facing the rising sun) in those complexes associated with the true pyramids. The fact that the step pyramid form was later incorporated within the body of the true pyramid may again indicate that the solar cult took over the architecture of an earlier cult.

The Step Pyramid was only the central feature of an entire complex. It was surrounded on four sides by an enclosure wall of white limestone which perhaps imitated the wall surrounding Zoser's palace. Within the enclosure there were many buildings of a religious nature, including a mortuary temple, shrines, storehouses, altars, courts, and subsidiary tombs. Most of the buildings duplicated features found in the royal palace; they usually occurred in the pyramid complex in pairs, suggesting that it was designed as a residence for the king after death. Provision was made here to allow kingship and other rituals to be performed simultaneously in two sets of buildings, for the king as ruler of both Upper and Lower Egypt.

Some areas are of particular interest. Part of the complex seems to have been designed for the re-enactment in the next life of the king's coronation. Jubilee festivals, commemorating the coronation and probably intended to magically restore the king's waning powers, were performed at intervals throughout the king's lifetime. At an earlier, less enlightened period, an ageing ruler had perhaps been ceremonially sacrificed at such festivals and replaced by a younger, more vigorous ruler who could ensure good harvests and prosperity for Egypt. Now, however, as with other barbarous customs, magical substitution and ritual replaced the taking of life. Jubilee festival wall scenes have been discovered at Saqqara, showing the king carrying a flail and running around a course; this was part of the ceremony in which the king was required to run around an open court, thus reaffirming his physical prowess and ability to rule. In this complex at Saqqara, there is an oblong jubilee court, surrounded on the east and west sides by a series of dummy stone chapels where Zoser could repeat his festival and reaffirm his right to rule in the next world.

A small enclosed room, known today as a 'serdab' from the Arabic word meaning 'cellar', was included in some of the mastaba-tombs and occurs in this complex. It provided a place, accessible to the living, where food offerings could be brought for the deceased. It contained the statue of the tomb-owner, and part of one wall was either removed or pierced with two holes to allow the statue to see the offerings; the deceased, through the medium of his statue, could then partake of the food. Here, there was originally a statue of Zoser, but this has now been removed to the Cairo Museum and a cast placed in the serdab; it is nevertheless still an eerie experience to peer through the eye-holes and to confront the majesty of Zoser.

The complex also incorporates a southern mastaba-tomb, built against the southern enclosing wall; this has a burial chamber too small to accommodate a body, and its use is uncertain, although it was perhaps intended to receive the king's viscera, removed during the process of mummification. Alternatively, it could have served as a royal cenotaph to provide the king with two 'tombs' in his capacity as ruler of the Two Lands. His place of burial, in the substructure of the pyramid, has long since been plundered, although the archaeologists discovered there some alabaster coffins, stone vases and dishes and the remains of statues.

Zoser's funerary complex was planned as a single unit, and most of the buildings have no known precedent. The design was never repeated but the buildings, many of which have been restored by the Egyptian Antiquities Service in collaboration with M. Lauer, display many unique and interesting features. They show that the artisans and craftsmen were inexperienced in working with stone; here, we can see their first faltering steps in translating earlier forms into the new medium. There is uncertainty as to how certain architectural devices will work, but the results already show the style which was to characterise the best work of the Old Kingdom. Earlier sacred buildings had been constructed of light wood, reed or mudbrick; the structural uses for which these materials had been employed were now transformed into stone. Bundles of reeds and the later wooden pillars provided the pattern for the stone fluted and ribbed columns. Perhaps uncertain as yet of their skill in using free-standing columns to support the roof, the architects included engaged columns; the massive stone blocks used so confidently in the later buildings are not found in this complex, but small stone blocks, imitating the earlier mudbrick constructions, were employed to good effect.

The kings who followed Zoser copied his precedent and built pyramids as burial-places, and through these we can trace some of the main stages of development from the first step pyramid to the true pyramid. Several other stepped or layered pyramids were built, but the Medum pyramid, which can perhaps be attributed to the reign of Sneferu at the beginning of Dynasty 4, illustrates the next stage. Originally designed as a small step pyramid, and then extended so that it incorporated seven or eight superimposed layers, the building finally became a true pyramid when the steps were infilled with local stone and the sides of the pyramid were faced with white limestone. Associated buildings were arranged in a sequence which became standard for the Old Kingdom pyramid complex.

Twenty-eight miles to the north of Medum lie the two pyramids of Dahshur which were also probably built in the reign of Sneferu. The southern pyramid was planned as a true pyramid, but for some reason there was a change in design, perhaps because there was anxiety about the original angle of its sides. Nevertheless, work continued to a point just beyond halfway up the height of the pyramid and then the angle of its incline was sharply decreased. This

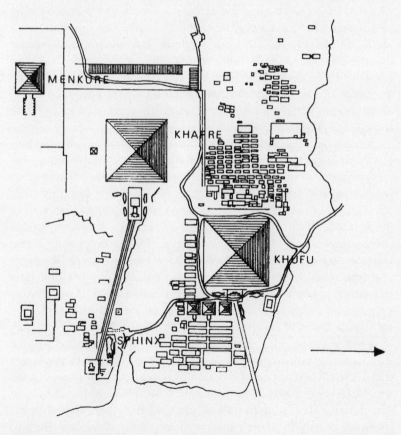

Figure 4   Plan of the pyramid area at Gizeh.

produced a blunted effect and the pyramid is now known by the term of 'Bent' or 'Blunted'. The northern Dahshur pyramid is the earliest known example of a true pyramid, conceived and executed as such.

However, it was Cheops, the son of Sneferu by Queen Hetepheres, who built the most famous of all the pyramids on the Gizeh plateau. He selected this hitherto unused site because of its proximity to Memphis and also because excellent limestone was available in the nearby quarries at Tura. Slightly elevated, this plateau provided him with every opportunity to build a dramatic and unrivalled funerary monument, and gave scope for extensive subsidiary buildings.

He did not waste this opportunity, and despite the pyramids which his descendants erected at the site as well as the encroaching suburbs of modern Cairo, the Great Pyramid still dominates the plain and conveys something of the grand scheme which its builder so carefully planned. It remains the monument to a king who enjoyed absolute control over the lives of his subjects and the resources of his country and who had the vision and disposition, albeit tyrannical, to direct the energies of the whole land towards the completion of a vast project.

As with the earlier monuments, the pyramid was only one feature in a complex of buildings; most of these have now partly or entirely disappeared but sufficient remains to indicate that the complex was built along the usual lines. It incorporated a Valley Building from which a causeway led to a limestone Mortuary Temple situated at the east side of the Pyramid. Outside the eastern enclosure wall of the pyramid, a number of rock-cut pits have been discovered. These are boat-shaped and although three have been found to be empty and one remains unexcavated, one pit contained a wooden boat consisting of planks and parts ready for assembly. The purpose of such burials remains uncertain, although in the Old Kingdom, they have been found in association only with royal pyramids. They may have been intended for the king's use on his ascent to heaven or for his journeys accompanying the gods. However, it is also possible that they were carried as part of the funerary procession and then buried nearby. At first it was thought that such burials were found only in association with the pyramids of the Old Kingdom, thus empha- sising the possibility of their solar function, but similar boat-pits have since been found in the vicinity of earlier mastaba-tombs, and this has prompted scholars to question their exact purpose and relation-ship to the sun-cult.

Another problem in interpretation is posed by the existence of three small pyramids at Gizeh; each has a small ruined chapel attached to its east face, and it has been suggested that these were given as burial places to favoured female relatives of the king. However, other examples occur of similar subsidiary pyramids and some would have been too small to accommodate a human burial. Other purposes for them have been suggested, including that of a secondary 'tomb' or cenotaph for the king, or of a burial place for the king's viscera.

Indeed, the most famous woman of Cheops' family – his mother Queen Hetepheres – did not have a pyramid at Gizeh but was buried in an unmarked tomb which lay south of the causeway, close to the first subsidiary pyramid. Discovered this century, the tomb was intact and contained fine funerary equipment including the queen's elegant bed and other furniture; the sarcophagus was also in the tomb, and although the queen's body was not there, the archaeologists discovered her mummified viscera preserved in a special wooden chest. This affords proof that the mummification process, including evisceration and dehydration, had already been developed and was in use at least for members of the royal family by Dynasty 4. Since this tomb had never been plundered, an expla-nation has been sought for the missing body, and it has been suggested that Hetepheres may have been buried originally with her husband Sneferu at Dahshur and that this burial site was later plun-dered and her body destroyed. Cheops may then have ordered the remainder of her funerary goods, perhaps providing her with addi-tional equipment, to be re-buried secretly at Gizeh, near his own pyramid; the viscera were perhaps overlooked in the tomb-plun-dering and were then transferred to the new site.

Other members of his family were buried in the fields of mastaba-tombs which occupied the areas to the east and west of Cheops' pyramid. The main branches of the family were buried here, being descendants of his wives and concubines, and he was surrounded in death by his favoured courtiers as he had been in life. The pyramid overshadows the rows of tombs and symbolises the gulf which existed between the god-king and even his closest relatives and honoured courtiers. Cheops' pyramid has aroused the interest and speculation of both ancient and modern travellers, and a succession of Classical, Arab and European visitors have paused to wonder at his great monument and to record their impressions and observations for future generations. This pyramid, as all others, had the simple and basic function of protecting the king's body, but for some people, such a straightforward explanation has been inadequate and they have sought to produce fantastic theories linking it with astrological and other lore.

The pyramid was, however, a quite inadequate concept for protecting the burial, and despite various changes in design including the removal of the burial chamber from the substructure to the interior of the pyramid, robbers still succeeded in entering and plundering the king's burial place. In front of the funerary area, land was set aside for the Pyramid City which was designed to house the funerary priests who attended to the tombs, brought offerings, and recited the mortuary liturgy in the temple for the king. These men and their families enjoyed exemption from taxation and were supported by endowments of agricultural land presented to them by the king. The tombs of the king and his courtiers were regarded as a great city of the dead and also required provisioning with food and drink; again, the king supported these from his bounty. The whole area rapidly became a great economic drain on the royal resources and presented considerable problems of organisation and maintenance. Unique in size and design, this great complex was never completed, and the purity of its concept was soon confused when, in Dynasties 5 and 6, the later smaller mastabas of the necropolis officials and mortuary priests were built between the original rows of tombs. This was compounded when, in Dynasty 26, believing proximity to the Gizeh pyramids conferred special benefits, others also constructed their tombs there.

Cheops' achievement was never surpassed in size or magnificence, although his son, Chephren, built his own pyramid next to that of his father. This still retains some of its outer limestone capping and the complex is the best preserved example of its kind. Some disturbance seems to have arisen at Cheops' death and his designated heir, Prince Kawab, was probably murdered by an usurper, Djedefre'. He was not buried at Gizeh, but started a new cemetery at Abu Roash, some miles away. Djedefre' himself may have met a violent end, and one of Cheops' sons, Chephren, claimed the throne and returned to Gizeh for burial.

His complex is modest by comparison with that of his father and

Figure 5 Figure showing various stages in the preparation and equipment of a mummy.

it did not include a family cemetery, his queens and children being buried in rock-cut tombs to the east of his pyramid. All the main features of a fully developed standard pyramid complex can nevertheless be seen most clearly here. In order to facilitate the king's ascent to heaven, it was essential that the correct rituals were performed at the time of burial; the body had to be preserved and reinvigorated for the king's use throughout eternity. Food offerings, on a regular and perpetual basis, had to be presented to the king at his funerary complex to sustain his spirit, and to accommodate these functions, the pyramid complex contained a sequence of important buildings.

Each pyramid was built on the edge of the desert but the adjoining buildings linked it with the river's edge, which not only enabled building materials to be conveyed to the site by river during the period of construction but also provided a landing stage for the funeral procession and for the subsequent food supplies. Each part of the complex played an important role in the funerary rites, but it is often difficult to determine the exact ritual purpose of some of these areas. The Valley Building, situated on the edge of the river, where the king's body was first received into the complex, may have been used for the royal embalming and purification rites, but it is possible that, although the rites were symbolically enacted here, the actual procedure of mummification was carried out elsewhere in a more temporary building, before the mummy was conveyed into the Valley Building.

It was during the early part of the Old Kingdom that the process known today as mummification – the preservation of the body by chemical means – was apparently first introduced, although its use was at first limited to members of the royal family. The nobility continued to simulate the contours of the body with stiffened pads and bandages, a practice employed for royalty in the earlier dynasties.

Mummies from later periods provide information relating to the procedure, although written accounts of the techniques involved have never been found in Egyptian literary sources. The most complete account of mummification is given in the writings of two Greek historians, Herodotus, who lived in the 5th century BC and Diodorus Siculus, who was writing some 400 years later. Herodotus described three methods available at the time when he was writing, and these will be considered in more detail below, but the most expensive and elaborate method which he describes was based on the technique devised and developed for preserving the bodies of Old Kingdom royalty thousands of years earlier.

First, the viscera were removed from the body through an incision made in the side of the abdomen; only the heart and the kidneys were left inside the body, the heart probably because it was considered to be the seat of the intellect and the emotions and the kidneys perhaps because their situation made them relatively inaccessible to the embalmer. The organs were then cleaned and dehydrated with natron. They were placed inside a box known as a canopic chest, although in other periods they were sometimes wrapped and either replaced in the abdominal or thoracic cavities, or placed in canopic jars, or laid on the legs of the mummy. After evisceration, the body was cleansed and rinsed, and the abdominal and thoracic cavities were packed with various packages containing spices to retain the bodily shape, and then it was preserved by a process of rapid dehydration. The sand which had produced this effect to a greater or lesser degree in the earliest pit-graves was now replaced as a dehydrating agent by natron, which is a salt mixture occurring in natural deposits. The natron contains a large proportion of sodium carbonate (washing soda) and sodium bicarbonate (baking soda), and sodium chloride and sodium sulphate are also present as impurities. Desiccation probably took some forty days to complete, and up to another thirty days were occupied with religious rites. Recent experiments support the belief that the body was not immersed and soaked in a natron bath but was placed between layers of dry natron. The body was removed from the natron bed, washed again to remove any remaining natron, and then tightly wrapped in layers of fine linen bandaging. Protective amulets were inserted between the bandages to assist the deceased on his final journey.

Once the body was preserved, it was necessary to perform upon it or a substitute statue the rite known as the 'Ceremony of Opening the Mouth'. This eventually came to be used for non-royal persons, as well as in connection with two- and three-dimensional art representations of the human being. The Egyptians believed that this ceremony would restore to the body (or statue or wall-relief) the life-force and would provide it again with the faculties of a living person. The ceremony involved censing, sprinkling with water, and touching the mouth, hands and feet of the mummy or figure with an adze to enable the spirit of the deceased to re-enter the body and to partake of the food-offerings. Twenty-three statues of Chephren were discovered standing around the walls of the T-shaped hall in his Valley Temple, and this ritual may have been performed on these statues at the time of his funeral.

The king's body was then taken along the roofed causeway which linked the Valley Building with the Mortuary Temple. This passageway was entirely enclosed to protect his body from contact with the outer world for, once the funerary procession had entered the complex, only the mortuary priests and highest officials were deemed sufficiently ritually 'pure' to see the final mysteries.

The final stages of the rites were performed in the mortuary temple which adjoined the pyramid; it had an entrance hall, an open court, five niches for statues, magazines for the storage of reserve food supplies and utensils, and a sanctuary with a false door in its west wall. Here, on a low altar, the priests made daily offerings to the king's spirit. The mortuary temple had two main functions – as an offering chapel for use after the king's death, and also to accommodate an important set of rites at his funeral when two sets of burial customs associated with the ancient cities of Sais and Buto were performed before the body was transferred to the burial chamber within the pyramid. The complex thus provided a sacred area, totally isolated from the outside world, where access was restricted to the priests. Other features of the Chephren complex included five boat-pits cut in the rock, and the unique Great Sphinx. This was carved from a natural outcrop of rock and given the body of a crouching lion and a human head, the features of which were said to resemble the face of the king. The original significance of the sphinx at this site, if it had any purpose other than to disguise this rocky protuberance, is now lost but it later came to be regarded as the guardian of the funerary area.

Mycerinus, Chephren's son and successor, was the last king to build a pyramid at Gizeh. It is smaller in size than its neighbours and was constructed of inferior materials when it was completed by the next king, Shepseskaf. This king, perhaps in an attempt to break the power of Re''s priesthood, broke with tradition and built not a pyramid but a variant of the mastaba-tomb, which is known today as the Mastabat Fara'un.

The kings of the next dynasty revived the custom of pyramid-building and moved the royal cemetery to Abusir and Saqqara. Their pyramids show marked differences from those of Dynasty 4, and probably reflect the general political and economic pressures of the time. The king's pyramid is no longer surrounded by a family cemetery; the tombs of relatives and courtiers in Dynasties 5 and 6 are arranged in more independent groups scattered over the necropolis area. Also, the standard of construction seen in the royal pyramids is markedly inferior to those of earlier periods; instead of solid internal construction, the core of small stones is now bonded with a mortar of Nile mud. Originally cased in Tura limestone, this

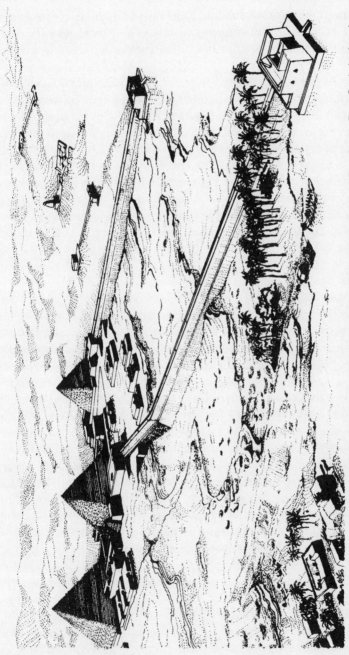

Figure 6 Reconstruction drawing of the pyramid complexes at Abusir (adapted from L. Borchadt, *Das Grabdenkmal des Konigs Ne-user-re'*, Leipzig, 1907, pl. 1).

has since been removed as building material by more recent generations, and the poorly constructed core is now exposed and shows
signs of such deterioration that these pyramids resemble piles of
rubble.

The first king of Dynasty 5, Userkaf, built his pyramid at Saqqara,
but those of Sahure, Neferirkare and Niuserre were constructed on
a plateau at the edge of the desert at Abusir. The temples of these
complexes were decorated with fine reliefs, but it is apparent that
resources had been devoted to the sun-temples at Abu Gurob rather
than to the kings' own funerary monuments. In the period which
followed, the decline in royal power and depleted resources ensured
that pyramid-building ceased, and although it was revived during
the Middle Kingdom for a short period, the kings were never again
able to equal the scope or magnificence of the early Old Kingdom
burial places.

The Pyramid Texts

As the kings of Dynasty 5 and the succeeding period built less elaborate tombs, they came to rely increasingly on magical means of
gaining entry to the celestial hereafter. During Dynasty 5 the spells
known collectively as the 'Pyramid Texts' were first inscribed on the
interior walls of their pyramids. These texts form the earliest body
of written material in the world, and it is generally assumed that they
represent a compilation of various elements from different periods.
They contain fragments of myths and legends, astronomy,
cosmology, geography, historical references, rituals and festivals,
magic and morals; essentially, they sought to provide spells giving
every possible means of access – wings, steps and ramps – by which
the king could reach heaven. The plundering of earlier tombs and
pyramids and the increasing economic problem of provisioning
royal burial places probably prompted the Egyptians to resort to
these magical formulae for protection and to guarantee the king's rebirth and resurrection. The king's immortality and survival were also
affirmed in the texts; in some instances, the gods were asked for assistance, and in others the king asserts his own strength. The most
famous example of this occurs in the so-called 'Cannibalistic Hymn',
which describes how the king devours the gods in order to gain their
powers for himself; an extract from this is given in Appendix A2.

It has been suggested that the texts are arranged in an arbitrary manner and that there was no attempt on the part of the compilers to order them systematically, or to clarify and amend features which are sometimes contradictory. This would accord with the Egyptian belief that all magic was potent and that such a collection of spells would enhance the efficacy of the magic. In this context, they would not have seen any benefit in organising the material to create a coherent body of texts. As with other areas of Egyptian religion, earlier concepts were retained and incorporated to provide as many avenues of approach as possible.

The texts were probably compiled some time between Dynasties 3 and 5, and provide one of the most important and comprehensive sources of early Egyptian belief. The texts were prepared by the priests of Heliopolis and the spells almost certainly embody at least three different elements. Older beliefs from the predynastic period are evident, originating as oral traditions which were then perhaps written on ostraca before their final incorporation in the Pyramid Texts. These refer to features of ancient kingly ritual, to the hostilities predating the unification of the Two Lands, and to the Cannibal Hymn in which mention is made of the practice of assembling the bones of the deceased – a custom which must have predated the first attempts at mummification in the Archaic Period.

Most of the spells fall into the second category and reflect elements of the royal celestial afterlife. It is possible that two important doctrines had merged at an early date, facilitated by their basic similarities. These were the stellar and solar cults, in which the king was identified as a star or was associated with Re'. The possibility that the absorption of a star-cult into the solar cult may be reflected in the architectural features of the step pyramids and the true pyramids has already been considered, and some of the Old Kingdom pharaohs may have attempted to assert their independence of the cult of Re' by breaking with the tradition of building true pyramids as tombs. Although the most notable example of such a break is provided by the mastaba-tomb of Shepseskaf, two other kings of Dynasty 4 – Djedefre' and Nebka – also built funerary complexes which may indicate attempts to return to earlier cults.

The third element in the texts reflects the growth of the cult of the god Osiris towards the end of the Old Kingdom. This had developed around the belief that Osiris, personified as an ancient vegetation god as well as king of the underworld, could promise eternity in his realm. At first only available to the king, this afterlife had become attainable to the nobility by the Middle Kingdom, and eventually people of all levels in society could aspire to resurrection after death if they worshipped and believed in Osiris and lived their lives according to a code of ethics. Osiris himself was believed to have been a human ruler who had experienced resurrection after being murdered and dismembered. Even by the end of the Old Kingdom, the cult of Osiris had gained popularity at the expense of Re'; the mythology of the god with its tale of human tragedy and suffering and eventual victory of good over evil had a widespread appeal, whereas the of official cult of Re' with its royal patronage and hier-archical priesthood had less personal impact.

The inclusion of Osirian elements in the Pyramid Texts may indi-cate not only the increased importance of this god but may also suggest that the Osiris cult was becoming an official alternative to the solar cult. However, it is difficult to accept that these official texts reflect any such religious rivalry or controversy, especially since they were first included in the pyramids of Dynasty 5 when the rulers were strong supporters of Re'. There is no other direct evidence that such a dispute affected the stability of the kingship or the state, and indeed, although Re' and Osiris had separate origins, both cults shared important features. They both offered survival after death – in the solar belief, this was symbolised by the daily rebirth of the sun, rising from the horizon after a nightime passed in the underworld, whereas the death and resurrection of Osiris was thought to be reflected in the annual rebirth of the vegetation after the inundation of the Nile had revitalised the parched land. Although Re' remained associated with the king's afterlife, resurrection through Osiris became widely available in the later periods, but both deities reflected the basic Egyptian belief that life, death and rebirth were cyclic and were apparent in the patterns of Nature.

Nevertheless, the two gods eventually developed very different roles, with Re' remaining a royal god associated with the priests of Heliopolis, who was regarded as a god of the living, whereas Osiris came to be seen as the god of the dead who was available and approachable to people throughout Egypt, although he had certain major cult-centres. Part of his considerable appeal was the fact that he could be worshipped as a funerary god by these people while they still retained their attachment to the local gods who had influence primarily over the affairs of the living.

While the Pyramid Texts probably do not reflect any direct

confrontation between Re' and Osiris, they may well indicate a desire on the part of the king, whose own divinity was by now eclipsed by the supremacy of Re' and his priests, to incorporate the Osirian elements in his funerary texts, for these affirmed that, as well as being the son of Re', the king also ruled on earth as the embodiment of Horus, son of Osiris and Isis, and that, upon death, he became Osiris and thus god and judge of the underworld. Therefore, although Re' continued to rule supreme in heaven, according to the Osirian doctrine the king retained undisputed power elsewhere.

Perhaps the best evaluation of the purpose of the Pyramid Texts is the suggestion that they incorporated beliefs and theologies which had never been resolved but that by placing these spells in his tomb, the king could hope to preserve and use for his benefit after death the magical powers which were derived from the various major religious systems.

The spells, placed on the interior walls of the pyramids, were perhaps arranged there in an order which reflected the sequence of part of the funerary service; as the priests passed in procession, bringing the king's body on its final journey to the sarcophagus in the burial chamber, they may have chanted these incantations in the order in which they appear on the walls. It may also have been envisaged that the king could see them and derive power and spiritual sustenance from them as he passed through the corridors and chambers of the pyramid to the burial room.

Unas, last king of Dynasty 5, was the first to place these spells in his pyramid at Saqqara, where they are carved on the walls of the vestibule and also in the burial chamber. They also occur in the pyramids of the Dynasty 6 kings Teti, Pepy I, Merenre' and Pepy II; in those of Pepy II's three queens; and that of Ibi who probably ruled during the First Intermediate Period. Most of the spells were placed in more than one pyramid, but very few are repeated in all the pyramids. Modified versions of these texts occur in later periods; during the Middle Kingdom, texts were inscribed on the coffins of the nobility (and are thus known today as 'Coffin Texts'), and eventually they became even more widely available as the basis for the Theban Book of the Dead. The purpose of these later texts was to ensure the safety of the deceased in his passage from this world to the next, as the Pyramid Texts (which were only used for royal persons in the Old Kingdom) had sought to protect the king. Considerable difficulties have been encountered in translating and understanding the religious content and context of these texts, but they nevertheless remain an invaluable and unparallelled literary source of early belief and practice.

The tombs of the nobility

There can be little doubt that the king's status was becoming increasingly undermined by the second part of Dynasty 5; corresponding with this, the nobility enjoyed a gradual but marked enhancement of their role, with increased opportunities to become even more independent of royal patronage. Nowhere is this better illustrated than in the nobles' tombs which were erected not only in the great royal necropolises but also in the provinces where some of these men held governorships.

The concept of the non-royal tomb remained unchanged from the Archaic Period through to the Old Kingdom. The main functions were still to house the body and the funerary equipment, and to supply a place on earth where daily provisions of food and drink could be brought in order to sustain the spirit or Ka of the deceased. The design included the burial-chamber in the substructure and the location of the tomb was marked by the superstructure where the offering place was also usually situated.

Technical advances (such as, for example, those in brick-making and stoneworking) were first used for the royal tomb, but then by royal favour they were extended to the nobles whose tombs, at least in the early years, clustered around the king's pyramid. Although the nobility were not permitted to construct pyramids, they made every effort to incorporate the new methods in their own tombs, to provide maximum security for the body and tomb equipment and to ensure that the tomb was provisioned in perpetuity. Although the classic mastaba-tomb of Dynasty 4 was still constructed of brick, the great advances in stone-working which had been achieved in pyramid-building from Dynasty 3 onwards, as well as the readily accessible limestone quarries and the availability of superb craftsmen at Memphis, soon encouraged the introduction of stone into the nobles' tombs, where it was used for the offering room and for facing some of the tomb chambers.

The mastaba-tomb continued to be used extensively for nobles' burials in the Old Kingdom; as well as Cheops' 'court' of subsidiary tombs at Gizeh, other similar fields occurred at Saqqara, Dahshur,

Medum and Abu Sir. However, rock-cut tombs, which attempted to maintain the outward appearance of the mastaba-tomb although the chapels were excavated in the solid rock, were introduced at Gizeh as early as the reign of Chephren, and towards the end of the Old Kingdom this type of tomb was increasingly used for the governors' burials in the provinces. As it no longer became imperative that the nobles should be near the king in death, they seized the opportunity to exercise their independence by preparing tombs in their own centres of power; here, they took advantage of the increased area of wall space to extend the decoration of the tombs.

Nevertheless, the mastaba-tomb remained the classic example of the Memphite style and was well designed for its required functions. The substructure continued to house the burial chamber and an access stairway or shaft; down to the end of Dynasty 4, various innovations had been introduced which included a deeper burial chamber reached by means of a larger stairway or passage or a vertical pit. Sometimes a second chamber and shaft were constructed for the burial of the tomb-owner's wife. The access shafts were filled with gravel and rocks and the internal doors were blocked with stone or bricks in an attempt to outwit the tomb-robbers.

Above ground-level was the superstructure which marked and protected the burial. The core was now made of solid masonry or of rubble which was contained within a bench-shaped wall; the brick cells found inside the superstructures of earlier periods had now been discontinued. The panelled brick facade which had once covered the outside of the superstructure was increasingly replaced with smooth limestone facings. Two false doors were set into the east wall of the tomb, intended to provide the deceased's spirit with a means of exit from the burial chamber and access to the food-offerings left daily outside the tomb. These gave the tomb the superficial appearance of a domestic dwelling, and indeed the tomb, known as the 'House of the Ka', was supposed to represent the home of the deceased in his continuing existence. Relief sculpture was used to decorate these false doors as early as Dynasty 2, and the two associated stelae were usually inscribed with the name and titles of the tomb-owner as well as the offering formulae.

Associated with the superstructure – either incorporated within it or added to it – were the offering chapel and the serdab. At first, the brick chapel, taking the form of an open enclosure, was built on to the east wall of the tomb, in front of the southern stela. Later, a flat or vaulted roof and a door were added, probably to protect the inner walls of the chapel from weathering and destruction, and by the beginning of the Old Kingdom, the complete structure was sometimes incorporated within the superstructure. As the chapel was extended, other compartments, including a vestibule, a portico and storerooms, were added. The serdab (enclosed room) was also included in the superstructure from Dynasty 4 onwards. It was eventually enlarged and also often connected with other parts of the tomb.

The provisioning of a man's tomb was considered essential to the continuation of his life after death. The Egyptian concept of the human personality which was probably formulated during the Old Kingdom included a number of elements. The body provided the essential link between the deceased and his former earthly existence; it enabled him to partake of food and drink and thus to sustain his spirit. The technique of mummification was developed and used for royalty and later for the nobility, to preserve the body from decay and to ensure that a likeness of the deceased survived. Further devices, such as magical formulae and architectural features, were introduced in an attempt to stop the plundering of tombs and their contents; in the event of the destruction of the mummy, statues of the tomb-owner and magical spells were placed in the tomb to provide a secondary method of sustaining the tomb-owner's spirit.

In life, the individual possessed a name by which he was known and which was also regarded as an integral part of his personality; knowledge of a man's name enabled good or evil forces to be directed towards him, and his body or statue were identified by an inscription as part of the funerary procedure. Also, his shadow, believed to be associated in some way with his procreative powers, was regarded as an element of his personality.

Certain forces, however, were considered to be spiritual elements, mainly concerned with a man's immortality. At first, these had belonged only to the gods, but they had then been extended to deified kings, and finally to all Egyptians. It is difficult to define these elements since, in the literary sources, the Egyptians seem to have interpreted them differently according to the context.

The insubstantial part of the personality – the 'Ka' – is perhaps most readily described as the 'spirit', although it was also regarded as the embodiment of the life-force, as the guide and protector of the owner, as well as his double, or the 'self' or personality of the individual which combined all the qualities and characteristics which make each human being unique. It is not clear how the Egyptians envisaged the relationship between a man and his Ka during his lifetime, but at death the Ka was thought to become a free, separate entity which achieved immortality but still played a vital role in the continuing association with earth. Usually depicted as a human with upraised arms, or simply a pair of upraised arms, the Ka was still considered to be dependent upon the body in the tomb, to which it could return to obtain sustenance from the food offerings placed there.

Another element which was believed to survive death was the 'Ba', which is loosely translated as 'soul'. Depicted as a human-headed bird, the Ba was an animating force which could leave the body and travel outside the tomb to visit places which had been enjoyed by the owner during his lifetime. Thus, the deceased had the ability to continue his association with favourite haunts. Finally, another element – the 'Akh' – was a supernatural power or force which could assist the individual after death.

Continuance of life after death was dependent upon the correct performance of the funerary rituals and upon the provision of all material needs. The 'Opening of the Mouth' ceremony, performed for the king in his mortuary temple, came to be carried out for the nobility and, eventually, for all who could afford an elaborate funeral. This ritual, it was believed, restored the life-force and the senses to the body of the deceased.

The provisioning of the tomb with food and drink was the duty of a man's heir and his descendants. However, this duty became increasingly difficult to perform for successive generations, and neglect of the tomb often ensued, threatening the Ka with starvation. Other methods of ensuring a food supply were gradually adopted and indicate that the procedure was considered to be of the utmost importance to the well-being and continuance of the deceased.

A custom was introduced whereby a Ka-priest was employed to place the daily provisions on the flat altar-table in the tomb-chapel and to recite the necessary prayers. A piece of land was set aside by the tomb-owner or by the king on his behalf and the produce from this estate was used not only to provision the tomb but also to provide payment in kind for the priest and his descendants who were expected to take on the commitment in perpetuity. Theoretically, such an endowment could be regarded as a guarantee that the Ka

would obtain eternal sustenance, but after a couple of generations
had elapsed, the priests often neglected their duties and other
methods of supplying food had to be devised.

Unlike the king, who was expected to enjoy his eternity in the
heavens, the nobility hoped to continue their existence on earth,
passing time in the tomb with access to the possessions and experi-
ences which had made life so pleasurable. This continued existence
was, however, expected to be free from danger, illness and worry.
From earliest times, the Egyptians had placed funerary goods in the
graves for the use of the deceased, but by the time of the Old
Kingdom, the contents and decoration of the nobles' tombs were
designed as a total concept, with the aim of obtaining the desired
hereafter for the deceased. The funerary service, and especially the
ceremony of Opening the Mouth, were believed to animate not only
the body but also all the statues, models, and wall scenes in the tomb
to provide for the needs of the deceased.

Aspects of his life which he had loved and enjoyed – his family,
his professional status, a fine house and estate with many servants,
and activities such as hunting, fowling, fishing and banqueting -
could be represented in the tomb by substitutes. These were either
objects used in life, such as clothing, tools and weapons, games, and
furniture, or models of servants or a boat to transport him on the
Nile. Increasingly, throughout the Old Kingdom, scenes carved and
painted on the walls of the tomb depicted the events which the
owner wished to enjoy. The scenes were augmented by inscriptions
which conferred benefits on the owner and often helped to guard
him against danger.

The most important scenes related to the production and provision of food; harvesting, slaughtering, brewing and baking were all
shown and an offering list was provided with the formula which
would ensure an abundance of food for the tomb-owner.
Accompanying the menu, there is often a scene showing the tomb-
owner seated at a table piled high with food. By including such
scenes, the Egyptians were able to provide a substitute source of food
for the deceased by means of magic and to lessen his reliance upon
either his family or the Ka-priest.

The decoration of the nobles' tombs can be traced from Dynasty
4 tombs at Gizeh; here, it was generally limited to the outer rooms
of the chapel and not placed in the offering chamber. In the early
part of Dynasty 5, the decoration and subject matter remained

simple and limited in scope, but later in the dynasty, the chapels became more complex and the number of rooms was increased; daily life scenes were now introduced into the interior chapel. A fine example of a tomb of this period is that attributed to Ti at Saqqara.

By Dynasty 6, the mastaba-tombs in the vicinity of Teti's pyramid show the development of multiple-roomed chapels which occupy a large area of the interior of the superstructure. An excellent tomb of this style is that of Mereruka at Saqqara, where a whole series of apartments were provided for the owner, his wife and son. The burial chamber is also painted now and the reliefs are bolder than in Dynasty 5 and include an offering list in addition to scenes showing the owner and his family engaged in aspects of everyday life.

The provincial governors of Dynasties 5 and 6 adopted the style of the decorated rock-cut tombs which had originated towards the end of Dynasty 4 at Gizeh. They built these tombs in their own provinces, high in the cliffs on the edge of the desert. In Upper Egypt, from the latter part of the Old Kingdom into the First Intermediate Period, they retained in these tombs the feature of the painted burial chamber. From Dynasty 6, two basic traditions persisted in the reliefs in the provincial tombs: the old traditions established at Memphis in the heyday of its glory continued, but with a diminished standard of craftsmanship, at such centres as Meir, Deshasheh, Deir el-Gebrawi, Naga ed-Der, Beni Hasan, and Akhmim, while in the lower class tombs of Dynasty 6 and increasingly during the First Intermediate Period, a second style developed. This was characterised by figures which were cruder and more angular in execution than those of the Memphite tradition, and occurred in tombs at Naga ed-Der, Sheikh Faras, Deir el Melek, Luxor, Edfu and Aswan. Nevertheless, it was the traditional Memphite style which established the pattern for all later tomb decoration and which best illustrates the principles which underlay religious art in Egypt.

Tomb art – the underlying principles

Unlike certain other early civilisations, the Egyptians enjoyed a predictable climate which displayed few freak storms or violent contrasts; the environment also held few surprises, with a landscape which is perhaps most remarkable for the regularity and even monotony of its main features. The art forms reflect the permanence and repetition which the Egyptians saw around them. The art of the Old Kingdom in particular displays the qualities of assurance and serenity; coupled with high standards of technical excellence, these attributes ensured that the art of this period approached most closely to the Egyptians' concept of perfection. The traditions were now established and successive generations sought to emulate the style and, although there were superficial changes at a later date, there was no real attempt to discover fundamentally new forms. The only significant break with tradition occurred during the religious revolution of Pharaoh Akhenaten towards the end of Dynasty 18.

Apprentices in later periods were trained on Old Kingdom models and there was no desire to improve upon the work of earlier artists. The artist worked to a set of principles imposed by religious belief, and although high standards were required in his technical skills, he was not expected to produce imaginative or original work. Nevertheless, in the achievements of the finest artists, they attained a level of excellence which places their work on a par with the masterpieces of other ages, although this is still produced within the framework of religious principles.

The artists were usually anonymous, working as members of a team whose task was to supply the tomb-owner with a magical substitute for the next world. The tomb reliefs or statues were not placed there either to beautify the building or to provide spiritual ecstasy but to preserve and sustain the existence of the tomb-owner by imitating as effectively as possible certain aspects of his life. The artist was a state official, employed to perform a task in much the same way as a fellow-technician – whether he was a carpenter, stonemason, quarryman or smith – was required to carry out his work. No special status or temperament was attributed to the artists, although the best were obviously in great demand both for their official work and for private commissions which would help to augment their income

In the Old Kingdom artists were employed by the king to equip and to decorate his tomb; according to the king's wishes, they could then be made available for this purpose to other members of the royal family or to favoured courtiers and nobles. These men served an apprenticeship, learning their skills by copying models and acquiring competence in certain basic and repetitive skills. The tomb was decorated by a team, each man being specialised in an aspect

Figure 7 *Tomb scenes showing food presentation*
Registers of wall scenes in tombs of all periods showed the production of food and its presentation to the tomb-owner. This was intended to ensure his food supply even when the duty of offering food at the tomb was neglected. Here, bearers bring cakes, fowl, fruit, vegetables and flowers.

of the work, under the supervision of the Master Artist. The tomb-owner, probably in consultation with the Master Artist, would select the series of scenes which he wished to be placed in his tomb from a set of subjects, and preliminary sketches would then be prepared on papyrus before the scenes were transferred to the tomb walls where they were outlined in ink. In the Old Kingdom, the most important necropolises were near to local quarries which produced excellent stone; it was possible to use this to face the internal walls of the tomb and to carve the scenes on it in low relief before the paint was applied to the walls. Later, in the New Kingdom, the main burial site at Thebes did not have access to fine-quality limestone and the local mudstone was so inferior that it was not carved but the scenes were painted on top of the prepared wall surface.

The preliminary sketches were drawn up according to a system which incorporated the traditional canon of proportions; this ensured that the proportions of the human figure were always constant in relation to each other, although these could be increased or decreased accordingly to change the overall size of the figure. In the Old Kingdom the system was simple – a series of guide-lines ran through the main points on the body - although by the New Kingdom a more elaborate grid system was employed. Towards the end of Dynasty 3 and the beginning of Dynasty 4, the fully developed wall composition of the Old Kingdom is evident, showing a large figure (the tomb-owner) dominating a series of horizontal registers occupied by subsidiary figures. Although no earlier examples have been found, this type of composition may in fact date from the end of Dynasty 2. The only large wall decoration which dates to the predynastic period, and which was discovered in a tomb at Hieraconpolis, is quite different, having small, scattered groups of figures instead of clearly defined registers.

The tomb of Ti at Saqqara presents a good introduction to the general layout and decoration of an elaborate Old Kingdom tomb. Ti was a wealthy nobleman, favoured by the king, and his tomb reflects his obvious success and status in life. It consists of a columned courtyard with a subterranean passageway leading to the inner chambers, an entrance passage, and an offering chapel with an adjoining serdab where Ti's statue was placed to look out through three slits in the wall on to the food offerings.

Some variation occurs in the wall decoration of nobles' tombs in the different dynasties, but in any tomb it is possible to discern a pattern which will incorporate offering scenes; activities on the owner's estate – harvesting, agriculture, herding cattle, marshalling wild and domestic animals, dairy work, and bird-netting; the pastimes of the owner, including hunting birds and spearing fish in a papyrus swamp, hunting wild animals in the desert, or occasionally being carried around the estate in a sedan chair; and finally a large scene showing the various stages in the funeral of the tomb-owner. Frequently, additional scenes are included, showing the activity of the craftsmen preparing the equipment for the tomb and the funerary procession.

On the eastern panel in the passage of Ti's tomb, there is a scene showing one of his statues being drawn along on a sledge by seven men; another man runs ahead of the sledge and pours a liquid under the runners to ease its passage. In the Offering Chamber, a variety of activities are depicted: on the South Wall, at the east end, a large figure of Ti is shown seated on a chair under which is his pet dog; he is accompanied by the much smaller figure of his wife who sits on the ground and clasps her husband's leg in a gesture of affection. The four horizontal registers over which Ti presides are occupied with workmen pursuing various tasks: in the upper register, goldsmiths are engaged in various processes of their craft; the second register shows a sculptor's workshop and a vase-maker; in the third register, carpenters and cabinet-makers ply their trades; and in the lowest register, there are several market scenes as well as other craftsmen including a tanner and a cylinder-seal manufacturer. This scene provides a good example of a convention which had become established by the Old Kingdom: the size of each figure indicated the status of the individual, and thus the tomb-owner was always the largest figure in a scene, followed by the figures of his wife and his children who, even if they had reached adulthood, were shown as infants with characteristic nudity and the plait of hair at the side of the head which was known as the 'Sidelock of Youth'. This hairstyle was worn until puberty. Servants, farm-labourers and other subordinates were represented on a smaller scale, often arranged as here in registers, to indicate their comparative insignificance. Thus the customary principle of perspective - that the largest figure in a scene is the one nearest to the viewer and the smallest one is most distant – is ignored in Egyptian tomb art in favour of a concept based on Egyptian religious belief.

Again, another use of the register in tomb art, where the available wall space was necessarily limited, was to show a sequence of action; the accompanying inscriptions, in addition to identifying the scene, also often give the conversational remarks of those depicted.

Animals and birds occur in the scenes in the centre of the South Wall; in the two upper registers, oxen are being led by a herdsman while in the lower register, men herd cranes. On the North Wall, the centre relief shows the traditional hunting scene; Ti stands in a boat and, accompanied by the smaller figures of the boatmen, he engages in a hippopotamus hunt. The location of this activity is set by the inclusion in the scene of the River Nile, teeming with many varieties of fish, and an assortment of birds and animals in a thicket of papyrus reeds. This was the method by which the Egyptian artist indicated background scenery; there is usually a tree or section of blue water to represent the environment, but no attempt to paint the features of the landscape in any greater detail. Again, the figures themselves are treated in a similar manner, almost as theatrical 'props'; they are shown performing duties or tasks or participating in some event, but the artist does not try to convey any display of emotion in the facial features of the men and women. Their expressions are stereotyped and there is no attempt to relate the thoughts or feelings of one figure to those of his neighbour.

The main aim was to provide a diagrammatic scene of a place, object or situation; this was based on what the artist knew to exist and not on his visual perception from any given standpoint. By creating such a scene, the desired object or activity could be 'brought to life' for the benefit or enjoyment of the deceased. When these principles were carried to extremes, however, the Egyptians produced some bizarre representations not only of the human figure but also of the surrounding scenery.

Since it was believed that the 'diagrams' in the scenes could be activated and turned into reality, the figures represented on the tomb walls always exhibited certain peculiarities. The important persons – the tomb-owner and his family – are therefore always represented as men and women who are young, without physical abnormality or imperfection, and with indistinguishable 'idealised' faces which conformed to the existing concept of beauty. Only the accompanying inscriptions distinguish the individual and give him identity after death. The body is shown held in a stiff, formalised manner; the head is in profile but only one eye is indicated, with the pupil positioned centrally; the torso is presented frontally, but the legs and

Figure 8   *Tomb scenes showing preparation for a banquet*
Wall scenes showed the upper classes attending banquets, a favourite
occupation enjoyed in life which they hoped to continue in the next world.
Here, servants (left) prepare their mistresses for the banquet, presenting
them with floral wreaths.

feet are in profile, with one foot in front of the other. This pose was
physically impossible, but the human figure was represented in this
way to ensure that it could be used to maximum effect when it was
magically activated by the tomb-owner. However, if the laws of
perspective had been observed, much of the symbolic power of the
body would have been lost; certain features such as the nose and the
feet would have appeared flattened and foreshortened if they had
been painted frontally, but others, such as the torso and arms, were
shown this way in order to ensure that, when the figure was 'brought
to life', the full strength of these parts could be revitalised. Following
the concept that this was a plan of the body, only one eye or breast
was indicated, with the assumption that both would be restored in
reality. Thus, in order to recreate a complete three-dimensional

figure or object with all the powers and functions of the original when the inanimate scene was magically imbued with life, the artist was required to show as many facets of the form as possible.

This principle was extended further: the contents of baskets and dishes were shown piled up on top of their containers, and houses and buildings, lakes and gardens were given in a diagrammatic form so that the fruit and vegetables as well as the containers would 'come to life', and three-dimensional buildings rather than their facades would be magically recreated. Similarly, the Nile was never represented by a thin blue line in the distance, as it would have been according to the principles of perspective, but was always shown in section, teeming with fish, so that when the scene was reactivated, the tomb-owner would be supplied with an eternal and ample catch of fish.

The lower register shows a procession of women bringing produce from Ti's estate to provision his tomb; this continues along the lower register of the West Wall. Above this another scene depicts herdsmen directing oxen, cows and a calf across a ford and protecting them from lurking crocodiles. In the upper register a cow-herd assists at the birth of a calf. Above the entrance in the North Wall there are two registers where we see herdsmen directing oxen, cows and a calf across a ford and driving a flock of rams. The East Wall is occupied in the north half with a number of harvesting scenes in the presence of Ti and his wife, while in the south half, a series of scenes illustrates a shipyard and the stages in building and assembling a ship.

The Egyptian artist was an accurate observer of animals and birds, noting the finest details of marking and colouring; in the reliefs, he was able to translate this knowledge into an imaginative treatment of the fauna which surrounded him. In these representations, the artist was at his best, untrammelled by the artistic conventions, and the birds and animals provide a marked contrast with the formal and stereotyped human figures. However, even in relation to the representation of the human figure, there were degrees of formality; figures of important personages, whether they were deities, royalty or tomb-owners, were treated in accordance with strict principles and conventions, whereas less important figures, such as those of servants and labourers, were often represented more naturalistically as some of the rigorous traditions were relaxed. This sometimes produced spontaneous and delightful results and from these minor subjects and from other secular art forms, we can gain an idea of the humorous approach which the artists adopted towards their work. The private tombs of the nobles provide a wealth of detail relating to the daily life not only of the nobility but also of the servants and subordinates who worked for them.

The decline of the Old Kingdom

The well-ordered and stable society which appears in the tomb reliefs was not destined to survive. In Dynasty 6 there was a gradual decline in the power and wealth of the king; pyramid-building was already declining in standards and the royal solar temples which had flourished in Dynasty 5 were no longer being erected, probably as the result of economic rather than religious factors. With the death of Pepy II at the end of Dynasty 6, there came a period of disorder and disillusionment when the beliefs and ideals which the Egyptians held most dear were threatened and the structure of this seemingly stable society crumbled and disintegrated. Outwardly, however, the rulers of Dynasty 6 were still prosperous; Egyptian power expanded in Nubia and the governors of Elephantine extended their control as far south as the Second Cataract, while in the north, trading contacts were increased with countries which bordered the Mediterranean. However, it was internal frictions, present for generations in the structure of the administration and in the fabric of society, which finally precipitated the disintegration and collapse. Social, economic and religious factors all contributed to the dissolution of the Old Kingdom.

The status and role of the king were central to the problem. At first, every effort was made to emphasise the chasm which was believed to exist between the king and his subjects. He married a royal princess so that the divinity of the line would be preserved; he was regarded as partly divine – a man who could nevertheless approach the gods as an equal; his burial in a pyramid, where he was surrounded by his 'court' of nobles in mastaba-tombs, underlined his unique destiny and individual eternity. Only through the king's bounty could the nobles hope to gain any chance of eternity, and they were dependent upon him for the gift of a tomb and of land from the royal estates which would provide food offerings for the tomb. The king's absolute power reached its zenith in Dynasty 4, epitomised in the great funerary complex of Cheops at Gizeh.

However, from Dynasty 4 onwards, there was a gradual equali-
sation of wealth, for over a period of years the king's economic
policies had had a disastrous result. Although in theory he owned
Egypt and all its people, resources and possessions, in practice this
great royal estate was gradually eroded as it was passed into other
hands. The crown land, presented to favourite nobles for the provisioning of their tombs and the maintenance of their Ka-priests, was
a continuous drain on royal resources. This land was also usually free
from taxation, further depleting the royal income, and as the circle
of inheritance widened, these estates were broken down into increasingly small units.

In addition, the expense involved in building and maintaining
each new pyramid complex was considerable; each funerary monument had its own endowment and had to employ and support a staff
of priests. Every king inherited the burden not only of providing his
own burial-place, but also of repairing and provisioning those of his
ancestors. He was also required to make gifts of tombs to members
of his family and to the great nobles at his court.

From Dynasty 4 onwards, royal decrees were published which
exempted from payment of tax and from drafts of enforced labour
not only the possessions and personnel of the pyramid mortuary
temples and nearby residence cities, but also the tombs and Ka-
priesthoods associated with the nobility.

As the king's economic power declined and the importance of the
nobility grew, the reversed situation was reflected in their burial
places. The royal pyramids, constructed now of inferior materials,
diminished in size, while the tombs of the nobles became larger and
more elaborate in design. The services of the best craftsmen were
employed in decorating these tombs with fine reliefs and in equipping them with superb statuary and funerary goods. Gradually, the
nobles who held governorships in the provinces preferred to be
buried in tombs in their own localities instead of at the foot of the
royal pyramid. This further emphasised their growing independence
and the impending collapse of the centralised government.

The nobles had come to regard the kings as less than divine. The
depleted economic resources of the royal family had encouraged
and perhaps forced the king to marry outside his immediate family
circle, and from the end of Dynasty 4, an increasing number of
marriages took place between the king and members of the wealthy

but non-royal nobility. As a result, the fiction of the king's divinity and his fundamental difference from his subjects could no longer be sustained; increasingly he came to be regarded as just one of many rulers who exercised power over a limited area of the country.

In addition, the absolute dominion and divinity of the ruler had been undermined by the powerful cult of the sun-god Re'. This deity was adopted as the great royal patron and state god, and the endowments and privileges of tax exemption which benefited the nobility and the funerary establishments were gradually extended to the god's temples. These centres and their priesthoods thus became wealthy and powerful but this was again achieved at the expense of the king. In particular, the Heliopolitan priesthood gained ascendancy and by some means, perhaps by supporting one line of prospective rulers against another, they were able to reduce the status of the kings of Dynasty 5 so that they were subordinate to Re' and accepted the title and role of "Son of Re'" whereas previously they had exercised their own divine power and equality.

The independence of the nobility was further enhanced by a change in policy in Dynasty 5 in the appointment of officials. The highest administrative posts were now no longer reserved for the king's relatives, and many men of non-royal birth were appointed. At first, these posts had been granted as signs of the king's personal favour, on a temporary basis or for the lifetime of the official. The king had thus aimed to win the loyalty of these men who were dependent upon his goodwill. However, the appointments to provincial governorships gradually became hereditary and the nobles no longer regarded themselves as beholden to the king. Economically and politically they no longer felt committed to him; his court at Memphis was distant from many of their provinces and he could no longer retain their allegiance either by threats of force or by termination of their appointments. The nomarchs (governors of these 'nomes' or provinces) came to exercise almost princely powers in their regions and no longer wished to be buried near to the king. By the end of the Old Kingdom, the process of decentralisation had advanced to the state where the country had virtually returned to the political situation which had existed before Menes united all regions under one control. Once again local rulers, supreme in their own areas, formed alliances and fought against each other.

Pepy I tried to win back the allegiance of the Upper Egyptian nomarchs by giving them titles, and by choosing his viziers from amongst the ranks of the provincial nobility. However, the measures gave only a temporary respite and the final collapse was inevitable. By the end of Dynasty 6, external threats to peace and security were also present; the Beduin nomads on Egypt's north-eastern border raided and infiltrated the country, doubtless encouraged by the internal weaknesses. This further undermined the king's ability to provide a strong, centralised state. The problem was finally exacerbated by the weak and ineffectual rulership which the reign of Pepy II would have produced. This king came to the throne as a young child and ruled for over ninety years. The seeds of destruction which had lain dormant within the system for so long finally flourished, destroying the finely balanced structure of the society and ushering in a period of turmoil and disaster.

3

The First Intermediate Period and the Middle Kingdom

Collapse of the society

The events which overtook Egypt at the end of Dynasty 6 are probably recalled in a text which is often referred to as the 'Admonitions of a Prophet'. In this a wise man named Ipuwer appears at the court of a king who is almost certainly the aged ruler Pepy II. The king, secure in his palace, is unaware of the dangers confronting his country, and Ipuwer describes the horrors that prevail, urging the king to combat them before it is too late. The extract from this text (given in Appendix A2) provides a vivid account of the situation in which the order of the Old Kingdom is overturned: the rich and the poor find their roles reversed; violence, robbery and murder are widespread, and people endure famine and disease. The government is harassed by foreign mercenary troops and the Beduin endanger Egypt's borders. The people themselves threaten the administration which gradually disintegrates, causing internal disorder and the termination of Egypt's once flourishing foreign trade. Here we have a picture of a society collapsing from within, where law and order are replaced by chaos, and neglect of the irrigation system brings about famine and economic disaster. Thieves and murderers take advantage of the social collapse to strike terror in the hearts of their countrymen.

The very people who had so wished to prolong the joys of life and to extend them beyond death now questioned the values of their lives and their society. As the god-king and the royal family fell into oblivion at Memphis and the provincial nobles seized power throughout the land, the accepted traditions and religious beliefs of the Old Kingdom were questioned and often discarded. In the

'Admonitions of a Prophet' the Egyptians are driven to wish that they had never been born, and to regard death as a welcome oblivion. However, peace could not even be found in death, for the materials were no longer available to provide fine burials, and the plundering of the great tombs and the destruction of bodies were frequent occurrences.

From this period a poem is preserved which is justifiably famous in Egyptian literature, for not only is its theme unique but it convincingly expresses the self-doubt and self-examination which the devastation inspired. The text is often referred to as the 'Dispute with his Soul of One who is Tired of Life'. It takes the form of a dialogue between a man and his soul; the man, weary of his existence, contemplates suicide – a possibility which was quite alien to the Egyptian mind in more secure and stable periods. It would have been unthinkable that such a literary composition could be written during the Old Kingdom, expressing the doubts felt by one man concerning his existence and his despair as he considered ending his life. The man's soul, however (regarded in the poem as a separate entity which stood apart from its owner), decides to leave the man because it does not wish to face the hardships it will invariably suffer after the man's death if no tomb is prepared and no food offerings are available. The poem (extracts from the text are given in Appendix A2) goes on to relate the man's attempt to persuade his soul to remain at his side; the conditions prevailing in Egypt are described and compared with the benefits which death would bestow. Finally, however, the soul wins the argument and persuades the man to remain alive until death comes naturally to him, so that eventually they may share a prepared resting place for eternity.

It is apparent that the old order had now been swept away. The 'Admonitions' state that the kingship was destroyed – 'Behold, a thing hath been done that happened not aforetime; it has come to this that the king hath been taken away by poor men'. The country was once again divided into warring factions, each under a local ruler, and the political situation must have resembled the conditions of the Predynastic Period. The wealthy found their positions and possessions seized by those of lowly stature, and all the old values were reversed. There is little doubt that the literary sources describe the general chaos and disintegration of Dynasties 7 and 8 when, although some semblance of authority was maintained at Memphis, the centralised government rapidly fell into a state of complete confusion. These dynasties, together with Dynasties 9, 10 and some-times 11, are grouped together and referred to as the 'First Intermediate Period', although Dynasty 11 is sometimes placed in the Middle Kingdom.

The complete collapse of royal authority now led the masses to question the king's divinity and especially his exclusive claim to enjoy the benefits of an individual eternity. A gradual process of democratisation in religious and funerary beliefs and customs occurred. At first, the great nobles who built and equipped their tombs independent of the king's bounty now aspired to individual immortality, but in time, all classes could hope to experience indi-vidual survival after death. This coincided with the emergence of Osiris as the supreme deity of the pantheon. A profound change affected all aspects of the religion, and this period of transformation and experimentation was expressed in the art forms. The perfection of the Memphite art was replaced by a variety of provincial styles. These showed a decline in the standard of craftsmanship, but the literary forms, expressing for the first time the pessimism and self-interrogation which now prevailed, indicate that, through suffering and tribulation, the Egyptians had at last reached maturity.

Restoration of political order

The political events of the next few generations gradually restored stability to Egypt. As in earlier times, one local family seized power and, by a series of alliances and by warfare, sought to bring the divi-sions under one control. Manetho's history indicates that the local rulers of Heracleopolis, some of whom were named Akhtoy, estab-lished their rule in Middle Egypt, between Memphis and Thebes, and formed Dynasties 9 and 10. In this area, they introduced a period of comparative peace, enabling local princes to prepare fine tombs for themselves in the vicinity of their own courts, at such centres as Beni Hasan, Akhmim and El-Bersha. However, this peace was short-lived, for a southerner from Thebes gradually expanded his influence northwards and came into conflict with the Heracleopolitans. This man, Mentuhotep I, was successful in defeating the princes of Heracleopolis and in establishing a strong centralised government. He was able to restore the unity of the land and to bring the warring princes under his control, thus establishing the foundation of the Middle Kingdom. He and his successors ruled

Egypt firmly and wisely throughout Dynasty 11.

Mentuhotep came of a family of Theban princes who traced their ancestry to a noble named Inyotef the Great. It seems that Mentuhotep adopted three different titularies to mark various successful stages in his career, but there has been some confusion as to whether they signify the different stages of his career, or whether they refer to three separate rulers. Mentuhotep I, founder of Dynasty 11, is usually known as Mentuhotep Nebhepetre.

This king first established the dominance of Thebes and raised it from its previous status as an insignificant town with merely local powers to a centre of national importance. This first step was ultimately to transform Thebes into the great capital of Egypt and its empire during the New Kingdom. Mentuhotep's ancestors were buried here, probably in row-tombs in north-western Thebes, and he chose a local site to build his unique pyramid-temple.

Little is known of Mentuhotep's methods of administering Egypt, but the local tombs of the nomarchs continued to be built and there is no evidence to suggest that he made any attempt to abolish the provincial nobility. He effectively gained their allegiance and perhaps reinstated the early Old Kingdom policy of appointing the nomarchs himself on a non-hereditary basis.

The king continued to reside at Thebes, his family home, and he undertook the restoration and improvement of temples at various sites. The neglect and destruction of the earlier period was evident throughout the country, but under his patronage, the arts revived and a new Theban style of art developed which was cruder and more angular than the classical Memphite form, but nevertheless marked the beginning of a distinctive southern school.

This great ruler, whom later generations regarded as the founder of the Middle Kingdom, passed on to his successors – S'ankhkare Mentuhotep II and Nebtowere Mentuhotep III – a country which once again enjoyed peace and stability. However, violent events marked the reign of Mentuhotep III and Egypt's history entered a new phase.

The Middle Kingdom

Mentuhotep III seems to have fallen at the hand of his vizier, a man named Amenemhe, who then seized the throne and, as Amenemmes I, founded Dynasty 12. He and his descendants, a line of determined and brilliant men, ruled over a country which again flourished and prospered and it is to their credit that, through ingenuity and innovation, they overcame the variety of problems which faced this dynasty.

Amenemmes I had usurped the throne, and he and his successors went to considerable lengths to ensure that their rule was accepted and confirmed. Amenemmes I was born the son of a commoner named Sesostris and his mother came from Elephantine in Upper Egypt. His statues suggest that an element of Nubian ancestry can be detected in his features. Lacking any royal blood or any real claim to the throne, he found it necessary to introduce measures to protect his own reign and to ensure a peaceful succession on his death. He transferred the capital from Thebes to a new site in the north from which the country could more easily be governed. Every attempt was made to create new conditions, and officials and artisans were moved from Thebes to the new capital of It-towy which was situated some distance south of Memphis. A new royal burial site was also started at nearby Lisht, where Amenemmes I revived the use of the pyramid for royal burials. Here, once again, the mastaba-tombs and pit-tombs of many of his nobles clustered at the base of his pyramid, but Thebes still retained its position as a great religious centre where the royal funerary temples were still maintained and cemeteries were provided for the burial of those priests and officials who either still worked there or who wished to return from It-towy to Thebes after death.

Amenemmes I also inaugurated a political system which dealt effectively with any attempt to place a rival claimant upon the throne after his death. His son and heir became his co-regent during his lifetime and probably took on some of the royal duties. Although Amenemmes probably died at the hand of a conspirator, the succession was ensured by this system of co-regency and his son Sesostris became king. Co-regencies were adopted by many later rulers as an effective means of securing the continuation of the family line.

The kings of Dynasty 12 found it necessary to deal with the problem posed by the provincial nobility. Amenemmes I, needing the active support of the nomarchs to counteract the dangers inherent in his position as a usurper, sought their allegiance by restoring many of their privileges which Mentuhotep had removed. Mentuhotep had also discarded some of the provincial governorships and again Amenemmes filled these positions with new appointments. The nomarchs were now able to build their tombs using fine materials and skilled craftsmanship and although some were buried near the king, others still elected to have tombs in their own localities; their local courts were reopened; they could both raise troops locally and they could establish the level of taxation on their subjects. They wielded considerable power, although the king monitored their activities and could, when the opportunity arose, demand troops and ships from the nomarchs. Nevertheless, the inherent dangers of independence and military uprising were still present, and a later ruler of Dynasty 12, Sesostris III, found his reign was disrupted by the nomarchs. He took decisive action, depriving the local rulers of their rights and privileges and closing the local courts. The great provincial tombs ceased to be built, and although it remains uncertain how the king achieved his ends, he ensured that the old threat was removed forever. The king was never again undermined by the political strength of the nomarchs. The old system was replaced by a new middle class, comprised mainly of craftsmen, tradesmen and small farmers, who owed a debt of gratitude for their advancement to the king. The new administration was from now on directly responsible to the king and his agent, the vizier.

With characteristic energy, these kings not only restored the systems which had lapsed at the end of the Old Kingdom, but also introduced new ideas and schemes. They renewed trading contacts with areas of Western Asia, particularly with Byblos and Phoenicia, and also with Crete; once again, expeditions set out for Punt in search of the highly valued incense trees which grew there, and the copper and turquoise mines in Sinai were re-opened. However, Egypt's right of access to Nubia, established so that hard stone could be acquired from there, was now barred. A new and more aggressive people had entered Nubia during the troubled period at the end of the Old Kingdom and Egypt now faced a confrontation in this area. The wealth of Nubia was so essential to civilised living in Egypt that the kings adopted a strong, aggressive policy and actively reduced the Nubians to submission. To impress upon them the might and authority of Pharaoh and to ensure the safe passage of the valuable commodities, the Egyptians built a string of large brick fortresses along the river between the cataracts in Nubia. These eventually became permanent stations, staffed by long-serving Egyptians, and they exerted a considerable influence on the surrounding district.

The kings also pursued active policies within Egypt. The efficient irrigation system which had fallen into disrepair in the troubled times was now restored, and Sesostris II and Amenemmes III carried out a great reclamation scheme of the land in the Fayoum basin, around Lake Moeris. There is evidence which indicates that Sesostris II was worshipped as a god in his own lifetime (a rare occurrence in Egypt, although all kings were believed to be part-divine), and that his cult continued into the New Kingdom. As late as the Graeco-Roman period, a legendary 'King Sesostris' was mentioned as the perpetrator of great deeds and although this figure probably combines elements of several famous rulers, there is little doubt that Sesostris II was regarded as one of Egypt's most effective kings. Amenemmes III is also remembered in Classical legend, attributed with the construction of Lake Moeris in the Fayoum, and although the lake was probably a natural feature, it is most likely that Amenemmes undertook an extensive programme of land reclamation here. He seems to have taken a special interest in the area, building a temple to the crocodile god Sobek there, and also probably initiating the construction of the famous Labyrinth. This legendary building aroused the enthusiastic comment of Classical writers, but it was only in AD 1889 that the site was discovered by Petrie. He uncovered the remains of this once great complex, near the king's pyramid at Hawara at the entrance to the Fayoum; designed as a labyrinth with interconnecting passages and chambers, the unique plan incorporated not only the pyramid mortuary temple but also administrative quarters and also possibly a royal residence area.

Religious developments in Dynasties 11 and 12

The kings of Dynasties 11 and 12 each in turn promoted the status of gods who had previously enjoyed only local significance. The omnipotence of Re' was replaced on the one hand by the cult of Osiris, and on the other, by deities who were of importance to the new rulers. The Theban rulers of Dynasty 11 elevated as state god their local falcon-headed god of war Montu, who was probably of southern origin; his principal cult centre was at Hermonthis and he had been worshipped locally at Thebes. In Dynasty 12, Amenemmes I emphasised his devotion to Amun, a local Theban god, by making him protector of the dynasty. During this period, the temple to Amun at Karnak in Thebes was developed as a centre of religious importance and this later became the greatest temple in Egypt. This king may also have founded a neighbouring temple to Amun's consort, Mut. His son Sesostris I erected a limestone shrine of exquisite beauty at Karnak, where the barque of Amun was set down to rest during the great festivals. This building marked the king's first jubilee festival. Other deities were not ignored, and building work was also carried out by the Dynasty 12 kings at the temples of Ptah at Memphis, of Hathor at Denderah, of Re'-Atum at Heliopolis, of Min at Koptos and of Osiris at Abydos.

Royal funerary monuments of Dynasties 11 and 12

The comparatively peaceful conditions which prevailed in these two dynasties enabled the rulers to give their attention to the construction of magnificent burial places. It is probable that the rulers of Dynasties 7 and 8, and also the Heracleopolitans, were buried at Saqqara. However, Mentuhotep I of Dynasty 11 preferred to follow his ancestors' example and be buried at Thebes.

The location and design of his funerary monument was dramatic. It was built against the awe-inspiring cliffs at Deir el-Bahri which rise on the west bank opposite the ancient city of Thebes. Unfortunately today there is little left of the building, for most of the stone was used either to construct the adjacent and much better preserved temple of Queen Hatshepsut in Dynasty 18, or for other building projects. Some of the features of the Dynasty 11 complex, and most particularly its striking location, were imitated in Queen Hatshepsut's monument.

Mentuhotep's complex, excavated by Naville and Hall for the Egypt Exploration Fund, and later by Winlock for the Metropolitan Museum of New York, was designed to contain both a tomb and a cenotaph for Mentuhotep, in addition to the customary temples found in a funerary monument. The plan was apparently changed several times and incorporated many new features. The king's burial chamber, lined with alabaster and containing an alabaster shrine, was situated in the bedrock. It was reached by means of a passage and was obviously designed for maximum security, but the excavators discovered only broken sceptres, two small boats and other debris.

Before the king's own area was completed, six women, probably queens or princesses of the royal harem, were buried in the complex. Six cubical limestone shrines, designed to contain the Ka-statues of these women, were built on the terrace, and behind each shrine there was a vertical shaft which led down to a small pit-tomb situated in the temple platform. Each tomb contained a finely carved sarcophagus, and on two of these reliefs were found which depicted the daily activities of the royal women. Other tombs were built in the complex for other female members of the royal household, including Neferu, the king's full sister; her tomb was visited as a place of national pilgrimage in the New Kingdom. Other tombs were included for his favourite wife, Amunet, and his eldest son. It is apparent that the complex was designed as a royal burial area and as a place where the funerary rituals could be performed in the mortuary temple, the sanctuary and the hypostyle halls. The tombs of the nobles of this period were cut into the cliffs to the north and south of the complex. In a unique manner, Mentuhotep therefore succeeded in bringing together the features of the Old Kingdom complexes, but he also introduced new and exciting concepts in architectural design.

The kings of Dynasty 12 were more conservative in their aspirations, and returned to the use of pyramid complexes which closely imitated the main features found in the Old Kingdom monuments. Amenemmes I built his pyramid at Lisht; it was mainly based on the Old Kingdom plan, although some new Theban features were introduced. The inner core of the pyramid was built of stone used for earlier monuments, and the complex incorporated buildings which were built on two levels – the pyramid (the only example in this dynasty to have been constructed entirely of stone) was on the upper terrace, while the mortuary temple, to the east of the pyramid, lay on the lower level. The main buildings were enclosed by a rectangular mudbrick wall, and some tombs of the royal family and the courtiers lay within the walled area while others were built outside. Although the complex indicated a return to the earlier custom of burying the nobility near to the king, the size and scope of Cheops' funerary city at Gizeh were never again attempted and indeed many of the courtiers and officials now preferred to have their tombs at Thebes.

Another king of this dynasty, Sesostris I, also built his pyramid complex at Lisht, but the other rulers chose different burial sites. Amenemmes II built at Dahshur, and Sesostris II selected Illahun, perhaps because of his continuing interest in the Fayoum; Sesostris

III also constructed a pyramid at Dahshur, and Amenemmes III built two pyramids – one at Dahshur (probably his cenotaph) and the other, where he was probably buried, at Hawara.

The last rulers of the dynasty – Amenemmes IV and Sobekneferu – were again faced with problems which beset the land, and their attempts to unite Egypt met with failure. Their burial places have never been identified, although it has been suggested that two ruined pyramids at Mazghuna, south of Dahshur, can perhaps be attributed to them.

The royal jewellery of the Middle Kingdom

In a number of the Middle Kingdom funerary complexes, the excavators discovered jewellery which, in execution and design, perhaps surpasses in excellence any other examples found in Egypt. Four shaft tombs, built for members of the royal family, lay to the south of Sesostris II's pyramid at Illahun; in one of these, the jewellery of the tomb-owner, the king's daughter, Princess Sat-Hathor-Iunut, was discovered by Petrie and Brunton in AD 1913. Most of these objects were taken to the Metropolitan Museum in New York, although a few items remained in Cairo Museum.

In the enclosure of the pyramid of Sesostris III at Dahshur, on the north side of the pyramid, another archaeologist, de Morgan, found a set of jewellery not placed on the bodies but hidden separately in the tombs. In the pyramid complex of Amenemmes II at Dahshur, he discovered a similar treasure belonging to the royal princesses; this is now in the Cairo Museum. Finally, in the enclosure which surrounds the second pyramid of Amenemmes III at Dahshur (probably the king's cenotaph), de Morgan came upon another set of exquisite jewellery belonging to the royal women.

These eight groups of royal jewellery, all belonging to the queens and princesses of this dynasty, illustrate the high standards of craftsmanship achieved by the goldsmiths and jewellers of this period and also indicate the type of decoration with which these women adorned themselves.

Jewellery was worn by the Egyptians and was placed in their graves for use and enjoyment after death from the earliest periods. It is interesting in terms of its concept and design because it was regarded not only as a means of adornment but more importantly as a religious and magical attribute. The gods and goddesses were presented with jewellery and insignia in the course of the daily and other temple rituals, to signify and enhance their divine powers. Jewellery was used by humans in a variety of situations. It was a means of displaying wealth and status, but might also indicate that the wearer was the recipient of royal favour. Some courtiers and even members of the royal family were rewarded with jewellery by the king as a mark of his esteem for their outstanding service or valour. The Order of the Golden Collar was presented to deserving courtiers for bravery in battle from the Old Kingdom onwards, and in the New Kingdom, military bravery was rewarded with the Order of the Golden Fly. Jewellery was also used to commemorate royal occasions – the king presented his bride with a gift on their marriage, and on the king's jubilee festival, he and his queen were presented with jewellery by their courtiers.

Although these pieces were undoubtedly decorative and desirable symbols of favour and status in society, the primary function of jewellery, worn by the rich and the poor in life and in death, was to provide magical protection for the wearer. It assisted him against mysterious hostile forces, including terrifying animals, disease, famine, floods and accidents, and it attracted, by the principles of sympathetic magic, good forces which would help him. Certain stones were believed to have special hidden powers, and carnelian, turquoise and the rare lapis-lazuli were especially favoured. The jewellery would frequently incorporate in its design the popular magical symbols which were believed to bring health and good luck to the wearer, and sometimes single amulets would be worn or carried to alleviate particular problems.

The Egyptians believed that inanimate objects had the power to affect their lives, and amulets were accredited with such potency that not only were they carried in life, but they were also placed on the dead to assist them in their future existence. Some amulets were thought to be universally beneficial while others had significance and power only for the individual owner. There were amulets which fortified the wearer as he passed through dangers, and those which directed thought to a weakness in the body and thus effected a cure. Some amulets were produced in the shape of limbs; it was hoped that these would either direct magical strength towards an afflicted limb and bring about its recovery, or that the disease in the limb would be transferred into the amulet 'double', thus also saving the limb. Great care was often taken to select stones for amulets which had the same colour as the original, since it was felt that, in some way, these would be additionally beneficial to the sufferer.

A number of amuletic forms were considered to be outstandingly potent. These included the Sacred Eye of Horus which was closely associated with the mythology of Horus and Seth; the ankh-sign which symbolised life; the djed-pillar and tit-symbol which represented renewal and fertility; and the scarab, signifying the eternal renewal of life. The flat underside of the carved scarabs had originally been inscribed with the name or title of the owner, and these were used as seals, but increasingly, they came to be regarded not so much as seals but as lucky tokens, borne by the living and the dead, and they display a variety of magico-religious decorations, including mottoes, figures of deities and animals, or spiral and geometric designs.

The jewellery placed in the tombs of royalty and the nobles was frequently elaborate, and there is every reason to suppose that much of it was prepared for this purpose throughout the lives of the owners. It is often difficult to distinguish accurately between funerary jewellery produced for burial and the treasured possessions which were worn in life and were then placed with the deceased. However, the funerary objects tend to be more traditional in design and also of a heavier type.

The Egyptians utilised their natural resources to produce exquisite jewellery for both purposes. Gold, of which there were immense deposits in Nubia and the Eastern Desert, was in most widespread use. The Egyptians loved its colour which resembled and reflected the sun, and also admired its durability. In early times, it was collected as granules in the sand and gravel, and then melted into ingots. Later, Nubia was forced to pay its taxes in gold, and it was stored for use in Egypt. Mining was introduced, and gold was extracted from the veins in the quartz rock. 'Electrum' (which incorporated proportions of gold and silver) was brought from the Eastern Desert as well as from Punt on the Red Sea coast, and silver, more rare and therefore more highly prized than gold, was mainly imported, being introduced from Asia into Egypt.

The gem-stones which were set into these metals were selected primarily for the magical properties ascribed to the various colours; unlike modern jewels, they were never chosen for their brilliance and refraction of light. Carnelian was obtained from pebbles found in the Eastern Desert, turquoise was mined in Sinai from veins in the sandstone, and lapis lazuli was imported from Afghanistan via the region around the River Euphrates. Other desirable stones included garnets and jasper, green felspar, amethyst, and obsidian. Artificial substitutes, using calcite or rock-crystal backed with coloured cements, or faience (soapstone coated with an alkaline blue/green glaze) which imitated lapis lazuli, or frit which was a form of glass, were also employed.

The craftsmen included different specialists – goldsmiths, workers in precious stones, faience-makers, necklace-stringers, beadmakers, and so forth. The goldsmiths were the most important group who were mainly employed by the king and the temples. The craft was limited to certain families, and Memphis was their chief centre, where Ptah was worshipped as the patron of goldsmiths. The highest grades of goldsmiths probably received a training as scribes before they specialised in gold-working and they held important and responsible posts, acquiring and organising the materials.

Apart from the examples of jewellery which have been found, additional information is provided by tomb scenes which show the preparation of funerary goods, where the men are depicted working together under the supervision of the overseers. The inscriptions accompanying the scenes, as well as defining the activities, also give the comments of the workers, referring to the heat and dirty conditions in which they found themselves. Their tools were simple and they relied mainly on the fine raw materials, their own skills and training, and an unhurried schedule to enable them to produce such excellent results. Their repertoire of techniques included repoussé work, chasing, engraving, moulding, soldering, casting and cloisonné work.

The jewellery of the Dynasty 12 royal women included exquisite crowns made of gold and inlaid with semi-precious stones or coloured glass, and some of the finest pectorals which are executed in gold, with designs representing the king and the gods. In these, semi-precious stones, glass and other materials are inlaid into the cloisons, and the design is repeated on the reverse side in repoussé. The pectoral belonging to Princess Sit-Hathor-Iunut included 372 pieces of inlay which had each been made separately.

Many professions and trades had their own patron deities, and Hathor, the cow-headed goddess of love, music and dancing, was also the patroness of jewellers and miners. Her cult extended beyond

Egypt into Sinai where she was worshipped by the mining community.

A pyramid workmen's village

Most of our knowledge of ancient Egypt is derived from material discovered in burial sites. This is because the tombs in the later periods were frequently built of stone, whereas the houses were constructed of mudbrick; also, whereas the town sites underwent constant destruction and rebuilding over the years, the tombs, despite plunder and theft, usually preserved some semblance of their original state. However, a rare opportunity to examine a complete town site was presented in the late nineteenth century, when the site of a workmen's village was excavated by Petrie. It had been built by Sesostris II near to his proposed pyramid at Illahun, to house the workmen required to construct his funerary monument. The site, known today as 'Kahun', was named 'Hetep-Sesostris' in antiquity. This was the first time that such a town had been discovered and excavated systematically, and the material from the town, now mainly in the collections of the Manchester Museum and the Flinders Petrie Museum at University College London, has provided scholars with unparallelled information concerning the everyday life of such a community. The town was occupied for only a short period during Dynasty 12 and then appears to have been deserted. It is possible that this evacuation occurred because, once they had completed the pyramid, no further reason existed for the continuation of the village. However, the workmen and their families left behind their domestic possessions – cooking utensils, furniture, weaving equipment, cosmetics, jewellery, toys and games – and their building and agricultural tools. It is perhaps unlikely that these possessions, especially the workmen's tools, would have been left behind if the families had departed to set up home elsewhere, and there may be some other explanation for the desertion of the site.

Petrie was able to examine the archaeological evidence to determine the layout of the town. The workmen and their families were accommodated in parallel rows of mudbrick houses, laid out in straight lines and enclosed within a thick wall. Priests and officials of the nearby temple were housed in larger dwellings. The site is also famous for the discovery of archival material which has provided additional literary evidence on aspects of the society.

Osiris and the democratisation of funerary beliefs

During Dynasties 11 and 12, the ordinary person came to expect an afterlife which was no longer dependent upon the king's favour but which could be achieved through the performance of the correct ritual and burial procedures and through devoted worship of the god Osiris. When centralised power disintegrated at the end of the Old Kingdom, men could no longer place their hopes on the state cult and they could not seek eternity through the king's bounty. As the king's absolute power was swept away, and nobles chose to be buried in their own provinces, they now sought to achieve immortality by employing some of the magical and religious devices which had assisted the king to join the sun-god in the earlier period. Wherever possible, those who could afford the expense now provided themselves with fine tombs and elaborate funerary equipment. However, many people were too poor to aspire to such material goods, but the process of democratisation in religious matters had penetrated so extensively in this period that even the lowest classes now pursued the hope of an individual hereafter. This reversal of funerary beliefs was closely associated with the development of the cult of Osiris whose popularity now placed him in a position of unrivalled importance.

Osiris, as we have seen, was identified in later Classical sources as a human king who ruled Egypt at an early period and who brought civilisation and agriculture to the country before he met an untimely end at the hand of his brother Seth. Later resurrected as a dead, deified ruler, Osiris was always represented as a dead king, wearing a long white cloak, the crown of Upper Egypt, and carrying the royal insignia. However, sources throw little light on his historical origin, and studies of his name – 'Wsir' in hieroglyphs – have produced various suggestions as to its meaning (perhaps 'Mighty One' from the verb 'wsr' meaning 'to be strong'), but no conclusion regarding his origin or home.

It is certain that Osiris was regarded as a god of vegetation, and this was perhaps his primary role. He personified the rebirth of the vegetation, and it was believed that his annual process of death and resurrection followed and symbolised the seasons of Egypt's agricultural year. Each year the land became parched, but this was followed by the inundation of the river which, through the irrigation channels, brought water to the desolate areas and gave rise to the rebirth of the vegetation. Each stage was seen to coincide with a chapter in the myth of Osiris.

From this role as life-giver and source of fertility, Osiris probably acquired the attributes of a divine judge and king of the underworld, and came to be regarded as the symbol of victory over evil. As a vegetation god, he annually triumphed over death, and as a king, this miracle was expressed in a wider sense as the triumph of life over death. This resulted in his installation not as a king of the living, but as the ruler of the dead and of the underworld, and this experience enabled him to promise eternal life to his followers, for, having successfully encountered his trial before the divine judges, he could obtain the same benefits for his followers.

In the Old Kingdom only the king could become Osiris upon death and the references in the Pyramid Texts to Osiris were all related to the king's personal resurrection. The Osirian cult, like the solar cult, had first been directed towards assisting the king's rebirth, and although Re' was a god of the living whereas Osiris was the god of the dead, the two cults had much in common. Both symbolised the divine ability to overcome death, and both reflected the cycle of life, death and rebirth in the natural phenomena. The cult of Osiris flourished even in the Old Kingdom and was perhaps given royal support to counterbalance the priests of Re'. The king identified himself at death with Osiris, and his heir became Horus, the son and avenger of Osiris. Osiris reigned supreme in the underworld but did not concern himself with the affairs of the living; therefore, his cult did not directly rival those of other gods, and he was able to attract worshippers from all levels of society simply because of his funerary nature.

After the Old Kingdom collapsed, the new rulers were seeking for a deity who could supplant Re' as the patron of the earlier kings and who had a sufficiently widespread appeal. Osiris, associated not only with the funerary cult but also with the divine rituals and the rites performed at the king's accession and coronation, was the obvious choice.

Gradually, the great provincial nobles adopted the funerary rites formerly associated only with the royal burials, and eventually the magic spells designed to ensure a safe passage to the next world became generally available. Whereas once only the king had been described as an 'Osiris' in the Pyramid Texts, now the name was applied also to the non-royal dead. The kings of Dynasty 12, although they revived some of the religious customs of the Old Kingdom, made no attempt to restore the former power of the sun-god Re' at the expense of Osiris.

From his agricultural role as a vegetation god, Osiris also came to be regarded as a corn-deity whose rebirth was symbolised in the growing grain. In this capacity, he adopted some of the features of an earlier corn-god, Neper. He also assumed the role of moon-god. His characteristics as a dead god who was associated with the growth of the vegetation have suggested a connection with other Near Eastern deities, namely Adonis, Dionysus and Tammuz. The mythology which surrounds these gods also emphasises other links with Osiris; they too are described as shepherd gods and are associated with a goddess who searches for the dead god and then bewails and buries him. Other aspects of the gods differ, however, and a common origin for Osiris and the other deities cannot be accepted without more substantial evidence.

Our understanding of the cult and mythology of Osiris is limited by the surprising scarcity of original source material. Although religious texts contain many references to the god, no extant Egyptian version of his myth has ever been found. Such a text perhaps awaits discovery, but it is possible that the myth was handed down only through oral tradition. The earliest and most complete version is preserved in Greek, in the writings of Plutarch, and dates to a much later period of history. Since this version is predominantly Greek in style, it is difficult to assess how closely it resembles an earlier Egyptian tradition. In the Egyptian inscriptions there are two other main sources relating to Osiris. The earliest references mentioning the role of the god are to be found in the Pyramid Texts, dating to the Old Kingdom, and inscriptions and reliefs on the walls of some of the temples provide information regarding the rites performed during the annual festivals held to honour Osiris at centres throughout Egypt. These, however, also date either to the New Kingdom or to the Graeco-Roman period.

Apart from these sources, an inscription, preserved on the Stela of Ikhernofret which is now in the Berlin Museum, describes another aspect of the cult. Ikhernofret, chief treasurer in the reign of Sesostris

III, was sent to Abydos to reorganise the cult of Osiris and to replenish his temple furnishings. He describes how he took part in the Mystery Plays which were enacted by the priests to celebrate events in the life and death of Osiris. These were held annually at Abydos from Dynasty 12 onwards and formed part of a festival held in the last month of inundation. This was a time of great rejoicing not only for the priests but also for the many ordinary people who travelled many miles to participate in the god's resurrection at Abydos. These pilgrims were known as the 'Followers of Thoth', after another deity who played a major part in the festival. They were able to watch some of the rites which were performed outside the temple precinct, but the most sacred rituals, designed to ensure the resurrection of the god and his followers, were enacted in secret by the priests in the most secluded area of the temple. The eagerly awaited inundation of the Nile and the renewal of the vegetation symbolised the triumph of Osiris and of the deceased king who had become Osiris.

By the Middle Kingdom, Abydos had come to hold a unique position in the god's cult. It was a centre of pilgrimage, and some people made special arrangements to be buried there, or to have their mummies transported to Abydos before returning for burial at home. Others who could not afford this expense set up stelae at Abydos or included model boats in their tombs which could be used to transport them to the sacred city after death. The area had long been associated with the royal burials and accompanying rituals performed for the kings of the earliest dynasties, but an even more important factor was the belief that the body of Osiris was buried at Abydos. It was therefore considered to be desirable to associate oneself in some way with Abydos, so that participation in the god's resurrection would enhance the chances of individual rebirth. By this period, Osiris had replaced the king as the symbol of eternity, but the god offered a chance of immortality to all, regardless of wealth or status.

Although Abydos held an unrivalled position as the god's cult centre, the location of Osiris' first place of worship in Egypt remains uncertain. A unique and largely unexplained building lies immediately behind the Dynasty 19 temple built by Sethos I at Abydos. This building, known today as the 'Osireion', was thought in antiquity to have marked the burial place of Osiris. In the well-preserved temple of Sethos I, which was almost certainly erected above a number of earlier temples, there is a unique set of rooms at the rear of the building, and directly in line with the Osireion. The scenes on the walls in this area depict the rites which culminated in the raising of the djed-pillar, which probably symbolised the climax of the festival, when the god was believed to return to life. It was probably in this sacred area of the temple that the annual ritual was performed.

Some evidence, including references in the Pyramid Texts, indicates that Abydos was the god's first centre; here, he absorbed and assimilated the attributes of an earlier god who was worshipped at Abydos. This deity was known as the 'First of the Westerners' and had close associations, as god of the necropolis, with the dead. However, there are also indications that Osiris' first centre was at Busiris in the Delta, which is referred to as his birth-place in later writings. In Egyptian texts, he is often called 'Lord of Busiris' and it was probably here that he acquired the features of an earlier deity named Andjeti, from whom he took his kingly insignia and attributes. At Busiris, Osiris acquired his famous cult-symbol – the Busirite Symbol or djed-pillar. The origin and meaning of this symbol remains obscure but the djed-pillar came to represent strength and permanence to the Egyptians and to be an essential symbol of the god's resurrection. Osiris also took a cult-symbol from Abydos which is shown as a decorated box on top of a pole. It is known as the 'Abydene Symbol', but its origin and purpose also remain uncertain, although it came to be acknowledged and worshipped as the embodiment of the god.

The temple built by Sethos I at Abydos followed a tradition of religious development at the site. The renewed interest in Abydos was perhaps encouraged by the kings of Dynasty 11 who no longer wished to stress the royal association with Heliopolis and the sun-cult. From this time onwards, Abydos became the centre of religious fervour in Egypt, particularly in connection with the funerary cult. The set of chambers dedicated to a special Osirian function in Sethos' temple were not found elsewhere, but the rite of raising the djed-pillar is known from other sources to have represented the culmination of the Festival of Khoiakh in which the death and resurrection of Osiris were celebrated as well as his installation as king of the dead. By the Ptolemaic period, it is known that this festival lasted for some eighteen days and was performed in all the major towns of Egypt. The priests, by thus dramatising the events in the life and death of Osiris and by celebrating the accession to the throne of the living king as the embodiment of Horus, the heir of Osiris, sought to ensure that the inundation, the growth of the vegetation, and a plentiful harvest could be brought into existence.

These rites were closely associated with the accession, the coronation and the jubilee of the king, and the cult of Osiris became of paramount importance in establishing and maintaining royal power, but the main reason for the widespread appeal of Osiris continued to be his ability to offer immortality to all his believers. Osiris reigned supreme in the underworld and entry to this realm was dependent first upon the observance of the correct burial procedure and provision of food, but increasingly, it also came to rely upon the divine judgment.

Every Egyptian now believed that upon death he was required to face trial before a tribunal of judges, made up of forty-two gods, as Osiris himself had done. Defended by Thoth, the deceased would be expected to affirm the purity of his soul by reciting the Negative Confession; he would address each of his judges by name and then declare his innocence of any serious crime during his lifetime. Sometimes, knowledge of magic or suitable spells enabled him to deceive the gods, but the second part of the trial involved further examination. In the presence of Thoth, the god of learning and writing, Ma'at, the goddess of truth, and Anubis, god of embalming, the deceased stood in front of a large balance; one pan held the feather of Truth and Anubis placed the man's heart (the seat of his intellect and emotions) in the other pan. The goddesses of fate and destiny testified concerning the man's character, and Thoth recorded the verdict. The deceased anxiously awaited the outcome, for if he was found innocent, his heart and the feather would balance each other in the scales and Thoth would declare him free from sin. The verdict would be accepted by the gods and he and his soul would continue together into the Osirian underworld. From Dynasty 11 onwards, it became customary to place the words 'true of voice' or 'justified' after the name of the deceased to indicate the successful outcome of his trial, and throughout the Middle Kingdom, the name 'Osiris' was written in front of the name of any deceased person. These titles lost something of their original religious significance and came to mean simply 'the deceased'.

Success at his trial ensured that the deceased avoided the dreaded fate which awaited the guilty – the hearts of those found unworthy of immortality were believed to be tossed to a mythical animal, composed of parts belonging to different animals, which is depicted on the papyri crouching near the balance in anticipation.

Although it was accepted that magic and knowledge of spells could assist one to pass into the next world, there was an increasing emphasis placed on moral fitness as a prerequisite for entry. The ordinary man, if innocent of sin and a follower of Osiris, could now cling to a hope of individual immortality. The Osirian realm to which even the humblest could aspire, entry not being dependent upon the ability to furnish and equip an elaborate tomb, was envisaged as a place of lush vegetation situated below the western horizon or on a group of islands. Referred to as the 'Fields of Reeds', this paradise experienced eternal springtime and unfailing harvests, and here the dead enjoyed the pleasures of their former earthly existence, without any of the pain and suffering. The realm of Osiris was also essentially democratic in structure, and rich and poor alike were given plots of land which they were expected to cultivate. Although this land of eternity must have seemed most desirable to the poor, the wealthy nobles and aspiring middle classes apparently felt that some of the delights of their present existence would be lacking and they thus sought to perpetuate for themselves some of the more sophisticated pleasures which they enjoyed in life.

The three main concepts of eternity which began to be formulated in the Middle Kingdom – the royal celestial hereafter still retained, although less rigidly, for the kings, continuation of one's existence within the tomb, and an eternity spent tilling a piece of land in the Fields of Reeds – were to some degree interchangeable, but essentially they reflected the aspirations of the main social groups within Egyptian society. To obtain the desired benefits, the wealthy continued to prepare and equip fine tombs, and to provide a means of escape from the arduous agricultural labours to be encountered in Osiris' kingdom, they placed sets of figurines in the tombs which were expected to perform the manual tasks on behalf of the deceased. These, known as 'ushabtis', were introduced in Dynasties 9 and 10; they are mummiform and carry agricultural tools which are painted or carved on to the figure. The material, style, decoration and inscription show some variation throughout the dynasties, but after its introduction for this purpose in Dynasty 18, faience is the material used most widely for these figurines. Each set included hundreds of ushabtis (it is often said that they numbered one for each day of the year) as well as a related group of 'overseer figures'. The ushabtis are frequently inscribed with the owner's name and the spell indicating willingness and readiness to perform these tasks on his behalf.

The tombs of the nobles during the First Intermediate Period and the Middle Kingdom

Fine rock-cut tombs were constructed for the provincial nobility throughout this period at their centres of influence along the Nile. Usually cut in rows into the cliffs which border parts of Middle and Upper Egypt, each tomb included a portico with columns or a terraced courtyard which led into a columned hall which was cut out of the rock. This gave access to a small room or niche which contained the tomb-owner's funerary statue, where the food offerings were presented. The burial chamber lay beyond the chapel and access was often provided by means of an opening cut into the floor of the columned hall. This hall was decorated with painted wall-scenes which, together with the funerary equipment discovered in the tombs, provide excellent information regarding the artistic techniques of the period.

Most of the funerary art from this period is non-royal, and the decentralisation of power at the end of the Old Kingdom resulted in the decline of Memphis as the leading centre of craftsmanship. Local talent was now used by the provincial nomarchs, although during the Heracleopolitan Period, there was some attempt to continue with the basic style and techniques of the Old Kingdom. A few examples survive of the tomb reliefs and these were either badly painted in a rough, incised technique, or they were executed in a flat, low, sharp-edged style. However, with the advent of Dynasty 11, a new vigorous Theban school of art developed which broke away from the Memphite traditions. This was characterised by a mixture of high and sunk relief, close attention to detail, and human figures which were shown with different proportions, having small heads and tall, slender bodies. With the renewal of centralised government in Dynasty 12, the Memphite or northern school again exerted a great influence over both royal and non-royal art, but the Theban tradition continued to be apparent in this new style. Many nobles returned to the custom of burial close to the king, but some still built great provincial tombs and the private funerary art of this dynasty exhibits a marked local influence and variation, with each district patronising a school of local craftsmen. These artists based the content of their tomb decoration on the patterns established during the Old Kingdom at Memphis, but new details were added and in this period, the influence which local schools exerted on funerary art forms reached its zenith.

Although the style of the noblemen's tombs and the execution of the wall decoration developed in several directions during these years, only superficial changes can be determined in the character of the funerary equipment which was placed in these tombs, whether it dates to the First Intermediate Period or to the Middle Kingdom.

Tomb equipment and furniture

Some of the funerary equipment of this period can be illustrated by examining a tomb-group of the late Middle Kingdom which is now housed in the Manchester Museum, University of Manchester. The rock tombs of Der Rifeh in Middle Egypt were excavated by Petrie with the assistance of Mackay; situated in the cliffs some eight miles south of Assiut, they formed the cemetery for the town of Shas-hotep where the ram-god Khnum was worshipped. Here, Petrie discovered an intact but undecorated tomb, its entrance concealed under debris and situated at the end of a courtyard cut into the cliff. The small burial chamber barely accommodated the coffins and funerary equipment which, in his book *Gizeh and Rifeh*, p. 12, Petrie describes 'as fine as anything known of this period'. The tomb belonged to two brothers who were wealthy local men but not of the nobility; however, its considerable interest stems from the fact that the tomb, its contents and the mummified bodies of the brothers were discovered intact and they have since been kept together as a group at the Manchester Museum. They provide a good example of the standards of design and craftsmanship which even a relatively modest person could now expect.

Each brother was provided with a rectangular wooden coffin; these had flat lids although some examples are vaulted. Such coffins were widely used by all classes until the end of the Middle Kingdom, and were usually made of wood although royalty and the great nobles sometimes prepared stone coffins which imitated the features of the wooden ones. The earliest decoration consisted of horizontal lines of inscription, but many coffins, including these, also display brightly painted geometric designs representing the facade of a palace or a house. It may have been thought that the coffin symbol-ised a dwelling for the deceased. A pair of eyes, painted on the east or left side of the coffin in the direction in which the body faced, were intended to enable the deceased to look out at the food offer-ings which were brought to the tomb. The coffins were sometimes decorated with paintings of food offerings in addition to the inscrip-tions. These, known as the 'Coffin Texts', were adapted from the spells written in the Old Kingdom pyramids and were now used for non-royal persons; they incorporated direct statements which negated death and affirmed life, and attempted to overcome any adverse situation which the deceased might encounter in his passage from this world to the hereafter. These spells included some new additions and were inscribed, in a cursive hieroglyphic script, on the rectangular coffins of this period. The use of the Coffin Texts is limited to the Middle Kingdom (except for a brief revival in Dynasty 26), when they provide our main source of funerary literature.

Anthropoid or body coffins were placed inside the rectangular coffins. It is believed that these developed from the cartonnage masks which had originally been used in the Old Kingdom when they were placed over the head of the deceased to serve as a substi-tute as well as a cover for the head and face of the mummy. The anthropoid coffins were at first made of cartonnage or of wood, but they were eventually carved entirely of wood. They were mummi-form, and the features painted on the exterior of the coffin – the wide bead collar, the girdle, bandaging and jewellery – imitated the items found on the mummy inside. The eyes were often represented by obsidian and alabaster inlays set into the wood, and the wooden false beard and uraeus – symbols of kingship and divinity – were added to indicate the status of the deceased as an Osiris. The coffins were given stylised facial features which were not portraits of the owners; they were produced as part of a stock of funerary furniture from which people could select their tomb equipment. However, the cases of the brothers are particularly interesting; the inscriptions state that their names were Khnum-Nakht and Nekht-Ankh and that they were the sons of a woman named Khnum-aa, although the name of their father is not given. Nevertheless, from anatomical and medical investigation, it would seem that Khnum-Nakht was negroid while Nekht-Ankh was not. It has been suggested that the brothers may have been related only through their mother and had different fathers, or that one 'brother' was adopted. The anthropoid coffin in which Nekht-Ankh's mummy was discovered has a black face, while the face on Khnum-Nakht's case is painted white. There is some confusion over the identification of the ownership of other items in the tomb, and the body coffins may also have been wrongly assigned, but even so, the coffins may not have been specially designed for the brothers, with respective black and white faces, since black was used in religious contexts to indicate rebirth and resurrection, in the same way that the 'Black Land' was annually reborn, and this may have been its significance here.

The coffins of Nekht-Ankh were inferior to those of his brother but, apart from one statuette, all other funerary goods in the tomb belonged to Nekht-Ankh. These included a wooden canopic chest which was brightly decorated with lines of inscription, painted false doors, and a pair of painted eyes; it contained four pottery canopic jars with stoppers carved and painted in the form of human heads. In two of these were stored the viscera of Nekht-Ankh. There was an increasingly widespread use of these jars amongst the middle classes. They were dedicated to the demi-gods known as the 'Four Sons of Horus'; these included Imset (human-headed) who was in charge of the stomach and large intestine, Hapy (ape-headed) who looked after the small intestine, Duamutef (jackal-headed) who cared for the lungs, and Qebhsennuef (hawk-headed) who was responsible for the liver and the gall-bladder. These demi-gods were respectively protected by the goddesses Isis, Nephthys, Neith and Serket. Human-headed stoppers (probably intended to represent the deceased) found on the canopic jars of the Old and Middle Kingdoms were replaced in Dynasty 18 by stoppers carved to represent the heads of a hawk, ape, jackal and a human. In Dynasty 12, the canopic chest was usually placed in a niche in the east wall of the burial chamber in the line of vision of the deceased.

Comparatively few examples of mummification remain from this period. The group of royal mummies of Dynasty 11, discovered in the pyramid-temple of Mentuhotep I at Deir el-Bahri, and those of the Two Brothers, which were unwrapped in 1907 and investigated then and subsequently in 1975 by teams of Egyptologists, and medical and scientific specialists at Manchester, provide evidence that the mummification techniques used at this period were less effective than those of the Old Kingdom. The royal mummies had not been eviscerated, and the dehydration process, using natron, appears to have been unsatisfactorily completed before the bodies were wrapped. The bodies of the brothers were also badly preserved; the skin tissue on Khnum-Nakht's mummy was very dry and disintegrated into a fine dust when the body was unwrapped and there was also very little skin tissue on the other mummy. It is probable that mummies of this period are so poorly preserved because the body was inadequately dried and resin was applied to the skin surface before dessication was complete; the remaining moisture in the tissues would have encouraged rapid bacteriological decomposition.

Pottery vessels and model figures and ships were also included amongst the tomb equipment. It became customary to place large numbers of models in the tombs of the wealthy at this period. A named statuette of the deceased was provided, which, by the power of magic, could be restored to life-size; this would then be available for use by the deceased in the event that his body had been destroyed. Sometimes this would be accompanied by statues of the dead man's family. Non-royal statuary of this period was rarely life-size; it was produced in large numbers and usually showed great variety in style, although the standards of craftsmanship were not always of the highest. However, the three wooden statuettes discovered in the tomb of the Two Brothers are fine examples, exquisitely carved and painted. Two of them are inscribed with the name of Nekht-Ankh and the other bears the name of his brother but, as noted by Dr Margaret Murray who directed the investigation in 1907, confusion has occurred over the identification of two of the statuettes and they are wrongly named. The more recent research project, which involved the reconstruction, using scientific techniques, of three-dimensional 'busts' of the brothers, has now enabled the statuettes to be compared with the reconstructions and accordingly identified correctly.

Tombs were now equipped with a variety of model servants, soldiers and animals. The simple figurines of the Old Kingdom, which were shown in different stages of food preparation, were now expanded into complete groups which included servants engaged in food production and preparation – working in the granaries, the breweries, slaughter-houses, and ploughing the fields or fishing in the river. In some tombs, model figurines of soldiers have been discovered, fully armed to protect the tomb-owner in the troubled times of local warfare. There were also complete models of the owner's house, estate and herds, and in this miniature world, the activities of the great land-owner and his employees are captured in considerable detail. Many of these carved wooden models are based upon the subject matter of scenes found on the walls of the earlier Old Kingdom tombs. These, in addition to the mummy and the wall scenes, were believed to 'come into existence' through the magic of the funerary rites.

In the tomb of the Two Brothers, wooden statuettes of girl servants were found, bearing baskets of food to ensure the continuation of a food supply, but other tombs contained a wider variety of figures. In Dynasty 11, these included 'dolls' which took the form of flat, wooden, 'paddle-shaped' figures. At a later date, there were also 'concubine-figures', made of stone, wood or pottery and often decorated with inlaid eyes and elaborate hairstyles. These catered for the entertainment of the tomb-owner, as did the model harpists and dwarves. The purpose of the animal models is less apparent; these included cats, dogs, apes, mice and hippopotami, and although some may have been intended as pets, others perhaps had a magico-religious significance.

'Soul-houses' developed from a circular stone offering table or rectangular slab or platter which was originally placed in front of the tomb stela to receive the food offerings. In time, the tray became of secondary importance as it gradually came to be regarded as the courtyard of a model house. Produced in pottery, the model house varied to some degree in design but usually incorporated a two-storeyed portico, a staircace leading to a flat rooftop and a cooking area in the front courtyard on which the offerings were placed. These soul-houses now became the offering tables associated with the tombs, and they also provide us with otherwise unobtainable information regarding the different types of domestic architecture during this period.

Although the tomb of the Two Brothers did not contain a soul-house, another kind of model which became an essential feature of funerary equipment was included. A pair of model boats, complete with sails, oars, deck cabins and crew, were found; one was designed as a sailing vessel for transportation up the Nile, while the other, its sail furled and the rowers pulling at the oars, was intended to travel downstream. It became important to include at least one boat model in the tomb, and many people supplied themselves with several, whilst the great nobles sometimes had complete model fleets, with vessels, such as kitchen craft, fishing boats, long distance boats and funerary barques, for different functions. It was probably intended that some of these should convey the deceased to his resting-place, or would provide him with the opportunity to travel, but the most important and original purpose for including a boat amongst the funerary equipment was to enable the dead man to make the pilgrimage to Abydos.

Articles of everyday use were also placed in the tombs – linen clothes, jewellery, mirrors, cosmetics, toys and games. Wealthy people took cherished possessions including jewellery which they had worn in life, but they also prepared special sets of funerary jewellery which was heavy and traditional in design. In some cases, small, crude tablets of clay or stone were included; these were intended to represent the enemies of the king or of the tomb-owner and they were inscribed with the names of the deceased's foes – either general evils, Egyptian enemies, or those of foreign origin who might present a threat to safety. The tablets took the form of bound captives, although, in some cases, small pottery bowls were used; by smashing these, it was believed that the enemies' power could be destroyed, and the fragments were then buried near the tomb. These important and interesting inscribed fragments are known collectively as the 'Execration Texts'.

The contents of these tombs provide a wealth of information which relates not only to the religious and funerary beliefs of the period, but also illustrates the domestic and agricultural life. The Middle Kingdom was also the 'Golden Age' of Egyptian literature and many compositions of this period were used as models by later generations of school-teachers. Notable religious writings included Wisdom Literature similar in style to that of the Old Kingdom but also frequently incorporating an aspect of political propaganda, in addition to the sacred dramas which were performed by the priests on the occasions of the great festivals. These had now become an established feature of religious life, and two of the most famous, the 'Coronation Drama' and the 'Memphite Drama', are preserved to us.

However, despite the great political achievements of the rulers and the standards of excellence which were attained in the spheres of official literature and royal art forms, the Middle Kingdom was essentially the period when Egyptians of all classes first sought an individual eternity and aspired to this through moral righteousness in life.

4

The New Kingdom

The period of Hyksos rule

The Middle Kingdom was brought to a close when Egypt was invaded by a group known collectively as the 'Hyksos', towards the end of Dynasty 13. This was the name given to them by Manetho, but they were probably made up of different elements including peoples of Semitic and of Indo-Aryan origin. It is most likely that they entered Egypt in small groups, infiltrating the Delta during the period of weak government in Dynasty 13, and there is little evidence to support the contention that this was a horde invasion. They established their rule over Egypt and, despite later propagandist writings which relate how they burnt the cities and the gods' temples, they seem to have adopted Egyptian customs, perhaps because they were not in themselves a cohesive racial or social group. They appointed Egyptian bureaucrats to continue to administer the country, and there appears to have been no major break in general organisation. The new rulers taxed the people and took tribute from vassal regions in the south, but still supported the native arts and crafts and ensured that temple building continued and literary composition flourished. The Hyksos adopted the role and powers of the Egyptian king and even selected as their own state god one of the deities of the Egyptian pantheon. This was Seth, who played an important if controversial role in Egyptian religion, but it is probable that his character now embodied the features of one of their own Asiatic gods rather than those of the evil deity in the mythology of Osiris and Horus. Seth was given a cult centre at the newly established capital of Avaris in the Delta. In addition to Seth, the Hyksos also sought the protection of the old royal god Re', and there is no evidence that they attempted to force any new or unacceptable religious beliefs upon the Egyptians.

The Hyksos Period (Dynasties 15 and 16), also known as the Second Intermediate Period, was nevertheless regarded as a disaster by later generations, although it resulted in the introduction of many new ideas and a more advanced technology in weapons and domestic equipment. This interlude profoundly altered the character and attitudes of the Egyptians, changing them from an isolated although brilliant society into a people who sought to impose their rule abroad not merely to ensure access to resources but to establish the first empire. The Hyksos rule forced the Egyptians to acknowledge that, unless they pursued an aggressive policy, other people would continue to regard their rich land covetously and to seize any opportunity to possess Egypt.

A direct conflict arose between the Hyksos rulers and the Egyptians, spearheaded by the line of princes who ruled at Thebes as vassals of the Hyksos. The Egyptians later glorified the names of these native princes and regarded them as the heroes who had expelled the Hyksos rulers and pursued them into southern Palestine where they were finally subdued. The Egyptian traditions had been kept alive at Thebes during this period of foreign occupation and these princes now established Dynasty 18 and founded the New Kingdom.

The role of Amen-Re' (Amun)

The Theban princes attributed their ascendancy over the foreigners to the support of the local god, Amun, whom they had worshipped since Dynasty 12. The god of the air and originally one of the Hermopolitan ogdoad, Amun also had close associations with Min, the ithyphallic fertility god of Coptos and Akhmim. Both gods shared certain characteristics including their representation in human form. Amun was brought to Thebes at some time in the First Intermediate Period, and in Dynasty 12 he replaced Montu as the great state god.

Amun was now attributed with the successful expulsion of the Hyksos and also with Egypt's subsequent military victories in Western Asia which laid the foundations for the empire. To ensure that their god had no effective rival, the Thebans now associated their deity with the old solar god Re', creating the omnipotent

Amen-Re'. Amun henceforth absorbed the characteristics of the sun-god, including his mythology and role as the protector of royalty. This combination gave the local god more extensive powers and indeed it was the solarised aspects of his nature which became most prominent.

Amen-Re' was at first regarded primarily as a war-god but by the middle of Dynasty 18, when Egypt's supremacy in Western Asia was well-established, he assumed a different role, placing more emphasis upon the universality of his nature as a creator and ruler not only of the Egyptians but also of the other peoples of Egypt's empire. His priesthood at Thebes now sought to promote his cult-centre as the original site of creation and to delegate the earlier cosmogonies to a secondary position.

THE THEBAN COSMOGONY

The new cosmogony incorporated earlier beliefs, but essentially it stressed that Amun, the god of air, was to be regarded as the invisible but all-powerful creator of mankind. Combining all earlier forms of creator gods within himself, Amun was believed to have begotten himself in secret, coming forth from an egg on the primaeval mound. From this creative act, all other gods and cosmogonies were brought into existence. His mythology emphasised his role as 'King of gods', and his rulership of all other deities, who were in any case only variant forms of Amun whose appearance he could adopt at will. His most important aspects included associations with Re', Min, and Ptah; the ram, symbol of fertility, was regarded as his cult-animal, and he was also sometimes shown as a goose. In the earlier Hermopolitan cosmogony, Amun had been provided with a consort named Amaunet, but in his role as great state god he was now associated with Mut, the vulture-goddess, and their son, Khonsu, the moon-god. Both shared his great temple complex at Karnak and together they formed a divine triad.

The Theban cosmogony, as well as establishing the primary significance of Amen-Re', also claimed that Thebes was the site where the primaeval island had arisen from the waters of Nun and where Amun had created mankind. Amen-Re' was now the royal god, protecting the kings and supporting their claim to rule Egypt, and Thebes as his cult-centre became the most important city in Egypt. In addition to its cultic status, it was also the royal residence city, the political capital of a great empire, and the site where the kings now elected to be buried.

RELATIONSHIP BETWEEN THE KING AND THE PRIESTS OF AMEN-RE'

New temples were built for Amen-Re' throughout Egypt and he established his supremacy at new centres at the expense of older deities. However, it was at Thebes, where his great temple at Karnak was extended and embellished, that his priesthood acquired great power not only in spheres of religion but also in political and economic affairs. His priests eventually adopted the titles of other important deities such as Re' and Ptah, and claimed the right to supervise the cults of other gods. The increased wealth and influence of this priesthood was the direct result of royal policy towards the god in the early years of the New Kingdom. In this period, the rulers restored Egypt's control over Nubia, and then turned their attention to the small states which made up Palestine. By attempting to gain their allegiance, the Egyptian forces came into conflict at several periods with two other great states – the Mitannians and the Hittites – who sought to limit Egypt's enterprises in the area. These military confrontations brought a degree of success to the Egyptians, enabling her rulers to establish the first empire in the Near East. This was a loose association of semi-independent small states who were ruled by native governors whose allegiance to Egypt was assured. At its zenith, Egypt's empire stretched from Nubia to the banks of the River Euphrates, and the Theban kings were the most powerful rulers in the Near East. The Egyptians returned from their campaigns with booty and prisoners-of-war, and additional wealth was provided by the gifts which other, lesser rulers presented to Pharaoh. The kings did not forget the debt of gratitude which they owed to Amen-Re' for expelling the Hyksos and establishing their line, and throughout the early part of Dynasty 18, they made lavish donations to his temple at Karnak. Large estates were set up to support the temples and their personnel, and raw materials and prisoners-of-war were assigned to the temple for the service of Amen-Re'.

However, towards the end of the dynasty, the results of this disastrous policy became apparent and the relationship between the king and the god's staff became increasingly strained. As in the Old Kingdom, the king's generosity to the state god had created a situation in which the priesthood rivalled the ruler in wealth and power. Although a strong king could probably have resisted the claims of the priests, the god's role as father of the king gave the priests considerable strength in selecting and supporting a particular candidate for the kingship in cases where controversy arose over the succession. In the New Kingdom, the fiction was emphasised that each king was the offspring of a human royal mother and Amen-Re', and the Great Royal Daughter played an often vital role in the succession. Marriage to this woman could enable a man to ascend the throne at the expense of his rivals, and controversial claims arose within the royal family, often from children of minor queens. Thus, by expressing or witholding divine approval, the priests of Amen-Re' could ensure that their candidate was successful

It is therefore perhaps not surprising that Amenophis III, a strong and long-lived king, eventually sought to contain the priests' powers and ambitions and, in doing so, prepared the way for his son, Amenophis IV-Akhenaten, to introduce his religious revolution at the end of Dynasty 18.

THE TEMPLE OF AMEN-RE' AT KARNAK

The complex of buildings known as the Temple of Amun (Amen-Re') at Karnak today presents an awe-inspiring and confusing spectacle. It was started in Dynasty 12 and was subsequently enlarged and altered many times by rulers who each attempted to rival the efforts of their predecessors. The visitor is overwhelmed by a vista of courtyards, colonnades, obelisks and pylons, but several main buildings can still be determined which date mainly to Dynasty 18. The most significant and impressive is the Great Temple of Amun; this is approached down an avenue of ram-headed sphinxes and the various areas of the building are then divided by six massive pylons or gateways. Pylons also form a processional avenue which leads to the nearby temple of Mut. Different rulers contributed by building sanctuaries within the Great Temple of Amun, but the soaring columns with their plant-form capitals of the Great Hypostyle Hall, built by the Dynasty 19 pharaohs Sethos I and Ramesses II, justify its selection as one of the wonders of antiquity. Other temples were erected inside the complex, including those dedicated to Mut, Khonsu, Ptah and Montu. These were originally separate sanctuaries but, either because these deities were members

of Amen-Re''s triad or because their own local significance might
otherwise have threatened Amen-Re''s supremacy at Thebes, they
were incorporated into his complex and thus brought under the
supervision of Amun's priesthood.

A main processional route also linked the Temple of Karnak with
another temple, dedicated to Amun, Mut and Khonsu, which lay to
the south. It is known today as the Temple of Luxor but, in antiquity, it was called the 'Southern Harem', since it was believed to be
the official residence of Amun's wife, Mut. The god paid an annual
visit to Mut in this temple, when the priests carried Amun's statue
from Karnak to Luxor, and this procession provided the opportunity for the great and colourful Festival of Opet. Scenes of this
occasion on the walls of the Luxor Temple recall the music, dancing,
incense-burning and general merriment which would have accompanied the procession which bore the statue in its golden barque to
the Southern Harem. The god remained with his wife for a period
of twenty-four days and then the statue was brought back to his own
residence at Karnak.

In the Temple of Karnak, we can appreciate the Egyptian temple
at its greatest, not only in the magnitude of the architecture, but also
in the apparent power which its priesthood wielded in the community and the state. However, because of its size and random
development, it is at first difficult to relate it to other temples in Egypt
where the main architectural and ritual features are more clearly
delineated. Nevertheless, Karnak still retains the same characteristics as all other Egyptian temples, and was built according to the
basic principles which governed all temple architecture.

The Egyptian temple

The great stone temples of historic Egypt retained all the elements
which were already present in the reed shrines of the Predynastic
Period, in which the chieftain had made offerings to the local deity.
The chieftain eventually became the king, the local god of the
strongest tribal ruler became the national deity, and, with the great
technological advances in building materials and methods, the reed
shrine was finally transformed into the stone cultus temple.

Because the Egyptians were a conservative people, preserving
beliefs and customs which had served them well in the past, they
continued to incorporate features designed for the reed shrine in

temples built some 3000 years later. The temples, like the tombs, were designed to last forever; known as 'Houses of Eternity', they were built of stone, unlike the brick architecture designed for domestic use. Nevertheless, our knowledge of temples today is based mainly upon the well-preserved examples which date from the New Kingdom and from the Graeco-Roman Period, since earlier evidence is limited to representations of reed shrines, the remains of mortuary temples attached to pyramids, and some examples of Middle Kingdom cultus-temple architecture at Tod, Medinet Maadi and Medamud.

There appear to have been two distinct traditions of temple architecture in Egypt, which may have had quite separate origins. The solar temples of Dynasty 5 seem to owe little to the reed shrines of the Predynastic Period, and although elements of the solar ritual were included in the later cultus temples, the concept of the sun-temple probably developed separately. Some of the features of the early solar temples were reflected in those built for the cult of the Aten (Sun's disc) at the end of Dynasty 18, but they fall outside the main development of the Egyptian temple.

The second tradition, which does appear to have descended from the reed shrine, culminated in the New Kingdom in two types of temple which we designate 'cultus' and 'mortuary'. Their uses were distinct, but in terms of architecture and ritual they were closely associated. The cultus temple provided a place where the god's statue could be housed and where, through the means of ritual, the priest could approach the god and establish a relationship from which both derived benefit. The mortuary temple had originally been attached to the pyramid and was regarded as a place of great sanctity, where the funerary rites could be performed and offerings could be placed for the continuing sustenance of the deceased. By the New Kingdom, the kings were no longer buried in pyramids; their tombs were excavated in the rocky and inhospitable terrain of the Valley of the Kings at Thebes. This new location no longer afforded the possibility of building mortuary temples or offering chapels attached to the royal tombs, and from the reign of Amenophis I at the beginning of Dynasty 18 the rulers of the New Kingdom had to build mortuary temples which were separate from their tombs. Many chose to build these temples on the west bank of the Nile, on the flat plain which stretches from the river to the area where the royal tombs were situated. These temples nevertheless served the same purpose as the earlier mortuary temples in providing a place where the dead, deified ruler could continue to be worshipped and food offerings could be presented to him by means of ritual. Even when the temple was completed during the king's lifetime, it would seem that the ritual was nevertheless performed, with the king making offerings to his future dead, deified self. The mortuary temples were also dedicated to the cult of the chief local deity and were therefore also cultus temples, incorporating rituals for both the deity and the king.

The cultus and mortuary temples all had the same basic layout and architectural features, with only minor variation in detail. They were of course dedicated to different deities throughout the various districts of Egypt, and to the individual kings who had built them, but a knowledge of the basic features would even today make any one of them comprehensible.

The basic form was determined by the underlying mythology and ritual requirements, so that even the temples built during the Graeco-Roman Period conform to the same pattern. In these later temples there are inscriptions known as the 'Building Texts', which summarise the history of the temple and provide details of the names and sometimes the uses of the various halls and chambers. The texts at the Temple of Horus at Edfu also give a full account of the mythological explanation of the Egyptian temple. They relate how an island emerged from the waters which covered the face of the earth, at a time when darkness and chaos reigned supreme. This mound of land provided a landing place for the first god who was represented as a falcon, and his arrival made the island a place of great sanctity. Eventually, walls made of reed were constructed around the stalk on which he had perched, and the subsequent subsidence of the waters and expansion of the island permitted the erection of additional rooms, also made of reeds, at the front, sides and rear of the original chamber. This room containing the bird's perch came to be regarded as the sanctuary, and because the bird had alighted on the highest point of the mound, this remained at a slightly higher level than the later rooms. The Egyptians believed that every temple was in effect this original island of creation, which provided shelter for the resident deity and became a centre of great magical and religious potency. The concept of a 'First Occasion' was deeply rooted in their belief – they imagined that this was the time when the gods had handed down the pattern for a stable society, including the principles of law, religion, ethics and the kingship. The universe and

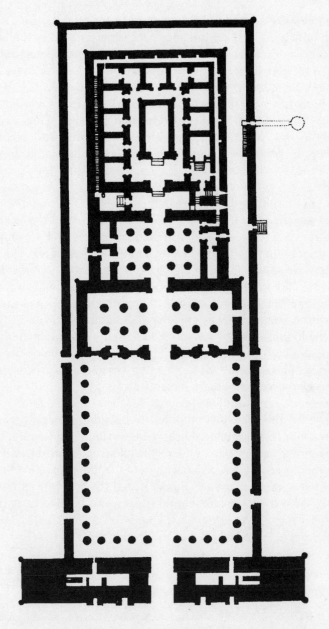

Figure 9 Plan of a typical cultus temple, based on the Temple of Horus at Edfu.

society were conceived as static entities and thus the guidelines and solutions provided on this First Occasion for the regulation of life would continue to meet all the needs of future generations. New answers were therefore not sought, and to derive benefit from all the forces put into effect on the First Occasion, it was deemed necessary only to re-create the environment and physical conditions which were thought to have prevailed on that occasion. Thus, each stone temple was designed to represent in its layout and architectural forms the physical conditions of the Island of Creation. Innovation in temple architecture was not only unnecessary but also undesirable.

In addition to this mythological concept, a secondary role was also attributed to the temple. It was the 'House of the God' where the resident deity was given shelter, protection and worship, in the same way that the mythical falcon had been cared for. The dead in Egypt possessed tombs which were regarded as 'houses' for their spirits, and similarly, the deities were provided with 'residences'. The requirements of the gods and of the dead – food and drink, washing, rest and recreation – were thought to be the same as those of the living, and they were supplied, in the case of the dead, by the funerary cult, and by means of divine rituals for the deities. Tombs and temples followed the same pattern as domestic architecture, and provided accommodation which was the equivalent of a bedroom, reception area, and storerooms for possessions. In the temple, however, this plan was modified to include a central processional route and to accommodate the various rituals, so that the building was elongated in plan. Other cosmological interpretations of the temple – viewing it as a microcosm of the universe or a reflection of the heavens, or a great coffin in which the sun-god slept and was daily reborn – were later embellishments to the two basic concepts

Figure 10   Section through a typical cultus temple.

of the temple as the Island of Creation and the god's house.

Every temple was rectangular in design and was enclosed within a mudbrick wall which was built in sections, decorated in wavy lines, and arranged in alternate concave and convex courses. These represented the waters which had surrounded the mythical island. In practical terms, the wall protected the temple from the gaze of townspeople who, in antiquity, had lived and worked in the immediate vicinity of the sacred enclosure. A great pylon (gateway) stood at the front of the temple; these were derived from the woven towers which had guarded the entrance to the reed shrine enclosures in the Predynastic Period. Beyond this lay one or two open courtyards, where wall reliefs depicted the king's prowess in battle and his relationship with the gods. It is not known whether the townspeople would have been allowed to enter these courts to offer up prayers or to watch the spectacle of the god's festival, but only the priests had access to the roofed area which lay beyond the courts. The open enclosure which had stood in front of the reed shrine was preserved in these courts.

From the court, one passed through a central doorway, situated on the main axis of the temple, into the hypostyle halls. The procession of priests would have followed this route, moving through the halls towards the god's sanctuary which was situated centrally at the rear of the temple. Subsidiary side-doors into the hall allowed the offerings of food and drink to be brought in. The brilliant sunlight of the outside world was immediately eclipsed on entering the hypostyle halls, which symbolised the reception area of the deity's residence. Roofed and dark, they were lit only by means of clerestory lighting and the flares which the priests carried. Heavy stone columns were arranged in groups, the central row being taller than the others to allow for the insertion of windows. The capitals were palmiform, lotiform or papyriform, and their primary function was to represent the lush vegetation of the Island of Creation and to ensure that this abundance could be magically reproduced in the surrounding countryside. The columns were placed here in such large numbers not merely to support the roof, which could have been achieved with fewer columns, but to symbolise the desired environment.

Similarly, the ceiling within the temple was decorated to represent the sky above the island, and plants were carved on to the bases of the walls, in the form of a frieze, to indicate the vegetation growing up from the island. The floor level inside the temple gradually inclined from the front of the building to the sanctuary at the rear. This not only increased the sense of awe and mystery as the god's resting place was approached, but attempted to reproduce the shape of the Island of Creation where the god's shrine had been positioned on the highest point. This feature was achieved in some temples by selecting a site which provided a natural incline; in others, the enclosed area of the temple, from the hypostyle halls to the rear, was built on a platform; and in a third group, the floor level was raised gradually from the hypostyle hall to the sanctuary and was then lowered again at the rear of the temple. This was achieved by constructing a series of pavements of different heights.

At the rear of the temple lay the sanctuary, the most sacred area of the temple where the god's cult-statue was placed in its shrine. This was a small, dark, rectangular room which retained the shape and characteristics of the early reed shrine. Here, the high-priest performed the rituals on behalf of the deity. A temple was usually consecrated to only one god, but in cases where other deities shared his temple, the sanctuary of the chief god was always situated on the main axis of the building and those of the lesser deities were placed on either side. In some temples, a subsidiary sanctuary was included to accommodate the god's barque and portable statue which were used for his perambulations during the festivals.

Other rooms were reserved for the storage of the god's possessions – his clothing, jewellery and insignia – and the vessels used in the rituals, while, in certain temples, special areas were devoted to particular aspects of the god's cult and mythology.

The rituals which were once performed in these temples are preserved in the scenes carved and painted on many of the walls within the enclosed areas of the building. Some of the scenes, which are usually arranged in two or three horizontal registers, are of a purely formal nature or they commemorate great events in the king's reign, such as his coronation or the foundation of the temple, but in certain rooms and chambers there is conclusive evidence that the scenes provide an orderly summary of the rites once performed within those areas. In the same way that the tomb scenes could be 'brought to life' by carrying out a religious ceremony, so too were the temple reliefs and accompanying inscriptions as well as the architectural features which symbolised the Island of Creation. This 'activation' of the temple was achieved, it was thought, when the newly built temple was handed over to the resident deity on the occasion of the Consecration Ceremony. Recharged with vital energy, the temple was then believed to assume the magical potency of the original island, and the rituals depicted on the walls would continue to be effective even if their actual performance was ever neglected or discontinued.

The temple rituals were of two main types. The scenes show the content of each rite, while the accompanying inscriptions provide the title of the rite, and the speeches of the king who performed the ritual and the god who received it. From these scenes we can therefore gain much information regarding this important aspect of the religion. One group of rituals were enacted regularly on a daily basis; these followed the same order for all temple deities throughout Egypt. The Daily Temple Ritual was performed in all cultus and mortuary temples from at least Dynasty 18 and provided a dramatisation of the commonplace events of everyday existence. Each morning the officiating priest entered the sanctuary, removed the cult-statue from its shrine, and took off its clothing and make-up. He then fumigated it with incense and presented different kinds of natron which could be chewed to cleanse the mouth; fresh clothing and make-up were then offered and the god's jewellery and insignia were placed on the statue, before the priest put the morning meal before the god and withdrew backwards from the sanctuary. Midday and evening meals were also presented, with the same ritual, and at nightfall the statue was returned to the shrine.

In the mortuary temples from the New Kingdom onwards this was extended, and a secondary ritual, known today as the 'Ritual of the Royal Ancestors', was performed after the conclusion of the Daily Temple Ritual. The food, removed from the god's table, was subsequently taken to another area of the temple where, after some preliminary rites, it was offered to the former kings of Egypt, whose support for the ruling Pharaoh was required. When he died and joined the Royal Ancestors, this continuing ritual in his temple would benefit him and perpetuate his name as well as ensuring that he had a food supply. The food, still intact, was finally removed from the altar of the ancestors and was taken outside the temple where it was divided amongst the priests as their daily food allowance. In cultus temples, this payment was made to the priests immediately after the completion of the Daily Temple Ritual.

The relationship which was believed to exist between the gods and mankind was based upon barter. In return for temples, perpetual food and other offerings, and the dedication of booty from the military campaigns, the gods gave the king his power, fame, eternal life and military prowess, and bestowed peace and prosperity on his subjects. The Daily Temple Ritual incorporated both Osirian and solar elements, and daily reaffirmed the god's rebirth. It was thought that this ritual revitalised the god's strength and any neglect of these duties would bring the return of primaeval chaos to Egypt.

The second group of rituals – the festivals – did not follow a single pattern, but varied from temple to temple, incorporating the mythology of each deity. They were held at regular, often yearly, intervals, and usually celebrated special events in the deity's life, such as the death and resurrection of Osiris, or the conjugal visits of other gods and goddesses. They were not performed in secret, although the most sacred stages of the festival were usually carried out inside the temple. The main event of most festivals, however, was the god's procession, when the deity's portable statue was paraded in a barque, amidst much noise and spectacle, amongst the crowds outside the temple. The festivals of the most important gods often attracted huge numbers of pilgrims from other parts of the country, and provided the only opportunity for the masses to participate in the worship of the temple deities.

The wall scenes in each temple show the king performing all the rituals for the god. As Horus incarnate, the son of Re', and the divine heir, only the king could act as the representative of mankind in the presence of the gods; the rituals and offerings were only efficacious if performed by the god's own son. He personified Egypt and represented every Egyptian in this role, and the gods had made him ruler so that he could execute their orders and attend to their welfare. It was therefore essential that the wall scenes should perpetuate the fiction that the king alone performed the rites in every temple. In earliest times, the tribal chieftain would have made the offerings to the local cult-statue in its reed-shrine, but as the ruler acquired increasing responsibility, he was no longer able to execute all the state and religious duties. Although he perhaps continued to perform the Daily Ritual in the main temple of the great state god, and was present at the consecration of each new temple, his duties in other temples were delegated to the high priests.

Each sizeable town possessed at least one temple, dedicated to the local deity, and in the capital city and the other great religious centres, there were large temples where the great state gods were worshipped. Nevertheless, although the temple played a vital role in the religious life of Egypt, it never became a centre of community worship, and the priests did not fulfil a pastoral role. The ordinary people had little contact with the temples, never taking part in the rituals and only perhaps visiting the outer courts to pray or to watch the great festivals. Apart from its essential role in ensuring the blessing of the gods and the continuation of Egypt, which were achieved by the repetition of the rituals, the temples had considerable economic, educational and social influence throughout the community.

Each temple owned estates, often of the best land, where livestock and crops were tended and vineyards and gardens were cultivated; these supplied food for the god's table and for the temple employees. Some temples also owned mines which provided the materials used by the temple workshops to produce cultic equipment. In addition to the king's presentation of booty to the temples, their economic power was also safeguarded by royal decrees which gave certain tax exemptions and privileges, and protected them from the extortions of crown agents, although the temples do seem to have paid some kind of tax. The temple also collected revenue from parts of the country; this was paid in kind, and included grain, oil, wine, beer, metals and other materials. At Karnak these dues were collected by the temple's own fleet of ships. Each temple also had extensive storehouses in its vicinity, where the revenue was received, recorded, stored and redistributed as payment to temple personnel.

The temple employed large numbers of people who were not only engaged in the religious duties but also in more menial tasks associated with the running of these great complexes. The Great Temple of Amun at Karnak was apparently run as a department of the royal administration which nominally came under the king, but the actual supervision and organisation of the temple, its personnel and its estates were entrusted to senior government officials who had extensive powers and duties. At Karnak, the top personnel were a major political force in Egypt, and the priesthood, a wealthy and privileged class, received a large proportion of the income from the god's estates in return for their services. This career offered young men a lucrative and promising profession, and the priesthood attracted the most able and ambitious in the land.

The priesthood

The priests, who acted as the king's delegates in caring for the god, were drawn from the highly educated levels in society. They were primarily responsible for ministering to the god's needs, and were called the 'servants of the god'. They were expected to understand the liturgy, and to study and teach their specialisations within the temple. They were not, however, required to give guidance or religious instruction to the community at large. The priesthood was usually held as a secondary profession; it was hereditary and could only be exercised by the male members of the family. These would be doctors, lawyers or scribes who held priesthoods related to their main professions, so that doctors could be priests of Sekhmet, goddess of disease and epidemics, and lawyers could be priests of Ma'at, the goddess of truth and justice. These men would practise their main profession in the community for nine months of the year and they could marry and raise families, but for three months of each year they were expected to live in the temple and complete the duties of a priest. As non-permanent personnel, they were divided into four groups and each group took a continuous term of duty within the temple for one month. The top positions in the temple hierarchy must have been permanent appointments, however, to provide continuity in organisation and management.

At the Temple of Karnak the most important post was held by the High Priest of Amun; this powerful position was usually held by a high-ranking courtier who had already pursued a highly successful political career at court, rather than by a man of great religious wisdom. The High Priest was able to affect the king's chances of survival and acceptance by offering or withholding the god's approval. His power was extensive and he owned a great house and estates which employed many servants.

The High Priests were known as 'First Prophets'; next in rank were the 'Fathers of the God' who included the Second, Third and Fourth Prophets of Amun. Below these were the ordinary priests or *w'bw* (Wabau); this title signified that they were ritually 'pure', an essential condition as they would, in the course of their duties, come into direct contact with the god's possessions, and everything pertaining to the deity was required to be 'pure'. While in the temple, the priests obtained ritual purity by the observance of certain taboos. They had to forgo sexual intercourse, wear garments made only of fine linen, shave their bodies and their heads daily, and cleanse their bodies in the Sacred Lake on several occasions in the day. Each temple possessed such a lake, where not only did the priests perform their ablutions but also the god's vessels and utensils were washed. It is probable that the water in these lakes was considered to possess special properties of purification. The lake was usually situated inside the temple enclosure, in the area where there were also priests' houses, magazines for storing the temple revenue, and the service quarters where all the activities which were not considered 'pure' – such as butchering and preparing the god's food – were carried out. Although it is not unknown for service areas to be included in the temple proper, it was obviously preferable to place them outside the sacred precinct.

Although the performance of the rituals was restricted to men, the singers and dancers who accompanied the services included women. At Karnak they seem to have been women of rank who frequently possessed fine coffins and funerary equipment, and were accorded the title 'Chantress of Amun'.

Apart from the full-time and part-time members of the priestly hierarchy, other full-time employees included the workers in the temples and on the estates. Among these there were the bakers, brewers and cooks to prepare the food offerings, the agricultural and textile workers, the craftsmen who produced the statuary and possessions of the god, and the servants who cleaned the temple. In the largest temples the number of staff required to organise and run these vast estates would have been considerable, and in general, the temples became the major employers of labour in the New Kingdom.

The role of religion in education

The temple also acted as the centre of highest education in Egypt. Some priests had specific skills and knowledge to contribute in such branches as liturgy, astronomy, astrology, the interpretation of dreams, geography, music, history and geometry, and students were sent to the temples to acquire instruction in medicine, law, architecture, and the skills necessary to become a scribe.

The system of education which existed in Egypt is nowhere clearly defined in the papyri, but the Wisdom Literature and other texts provide some information on their educational aims and practices. Until four years of age most children were under the complete control and guidance of their mother, and probably lived in the harem, or women's quarters of the house. They were expected to be obedient and to show great respect to their mother. After this their education was supervised by their father and, for some children at least, a formal education was provided until they reached the age of fourteen. Since a child was expected to follow his father's profession or trade, they were trained accordingly, and some attended the village school while others pursued more specialised courses. Education was not free, and each family was expected to pay in kind; in the country areas this often took the form of land produce. School lunches, consisting of 'three rolls of bread and two jugs of barley wine', were taken to the school by the mothers.

The curriculum included sports such as swimming, boating, wrestling, ball games, and shooting with bows and arrows, as well as instruction. For those who intended to pursue further education, writing was taught to train the character, as well as mathematics. Corporal punishment was considered to be desirable as a corrective measure for laziness and disobedience. In general, the Egyptians taught their children good manners and morals, self-control, and the ability to live in their society. The educational system encompassed not only scientific or scholarly learning but also aimed to instil manners which would make the person acceptable on all occasions. Indeed, in later times, the Greeks praised this system very highly.

The sons of the peasants followed their fathers into the fields, while those of craftsmen were apprenticed when they were about ten years of age, and the sons of professional men undertook further training. Only the boys intended for the priesthood or civil administration seem to have received an academic training. Some of the sons of the great nobles probably attended the classes taught by tutors for the royal children, whereas others went to a school where future officials were trained. At fourteen, those intended for a career as a doctor, lawyer or scribe were sent to undertake further studies at the temples.

The temples possessed fine libraries which housed papyri relating to many branches of learning, and the priests provided a range of teaching facilities. The training of the students was probably both theoretical and practical, and instruction may have taken place in the area of the temple known as the 'House of Life' where texts were copied and probably stored. Medical training may have involved treatment of patients from the surrounding district. We know almost nothing of the form which this education took, and whether it involved examination of the students, but it seems that the students provided their tutors with some social problems, as described in the following comments from a scribe to his pupil:

> I am told that you neglect your studies and devote yourself entirely to pleasure. You trail from street to street, smelling of beer. Beer robs you of all human respect, it affects your mind, and here you are, like a broken rudder, good for nothing. . . . You have been found performing acrobatics on a wall! Ah, if only you knew that wine was an abomination, if only you would renounce liquor, and think of something other than tankards of beer!

Education for girls was minimal and, apart from some of the princesses, it is unlikely that many received any further education or could read or write. Their role was in the home, where they acquired the necessary skills by assisting their mothers.

The role of religion in the law

Religious beliefs and practices permeated every aspect of life in ancient Egypt. There was no division between church and state and the gods were responsible for the establishment and continuation of all aspects of the political system, including the kingship and the law. Compared with other ancient civilisations, Egyptian law has yielded little evidence of its institutions but enough is known to indicate that it was governed by religious principles.

It was believed that the law, together with all the other tenets of the society, were handed down to mankind by the gods on the First Occasion. Law was personified by the goddess Ma'at, who governed truth, justice, righteousness, and maintained the correct balance and order of the universe and its inhabitants. The king upheld the law, but he too was subject to Ma'at, while the vizier, who was head of the law courts as the king's delegate, was the high priest of Ma'at. This legal system had developed from a primitive to a civilised form before the earliest extant texts were written during the Old Kingdom, for in these it is obvious that it had already become a formalised procedure. Many transactions deal with situations relating to funerary property or arrangements such as the settlement of land on Ka-priests. In theory the king was an absolute monarch and the sole legislator, with full powers over the life, death, labour and property of all his subjects, but in practice private law existed, and property could be the subject of private legal transactions. In general, although punishments were severe, the laws were more humane than those of other ancient societies, and great protection was afforded to women and children.

In Dynasty 19, however, a deterioration occurred in the method of judgment. Law courts were of two kinds – the local courts (Kenbet) were comprised of local dignitaries under the chairmanship of an official and these could deal with most cases; the High Court, which sat at Thebes under the presidency of the vizier, exercised judgment in capital offences.

All kinds of evidence were admitted and considered by the judges, and a verdict had to be followed by a declaration of submission by the defeated party. However, from Dynasty 19 onwards, a verdict was sometimes obtained by the use of an oracle. The statue of a god became the judge, and the god's will was obtained by means of a ceremonial performed before the statue. The inquirer would stand in front of the statue and read out a list of named suspects, and the statue was believed to give a sign as the name of the culprit was read out. Such practices were obviously open to corruption and abuse.

Texts from Dynasty 20 provide further information about legal and related matters in the New Kingdom. We learn not only of strikes and industrial unrest which occurred amongst the workmen engaged on the royal tomb in the reign of Ramesses III, but also of a conspiracy which threatened the king's life. In a papyrus which may have been housed originally in the temple library at Medinet Habu, an account is given of how the major-domo and the women of one of the royal harems, together with various harem officials, conspired to kill the king, possibly with the intention of placing a rival on the throne.

Another papyrus relates the means by which they hoped to achieve this – by writing magical spells and making waxen images which they attempted to smuggle into the harem. The plot was unsuccessful and the culprits were severely punished. A series of well preserved papyri provide details of further trials which began in the reign of Ramesses IX and continued for many years. Social conditions had become so depressed and poverty was so widespread by this period that tomb-robbery, always a common practice, had increased to the extent where the kings were prepared to take legal measures against the criminals and to bring them to trial.

The role of religion in medicine

The treatment and care of the sick were also based to some extent on magico-religious principles. Medical practice was a mixture of measures which were either objective and scientific, based upon observation of the patient, knowledge of anatomy, and general experience of disease, or which relied upon the use of magic. It was thought that, although these were separate approaches, they could both contribute to healing the patient. It was assumed that each person was born healthy and that all disease had a cause; this might be an outward, visible cause which could be remedied by rational medicine, or an inward, hidden cause, which was attributable to a 'devil'. This was regarded as the result of the malevolence of the dead, or the punishment of the gods, or even the ill wishes of an enemy. For such cases, every attempt was made to extract the 'devil', by the use of spells and incantations, accompanied by a ritual in which the practitioner imitated acts and gestures upon a figurine. In earliest times, the tribal chieftain had performed this magic for his people, and the kings were later believed to possess special magical powers. However, eventually, these skills were delegated to the priests who, by trial and error, developed the ability to make rational diagnoses and to treat patients who sought cures, thus establishing the foundations of a medical science.

Various deities supervised different areas of medicine. One of the most important was the goddess Sekhmet, the lioness who brought epidemics and disease and who could therefore be petitioned to remove them. Thoth, the ibis-headed god of scribes and learning, was worshipped as the inventor of the healing formulae, while Isis, who had reassembled the body of her husband Osiris, was patroness of magicians. Horus and Amun were oculist gods, and Tauert, a lowly but popular household goddess, cared for women in childbirth. Imhotep, the architect of the Step Pyramid at Saqqara, was also probably the physician of King Zoser, and he was later deified for his powers of healing, and identified by the Greeks with Aesculapius, their god of medicine.

The men who were priest-doctors had originally perhaps mediated between patients and Sekhmet in a purely religious function, but over the years, their practical medical skills developed, based on observation of the sick, and they were able to offer practical help. They were known as *w'bw* (Wabau) and worked in the temples, where they headed the medical hierarchy. Little is known of their medical training, but some temples certainly acquired special reputations as medical centres. In the Ptolemaic Period it is known that the temples at Denderah, Memphis and Deir el-Bahri were notable for their treatment of the sick and especially for the cure of the mentally and emotionally disturbed. The treatment which was offered may in fact have been practised in Egypt at earlier periods although no evidence has survived. At Denderah, a building constructed near to the temple acted as a sanatorium in which petitioners were accommodated during their quest for miraculous cures. They prayed to the god, consulted the oracle to find solutions to their problems, and underwent a form of treatment known as the 'therapeutic dream'. They were prepared by isolation, silence and the use of lamps, and then induced into a dream state described as 'Nun', the great ocean from which life had originally emerged. In this state they contacted the gods and obtained interpretation of their dreams. For some, at least, it seems that this isolation and therapy brought the desired cure.

A lower grade of doctors were known as *swnw*. These were state employees, appointed to serve either on building sites, or with the army, at burial grounds, or elsewhere. There were also magicians, and assistants such as nurses, masseurs and bandagers. The treatment of the sick was enlightened and considerate; there were ethical standards of practice and no patient, whatever his disease, was considered to be untouchable. The Egyptians had a good knowledge of anatomy because, unlike some other countries, their long association with the processes of mummification ensured that there was no taboo on dissecting a corpse. Indeed, they gained much knowledge from mummification procedures, but because deep surgery was never attempted on the living, their understanding of the functions of body systems was often inaccurate. Nevertheless, surgery was performed on surface wounds and tumours, and there was considerable expertise in the setting of dislocated and fractured bones. Circumcision of males was also commonplace. But one type of growth, known as the 'tumours of Khonsu', was regarded as incurable unless the god's intervention could be obtained. Other specialisations included gynaecology and the treatment of eye diseases; the existence of a dental profession is still disputed, but skeletal and mummified remains show evidence of severe dental problems.

Pharmaceutical treatments were also offered – aromatic oils and pleasant substances were believed to attract good gods and to repel evil. Drugs included mineral, vegetable or animal substances, and some medicines contained disagreeable substances such as dung or urine, in the hope that these would expel the evil from the patient. The treatment of some complaints involved the use of 'transfer'; one example was the migraine headache, when the head of the sufferer was rubbed with that of a fish, to transfer the pain.

There are several sources of information relating to medicine in Egypt. These include the medical papyri which give examples of the symptoms, diagnosis and treatment of a wide variety of illnesses; some of the tomb scenes which show servants and workers with physical conditions; stelae which belonged to physicians and which detail their titles and career advancement; some instruments which probably had a medical and surgical application; and a wall scene on the temple at Kom Ombo which may show a set of surgical instruments. Such sources are limited in scope, and further information may await discovery.

Nevertheless, sufficient evidence remains to confirm that later medical systems in Europe and the Near East derived their principles from Egypt, for it was here that, despite the continued use of magic as an alternative method, the basis of a medical science and profession was established. To Egypt, and in particular Alexandria, the later Greek physicians came to receive training in systematic dissection and medical principles, and in medicine, as in other fields, the Egyptian temples made a major contribution to society.

Household gods and personal piety

Although the ordinary people perhaps understood something of the god's role within the temple, and enjoyed the great festivals, their contact with these deities was minimal. They devoted their prayers and personal requests to a group of minor gods and goddesses who are now referred to as 'household deities', for they possessed no temples or divine cults but were worshipped at small domestic shrines. These deities could be approached for help and guidance in everyday matters and were worshipped widely throughout all levels of society. The most popular were Bes, who is shown with the body of a grotesque dwarf and who was the god of love, marriage, dancing and jollification, and Tauert, who appears as an upstanding, pregnant hippopotamus. She was the goddess of fecundity and childbirth and gave assistance to women of all classes at the birth of their children.

Since the state gods had little effect upon the lives of the ordinary people, it is surprising to find that Amen-Re', the most powerful and universal of the state gods, was worshipped by at least one community as a personal deity. A special relationship existed between the people of Thebes and their local god, Amun, before his elevation as a state deity, and in the New Kingdom this still continued in at least one community in the area. On the west bank at Thebes, situated in a remote area some distance from the royal burial sites of the New Kingdom, the early kings of Dynasty 18 had built a village to accommodate the workmen and their families who were engaged in the preparation of the royal tombs. This village, known today as Deir el-Medina, contained some seventy houses and a temple; the villagers were eventually buried in the neighbouring cemetery. Excavation of the site has revealed detailed and fascinating information about this community – the working conditions of the men, including their hours of labour, their equipment, payment and so forth, and an insight into their political and religious beliefs as well as their social organisation.

The village was occupied throughout Dynasties 18, 19 and 20, when the Valley of the Kings continued in use for royal burials. Once the king's tomb had been completed, the workmen were sent by their royal master to decorate the tombs of favourite queens, princes and high-ranking officials. They also found time to undertake private work for wealthy clients, fashioning desirable toilet articles and other trinkets, and were often able to prepare elegant tombs for themselves at Deir el-Medina, incorporating miniature pyramids on top of the adjoining funerary chapels. The skills of these men were handed down from father to son in this close-knit community, and the surviving evidence indicates that they had an amazing degree of autonomy in certain religious and legal spheres. The workmen carried out subsidiary duties as priests at Deir el-Medina, and the legal disputes were settled by the villagers in a local law-court, only submitting a case to the vizier's court if it was a capital offence. Limestone ostraca, decorated with quick sketches, have

1 *Anthropoid coffin (upper half) of Nekht-Ankh*
This finely painted wooden coffin belonged to a priest. It provides a good example of the geometric style of decoration which characterised Middle Kingdom funerary goods. The false beard and painted bead collar are notable features. From the Tomb of Two Brothers at Rifeh. Dynasty 12, *c.*1900 BC.

2 *Stucco portrait mask*
This stylised portrait mask on a flat board, representing a
woman, originally covered the face of a mummy. The
crimson garment and moulded gold jewellery are painted to
simulate the originals. From the Fayoum, Roman Period,
*c.*150 AD.

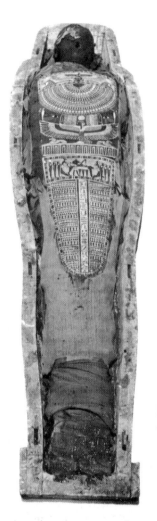

3 *Anthropoid coffin*
Painted with intricate scenes and inscriptions intended to ensure the owner's continued existence, this wooden coffin belonged to a young woman, aged about twenty-five, whose mummy was placed inside. The coffin has a gilded face, and probably dates to the Ptolemaic Period, *c.*300 BC.

4 *Mummy inside an anthropoid coffin*
This mummy of a young woman was found inside a body coffin (photograph 3). There is a cartonnage cover over the chest, decorated with the winged goddess Nephthys and scenes and inscriptions to ensure the owner's continuation. X-rays of the mummy revealed a partly metallic amulet beneath the bandages in the pelvic region. Probably Ptolemaic Period, *c.*300 BC.

5 *Wooden panel portrait*
Placed over the face of a mummy, this portrait shows the owner as a bearded man. It is encircled by a cartonnage headcover which extends over the breast and imitates a white cloak covering the head and bust.
From the Fayoum, Roman Period, *c.*150 AD.

6 *Mummy of a child (upper half)*
Excavated by William Flinders Petrie, this has a cartonnage cover with separate gilded pieces for the head, chest and feet. The eyes are inlaid and the moulded imitations of jewellery include snake bracelets and are set with glass to represent semi-precious stones. A bunch of flowers is held in one hand. From Hawara, Roman Period, *c.*170 AD.

7 *Mummy of a child*
Wrapped in a reed mat tied with ropes at each end, this is an example of a poor person's burial. The body of the infant is in a fair state of preservation, and x-rays have revealed that the child was just under three months of age and had suffered illness. From Gurob, Dynasty 18, *c.*1450 BC.

8 *Linen and stucco cover from a mummy*
This is painted with the representation of a young boy, and originally enclosed the body of a child. It shows the geometric pattern on the child's wrapper, and gilded stucco is used to represent the necklace and anklets. The child holds a bunch of red flowers in one hand. Roman Period, *c.*120 AD.

9 *Wooden panel portrait*
Portrait of a man, painted in wax on a wooden panel. This unique example was obviously first hung in the house during the owner's lifetime. It was subsequently discarded, the panel reversed and a portrait of a different man painted on the other side. Later, it was cut to size and placed over the face of a mummy. From Hawara, Roman Period, *c.*150 AD.

10 *Gilded cartonnage mask*
Originally placed over a mummy, this mask incorporates painted
representations of a feathered headdress and a bead collar. In the later
periods, the mummy was no longer buried with treasure, since in the past,
this had often been removed by plunderers; instead, this was simulated
with moulded plaster and inlaid 'glass stones' which decorated the face
mask. Ptolemaic Period, *c.*300 BC.

11 *Stone offering stand*
Found in the houses of a pyramid workmen's town, these stands were probably used to support dishes holding bread and other food offered to the gods in a regular household ritual. This shows two primitive figures of men, standing back to back. The unusual design of these stands may indicate either the presence in the town of foreigners with different religious customs, or the introduction by the native Egyptians of a local and distinctive style. From Kahun, Dynasty 12, *c.*1895 BC.

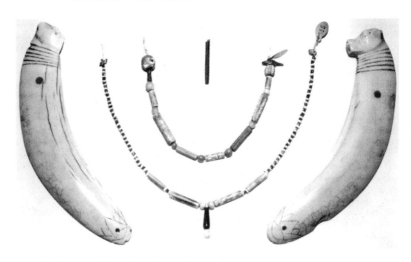

12 *Selection of beads and a pair of ivory clappers*
Found in the houses of a pyramid workmen's town, the ivory clappers were discovered buried in a hole in the floor of a chamber, together with a wooden figurine of a dancer representing the household deity Beset. They may have been part of a local magician's equipment. From Kahun, Dynasty 12, *c.*1895 BC.

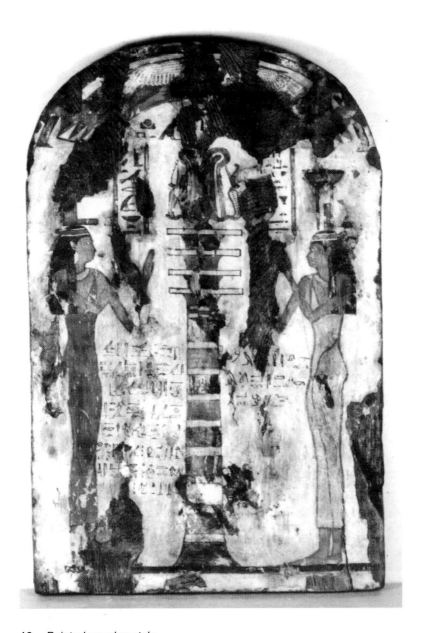

13 *Painted wooden stela*
This shows figures of the goddesses Isis (left) and her sister Nephthys
(right) adoring the Djed-pillar which represented Isis' husband, Osiris.
Stelae were set up in tombs and elsewhere to commemorate the deceased
owner and ensure his continued existence. Dynasty 18, *c.*1450 BC.

14 *Wooden statuette of Ptah-Sokar-Osiris*
Representing the god of the underworld, these figures were part of the funerary equipment in the later dynasties. A papyrus, inscribed with spells from the Book of the Dead to ensure the deceased's continuation in the afterlife, was placed in the box on which the figure stands. Late Period, *c.*525–*c.*332 BC.

15 *Bronze statuette of Isis and Horus*
These statuettes, originally mounted on a wooden base, represent the goddess suckling her infant son, Horus, who is shown wearing the Sidelock-of-Youth and the royal uraeus on his forehead. Isis wears a heavy wig surmounted by the sun disc and cow's horns. Dynasty 26, *c.*600 BC.

16 *Faience amulet of Bes*
This represents the popular 'household god', Bes, and was worn to protect the owner against evil and to bring good luck. Bes, in the typical pose as a dwarf wearing a feathered headdress, was widely worshipped as god of love, marriage and jollification. Late Period, *c.*600 BC.

17 *A pectoral found on a mummy in a tomb*
This chest ornament is a fine example of cloisonné work. Made of gold, the front (left) is inlaid with turquoise, lapis-lazuli and carnelian, while the same design is incised on the reverse (right). It incorporates the Sacred Eyes (top) which flank the sun's disc, and two hooded crows, each standing on the hieroglyph meaning "gold", on either side of the sceptre of dominion. From Riqqeh, Dynasty 12, *c.*1900 BC.

18 *Hypostyle Hall of The Temple of Luxor at Thebes*
An early 20th-century photograph showing the temple known as the 'Southern Harem', where the goddess Mut was worshipped. It was the setting for the annual festival of Opet when the statue of Amun, Mut's consort, was brought from the neighbouring Temple of Karnak. The lotiform capitals of the columns are clearly visible here. New Kingdom, *c.*1450–1200 BC.

19 *The Great Sphinx, Gizeh*

An early 20th-century photograph showing the Great Sphinx at Gizeh, adjacent to the pyramid of Chephren, whose appearance may be reflected in the Sphinx's face. The Sphinx was later regarded as the guardian of the Gizeh necropolis, but it was originally carved from a natural knoll of rock which was too friable to be used for blocks to build the pyramid. Old Kingdom, Dynasty 4, *c.*2550 BC.

20 *The Ramesseum at Thebes*
An early 20th-century photograph showing the mortuary temple of
Ramesses II, known as the Ramesseum. Regular services and rituals were
performed here by the priests to ensure the continued royal existence of
Ramesses II, who was buried in a tomb in the nearby Valley of the Kings.
New Kingdom, Dynasty 19, *c.*1240 BC.

21 *Wall Relief at the Temple of Hathor at Denderah*

On the southern rear outer wall of the temple, this scene shows Cleopatra VII (far left) and her son Caesarion (the child of Julius Caesar), who stands in front of her and offers burning incense to the gods of Denderah: Hathor (wearing the sun's disc and cow's horns), preceded by her son Ihy and followed by her falcon-headed husband, Horus. Graeco-Roman Period, c.30 BC.

22 *Stone 'false-door' from a tomb*
Inscribed with the names and title of the tomb-owner, a false-door was
intended to allow the spirit of the deceased owner to enter the tomb at will,
to take possession of the mummy and absorb spiritual sustenance from the
food offerings. From Saqqara, Old Kingdom, *c.*2500 BC.

been discovered in the village rubbish heaps; these often show caricatures of the nobility and their servants in which the nobles are depicted as mice while the servants who attend them are cats. These sketches, hastily drawn by the artists for their own amusement, and then discarded in the rubbish heap, indicate something of the independent attitude of this community.

It was this same community which, in Dynasty 20, ceased work on the royal tomb because their food rations were long overdue. This protest – the first recorded action of its kind in antiquity – occurred in the last years of Ramesses III's reign (c.1165 BC). Because of the importance of their work on the royal tomb and the pressing need to complete it, the authorities took special action, and the vizier made strenuous efforts to obtain their food rations from elsewhere, and so persuaded them to return to work.

The village was founded by Amenophis I, the first king to build a tomb in the Valley of the Kings at Thebes, and he was later deified and worshipped by this community at Deir el-Medina. Although some examples do occur, it was rare for kings or men to be deified and offered a personal cult in Egypt. However, the archaeological evidence indicates that Amen-Re' was also worshipped at Deir el-Medina, not as a great state god, but as a personal deity who championed the poor and the needy. Mottoes inscribed on scarabs which were worn by the people here confirm that he was regarded as their personal friend and protector who gave life and assistance, and who sustained the lonely. His role as the supporter of the poor against the rich and the rescuer of the weak and fearful from the oppressor is also emphasised in the official hymns. It is another aspect of the nature of this omnipotent god.

Advice was obtained from the gods on a whole range of everyday matters and this contact was often made through the use of an oracle which took a variety of forms. In this way, the villagers here and in other parts of Egypt derived help and comfort from a personal relationship with their deities.

The relationship between Egyptian and foreign cults and deities

During the New Kingdom, expansion brought Egypt into contact with religious cults and ideas in many other lands. Until this period, there had been an exchange of ideas with three main areas. The

Libyans who lived in the region to the west of Egypt had contributed
to the early 'cultural' processes in Egypt, although the extent of this
is still uncertain. Nevertheless, certain elements in the king's ceremonial costume – the animal tail on his headdress and the uraeus on
his crown – may have been derived from a general North African
culture which filtered down in both Egyptian and Libyan customs.
Some early Egyptian deities may also have had Libyan origins, such
as Neith, the ancient goddess of hunting, and Ash, a god who personified the desert and was later equated with Seth.

To the south, Egypt had long pursued a policy of colonising the
Nubians. Here, they stressed their own superiority. The gods of
Nubia were not, however, repressed by the Egyptians, but were
incorporated in the Egyptian pantheon, ruled over by the major
Egyptian deities. Thus, the Nubian deities were brought within the
control of Pharaoh, and absorbed in much the same way that the
predynastic tribes had taken over the deities of the conquered neighbours. Egypt regarded Nubia as an enlarged territory for her own
gods, and the kings built many sanctuaries there to Amun, Re' and
Ptah, to impress their importance upon the local population. The
Nubians came to worship these deities with fervour and devotion,
and they also deified and provided a divine cult for several Egyptian
pharaohs, including Sesostris III, Amenophis III and Ramesses II.
The latter built a temple at Abu-Simbel which was dedicated to Re'-
Harakhte and illustrates the continuing religious policy of the
Egyptians towards Nubia. Only one significant Nubian deity was
adopted by the Egyptians; this was Dedun, originally a bird of prey,
who was brought into the Egyptian pantheon and associated with
Horus as early as the Old Kingdom. By the later periods, he was
worshipped as the guardian of the fortresses which Egypt built in
Nubia to retain control of the surrounding area.

By the New Kingdom, Nubia had become merely another administrative district of Egypt, controlled by the Viceroy of Kush, an
Egyptian official who was directly responsible to Pharaoh. In
general, the Nubians had no command of their own resources and
found their culture dominated by that of their powerful northern
neighbour. No outstanding leader emerged there to challenge the
supremacy of Egypt, and local Nubian chieftains appear in
the Egyptian records merely as rebels who were to be subdued. It
was not until Dynasty 25 that the southerners were able to reverse
the tables and to overcome Egypt, but then they brought with them

the religious beliefs and cults which the Egyptians had introduced to Nubia many generations previously.

Egypt's relations with her northerly neighbours were very different. Contact with Palestine, Phoenicia and Syria had increased since the Middle Kingdom, and by the New Kingdom, Egypt's empire exerted a considerable influence throughout this area. However, no attempt was made to replace local rule with a purely Egyptian system, and local dynasts remained effective rulers of their areas, responsible to Pharaoh through a limited top administration. The practical test of loyalty to Egypt was the prompt and correct payment of tribute to Egypt. In this area, the population had already evolved a social, political and cultural system by the time they came into contact with Egypt, and this region never became an appendage to Egypt in the way Nubia had done. In religion and other matters there was a two-way exchange of ideas, and Egypt's effect upon these areas was also limited by the fact that, unlike Nubia, they were not geographically isolated but formed a crossroads for beliefs and concepts from other major powers. Nevertheless, the theory that the Pharaoh was the protector of the Egyptians was now extended to cover other peoples in the area who were subordinate to Egypt. However, although Pharaoh was considered to be the supreme ruler of the area, other leaders were also acknowledged as men of political significance and status. This attitude was reflected in religion, and although the Egyptians sought to promote their own state god Amen-Re' and to emphasise his role as the creator of all men, the chief gods of other countries were also regarded as the ruling powers of those areas. Indeed, when the Pharaohs erected and dedicated temples abroad, they were usually dedicated to these native deities.

It was believed that by absorbing the gods of conquered lands into its own pantheon, Egypt could acquire the additional powers of those deities for her own benefit. Some of the Syrian gods who possessed martial powers were therefore introduced into the Egyptian pantheon and were probably worshipped there by both Egyptians and non-Egyptian residents. Given Egyptian clothing and attributes, these deities now concealed their alien origins and rapidly became absorbed into the society. There were cults of Ba'al and Astarte and Resheph at Memphis; Hurun was worshipped at Giza; 'Anat, Astarte, Hurun and Seth as Ba'al had cults at Pi-Ramesse; Ba'alaat had a centre in the Fayoum, and Resheph and Qudshu were found at Deir el-Medina. The form which the cults of these foreign deities took is uncertain. They were invoked on stelae as purely Egyptian gods and the arrangement of their temples at the above sites showed no variation from the typical Egyptian pattern, while the names of the priests' ranks also comply with the Egyptian system. It is possible that foreign residents in Egypt had small household shrines for different sets of rites but none have as yet been discovered. Not only the warlike qualities of these gods were revered; some were also attributed with healing qualities, the most famous example being Ishtar of Nineveh whose statue was sent by King Tushratta of Mitanni to the Egyptian Court in the hope that she could relieve the suffering of Amenophis III.

In general, the Egyptian deities are not found in the Syrian pantheon, but Egyptian forms of local deities occur. Examples include Ptah-south-of-his-wall, who was Lord of 'Ankh-tawy and the Great Chief of Askelon, and the temple at Byblos in Phoenicia which was dedicated to 'Hathor, Lady of Byblos', as well as the temple dedicated to Amun at Gaza. Evidence suggests that Egyptian influence on ritual in Syrian and Palestinian temples was negligible, but Egyptians visiting abroad did dedicate stelae to local gods in Ugarit and Beth-shan.

Because of the limited and fragmentary nature of the available material, especially from the Syrian sources, it is difficult to assess the impact which the two societies had upon each other. There was obviously considerable contact between the royal courts, emphasised by the increasing number of royal marriage alliances towards the end of Dynasty 18, and between the ruling classes who met as envoys and men of letters. Amongst the lower levels of society, some of the itinerant artisans would have been aware of different concepts, and ideas were spread by prisoners-of-war and by mercenaries. However, present knowledge makes it difficult to assess the extent of religious and cultural exchange, and there is little evidence that any impact was made upon Egyptian theology, except to extend the king's role and powers over foreign peoples. It is probable that the introduction into Egypt of new deities and beliefs was more apparent than real.

Funerary beliefs and practices in the New Kingdom

The funerary customs remained basically unaltered from earlier periods, although some of the nobles' tombs indicate a more

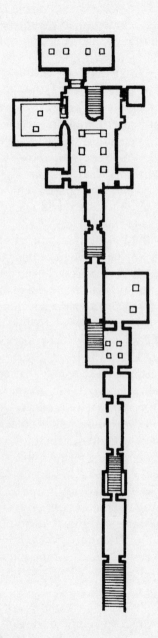

Figure 11 Plan of the tomb of King Sethos.

cosmopolitan atmosphere in the society, showing scenes of foreign peoples, notably Syrians and Aegean islanders, bringing tribute to Egypt.

From the beginning of Dynasty 18 onwards, the kings chose a new burial place situated in the bleak and desolate hills which dominate the west bank of the Nile at Thebes. This action was probably prompted by the continuous plundering of the pyramids leading them to look for a less ostentatious site. The place which they chose – a barren, narrow and rocky valley – is known today as the 'Valley of the Kings'. The natural shape and colour of the Theban hills are reminiscent of a pyramid and the highest point, called the 'Peak' by the Egyptians, was revered as a goddess who protected the dead buried in the narrow, arid valleys below. Perhaps because it recalled the appearance of the pyramid and also because it was near to the city of Thebes and yet isolated enough to be guarded, this site was chosen, and here the kings were buried in deep rock cut tombs which descended for many feet into the side of the mountain.

In the early part of Dynasty 18, each one consisted of an entrance stairwell cut into the rock and a long tunnel which sloped down to a rectangular ante-chamber; from this, a second stairway and corridor led to a pillared hall which accommodated the burial in a sarcophagus which was mounted on an alabaster base and stood at the inner end of the hall. As many as four storerooms opened off the sepulchral hall. These tombs were designed to defeat the tomb-robbers, but all the known royal tombs in this valley, with the exception of Tutankhamun's burial, which was entered in antiquity but escaped massive plundering, were robbed and the contents stolen and the mummies desecrated as the plunderers stripped them of their amulets and jewellery. Only from the wall scenes which decorate these tombs can the visitor now gain some idea of the original beauty and magnificence of these royal tombs. These represent rites taken from the Book of Amduat ('What is in the Underworld'), which provides an illustrated record of the journey which the sun-god took through the underworld when, for the twelve hours of the night, he combated the evils and demons which lurked there. This was obviously placed in the king's tomb to assist him in defeating the dangers which he would encounter during his own subterranean journey. In some tombs there are also other features, including excerpts from the Litany to Re' and scenes showing the king in the company of other deities. Some distance away from the valley,

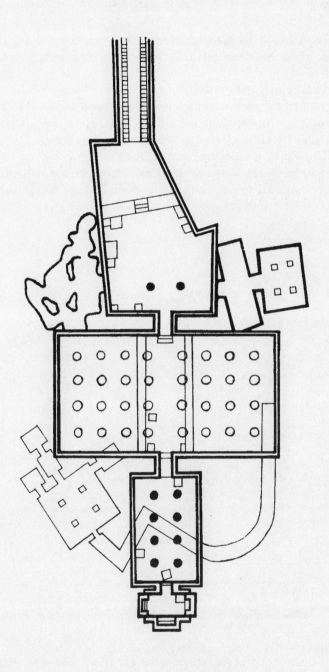

Figure 11 Plan of a New Kingdom nobleman's tomb.

situated on the flat plain which stretches towards the Nile, the kings built their mortuary temples where their funerary cults were performed.

In a nearby valley, known today as the 'Valley of the Queens' slightly less elaborate tombs were built for some of the favourite wives and princes of the royal household, but it seems that during much of Dynasty 18, no one area was reserved for the burial of the queens whose tombs were scattered across the whole region and, in the case of Queen Tiye, she was apparently buried with her husband Amenophis III in his tomb in the Valley of the Kings, while her parents were also given the unusual honour of a tomb there. In the

Figure 13 *Tomb scene showing anointing with perfume*
To prepare women of the upper classes for banquets and entertainment, the servants (left) anointed them with perfumed ointment. The noblewomen also wear scented wax cones on their heads.

tombs in the Valley of the Queens, the decoration on the walls again concentrated on the relationship between the deceased and the gods and the successful completion of the final journey.

The tombs of the favoured nobles of the period were situated in groups in the vicinity of the royal burials, but in these, the wall scenes depicted events and activities which the deceased had enjoyed in life. The typical Theban tomb of Dynasty 18 consisted of a rectangular courtyard behind which lay an inverted T-shaped chapel cut into the rocky hillside. At the rear of the chapel, or in a corner, there was a hidden shaft which descended to one or more subterranean chambers which accommodated the burial. In some cases, the walls of the burial chamber were decorated with inscriptions from either the Pyramid Texts, the Book of the Dead, or the Book of Amduat, but it was usual for only the chapels to have scenes painted on the walls. The chapel consisted of a transverse hall, a passage which ran longitudinally from the centre of the hall back into the mountain, and at the far end of this passage, a small sanctuary which contained a niche for statues of the tomb-owner and his wife. Sometimes there was also a false-door stela here. These tomb-chapels were directly derived from the portico tombs of the Middle Kingdom nobility, and although there were many variations, this plan remained the pattern for all such tombs built early in Dynasty 18, and can also be recognised in the later designs. Unlike the tombs of the Old Kingdom, the Theban tomb-chapels were frequently just painted, since the local supply of stone is poor although some examples occur of sculptured relief. The paintings were applied to the walls, which were coated with stucco and mud-plaster, using the gouache technique, and the scenes were arranged according to a logical sequence. In the front hall there are scenes showing the daily activities of the owner and on the rear wall they concentrate on his profession or career and emphasise his duties for the king, while aspects of his family life – devotion to the gods, sports and recreations, his family, social activities, and life on his estates – are found on the other walls.

In the passage and the sanctuary, the scenes depict the funerary preparations of the deceased, including his procession, the burial ceremonies and the presentation of the funerary offerings, and the funerary banquet, as well as his existence after death, when he meets the gods of the underworld and makes the pilgrimage to Abydos. Thus, we gain information from these tombs not only of the religious and funerary rites but also of the agricultural and domestic conditions, all set against the wider background of Egypt as a wealthy society with a sophisticated and cosmopolitan lifestyle.

These tombs were lavishly equipped with all the goods needed for a continued existence. Advances were also made in the process of mummification, in an attempt to produce an even more lifelike appearance. Much of our information regarding mummification during this period is derived from the bodies of members of the royal family. During Dynasty 21, the priests rescued the remains of the New Kingdom rulers whose tombs had been plundered and, so that at least the mummies would be preserved for continuing use by the deceased, they were hidden in two caches at Thebes. These were discovered between AD 1881 and 1889 and have since been examined by experts in various disciplines; they provide an invaluable source of information regarding disease and diet, as well as funerary customs, although this evidence comes only from one class of the society. Various methods of removing the brain had now been intro-

Figure 14 *Tomb scene showing noblewomen at a banquet*
These women, wearing floral wreaths and perfumed wax cones, represent the fashions and styles of the New Kingdom (*c.*1400 BC). According to the traditions of formal, religious art, they are represented in profile.

duced, and the skull cavity was subsequently packed with resin-soaked strips of linen. Also, the positioning of the hands varied according to the sex and date of the individual, and during Dynasty 18, there was a change in the location of the abdominal incision for the removal of the viscera. However, the most notable advance was the introduction of a number of techniques which were designed to restore a lifelike appearance to the mummy. The first attempt to introduce subcutaneous packing is apparent in the mummy of Amenophis III of Dynasty 18. This elderly king was obese in life, and it was probably a wish to preserve the original rounded contours of his body rather than the shrunken form which the mummification procedure produced, that resulted in experimentation with this technique. By Dynasty 21 subcutaneous packing, whereby material was inserted under the skin through insertions, was used for many mummies of the upper classes, and a peak of achievement was now reached in mummification, with every attempt being made to reproduce the features of the person in life. The neck and cheeks were packed, with the facial stuffing being introduced through the mouth, and artificial eyes were often inserted in the eye sockets and false tresses were added to the existing hair of the deceased. The surface of the face and often of the whole body was painted with red ochre (for men) and with yellow ochre (for women), to restore the colouring apparent in life.

The court of Amenophis III

During the long reign of Amenophis III, Egypt reached the height of prosperity; diplomatic links were well-established with other countries of Western Asia and Egypt was acclaimed the greatest nation in terms of wealth and power. Amenophis III carried out an extensive building programme, concentrating his efforts at Thebes, where he added to the Temple of Karnak as well as starting work on a vast mortuary temple on the west bank, and on the Temple of Luxor which lay not far from Karnak. Also on the west bank, south of where the Temple of Medinet Habu still stands, he built an extensive palace complex at the site known as Malkata. It covered an area of over eighty acres of land, and included a number of palaces used by members of his family, administrative quarters for the officials engaged on royal business and matters of state, the houses of senior officials as well as those of palace servants, and a harem where the

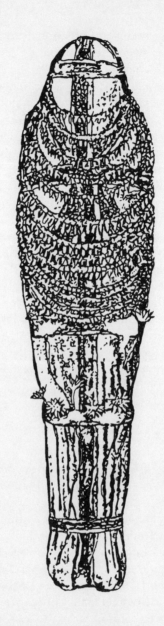

Figure 15 *Mummy wrapped in bandages*
Flowers were regarded as an important element in religious rituals
associated with both the living and the dead. Floral wreaths were placed
on mummies at the time of burial, since they symbolised rebirth and
renewal.

minor royal wives and concubines were accommodated. Some chambers were decorated with painted scenes of plants and animals and motifs which suggest that some of the artisans employed here may have had a Mediterranean origin.

Amenophis III was the son of Tuthmosis IV and his Great Royal Wife, Mutemweya. This marriage marked a break with earlier tradition when the kings had consolidated their claims to rule Egypt by marrying the royal heiress who was usually the king's own sister or half-sister. Perhaps because the dynasty was now firmly established, and there was a greater need to consolidate foreign alliances by diplomatic marriages, Tuthmosis IV took as his chief wife and the mother of his future heir a princess from the land of Mitanni, which had been one of Egypt's main military combatants. It is possible that, even at this stage, such an alliance was an attempt on the part of the king to curb the power and interference in his domestic affairs of the priests of Amen-Re'. Their patronage had been so important in the selection of the royal successor, and they undoubtedly would have supported a traditional marriage between the royal heir and the Great Royal Daughter. The reason for Tuthmosis IV's choice remains obscure, but his son Amenophis III followed this lead and took it one stage further by marrying as his chief wife a girl who was not only not a member of the Egyptian royal family but was the daugher of commoners. Tiye was the child of Yuya, a Prophet of Min and Overseer of Cattle at the town of Akhmim, and his wife Thuya. Amenophis III emphasises the non-royal origin of his wife's parents on the commemorative scarabs which he issued to mark the occasion of his marriage. Soon, however, Tiye became Amenophis III's Great Royal Wife, and her son, Amenophis IV, eventually became his father's heir. Tiye's parents, although commoners, were afforded the rare privilege of a small but richly furnished tomb in the Valley of the Kings, and Tiye retained her powerful position at court although her husband added many Egyptian women to his harem and also cemented foreign alliances by marrying princesses from other major royal families. In year 10 of his reign he received Gilukhepa, the daughter of the king of Mitanni, and later Tadukhipa, daughter of the next Mitannian ruler, came to Egypt as the bride of Amenophis III. He also apparently married Sitamun, his own daughter by Tiye, before the thirty-first year of his reign and gave her the additional title of 'King's Chief Wife'.

Prince Amenophis, son of the king and Tiye, passed his youth in the palace at Malkata. His elder brother, Thutmose, destined to succeed his father on the throne, died prematurely, and Amenophis was selected as the ageing king's heir. One aspect of this period which has attracted much discussion is the possibility of a co-regency between Amenophis III and Amenophis IV. One argument maintains that Amenophis III shared his throne with his son for as long as twelve years, while another suggests that it was for only a few months. Other scholars entirely discount a period of co-regency and

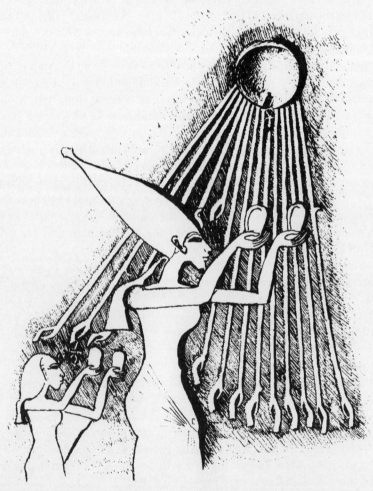

Figure 16   Scene showing King Akhenaten worshipping the Aten.

claim that Amenophis IV succeeded to the throne only upon his father's death. These theories are based on inconclusive evidence, but one of the main advantages of a co-regency at this time would have been to ensure that the priests of Amen-Re' had less opportunity to introduce and support a rival claimant against the son of Tiye.

If such a co-regency did exist, then it would have been spent at Thebes, with both kings residing in separate palaces at Malkata. Amenophis IV had by now married Nefertiti, the queen whose great beauty is captured in various art forms of the period. However, few details of her family background are known, and her origin is completely obscure. Attempts have been made to identify her with Tadukhipa, the Mitannian princess who came to marry Amenophis III, but it seems more likely that Nefertiti was a non-royal Egyptian, perhaps the daughter of a prominent courtier. One theory suggests that she may have come from the same family as Queen Tiye, but although we know that she had a sister named Mudnodjme, who appears in scenes in the role of the queen's lady-in-waiting, and that her nurse or tutor was called Tey, other details of her background are missing.

History of the Aten

It was during his final years at Thebes that Amenophis IV began to promote the cult of the Aten (Itn), a hitherto unimportant deity symbolising the disc of the sun. At one time historians regarded Amenophis IV as the originator of this god and as the sole force behind the religious revolution. Now, however, although it is recognised that his interpretation of the cult and his zealous attempts to elevate the Aten as the sole god of Egypt were unique, it is accepted that the Aten was in existence at a much earlier date and that the cult had been given some prominence in the reign of Amenophis III.

Amenophis IV, however, attempted to impose on Egypt a form of solar monotheism which was based on the worship of the lifeforce present in the sun. This differed from the earlier sun-cult in several respects – the Egyptians had previously worshipped the material form of the sun and not the life-force and energy emanating from it, and the supporters of Re', although seeking pre-eminence amongst other deities, had never claimed that the people should pay their god exclusive homage.

The Aten is mentioned as early as the Middle Kingdom, but it is not clear when it first received a cult as a separate deity. It gained in influence during the early part of Dynasty 18, but it was only during the reign of Tuthmosis IV that evidence exists to show that the Aten was identified as a distinct solar god and not merely a variant form of Re'. In the reign of Amenophis III references to the god increase and a cult to the Aten was apparently established and promoted by the king, perhaps as an attempt to provide a rival to the omnipotence of Amen-Re'. By making the Aten a creative force, the god could be envisaged as a universal deity, with powers beyond Egypt, and he could thus threaten the international role which the priesthood claimed for Amen-Re'. Nevertheless, Amenophis III did not neglect the other gods and there is no evidence that he made any move to promote the Aten as an exclusive deity.

THE ATEN AT THEBES

During the years he spent at Thebes, Amenophis IV took on the role of supporter and promoter of the Aten, while, at least outwardly, he still respected the traditional deities. During this period, he erected at Thebes a number of buildings which included temples to the Aten. A recent study of these buildings has introduced a new opinion of this period. They were dismantled by later rulers who used them to fill in new constructions in the Temples of Karnak and Luxor, and recent dismantling of these later buildings has revealed the existence of some 36,000 decorated blocks from the Aten buildings. The blocks have been examined by a team of scholars and, wherever possible, pieced together in relief scenes, using a computer to assemble the elements of each scene. It remains uncertain how many buildings were constructed from these blocks, but there were probably at least two temples at Karnak and at Luxor, and also possibly a palace. Some important conclusions have emerged from this project, including the recognition that Nefertiti held a position of unprecedented importance in this cult, the role of the queen perhaps equalling that of her husband. Also, it has shown the influence and significance of Amenophis IV's early years at Thebes, and the extent of his promotion of the Aten in the cult city of the traditional god, Amen-Re'. The relative importance of the Aten at this period was not hitherto fully appreciated.

THE MOVE TO EL-AMARNA

Possibly because the relationship between Amenophis IV and the priests of Amen-Re' became increasingly strained, as funds were diverted from the royal resources towards the building of the Aten temples at Thebes, Amenophis IV next made a series of unprecedented moves. In the fifth year of his reign he made it apparent that he was determined to establish a monotheistic cult in Egypt, based on the worship of the Aten.

The names of all other deities were expunged from their monuments, their priesthoods were disbanded, and the income was diverted from their temples to support the cult of the Aten. Finally, Amenophis IV publicly denounced any further association with Amen-Re' by changing his name from Amenophis to Akhenaten (probably meaning 'Servant of the Aten'). Nefertiti also took a new, additional name – Neferneferuaten – which probably meant 'Fair is the goddess of the Aten'. The tensions at Thebes now made it necessary for the king to move his residence and his religious capital to another site which would be untainted by previous associations with other gods.

Acting on the god's instructions, Akhenaten selected a virgin site, situated between the river and the encircling eastern mountains at a place roughly equidistant from Thebes and Lower Egypt. The city was built over some eight miles of land along the course of the Nile, and Akhenaten set up fourteen large boundary stelae to mark out the perimeter of the city and its surrounding land. These were inscribed with the conditions of founding and establishing the city and in one, he expressed a wish that, if he died elsewhere, he should be brought back to this city for burial; this was also extended to members of his family, and he also claims that he would never extend the city beyond the original boundaries marked by the stelae.

The city was given the name of Akhetaten (meaning 'Horizon of the Aten'), and it grew rapidly. The buildings, often hastily and poorly constructed of plastered mudbrick, included all the elements of a political and religious capital – palaces, administrative headquarters, military barracks, records office, houses for all ranks of officials and craftsmen, and the large sun-temples erected for the worship of the Aten. These, and the earlier Aten temples at Thebes, differed in many respects from the traditional cultus temples and are much closer in concept to the solar temples of Dynasty 5. Although they incorporated pylons and a succession of courts which led to the sanctuary, the temples were unroofed; there was no cult-statue because the Aten was represented by the sun's disc in the sky, and the god could thus enter directly into his temple to receive the cult. The exact nature of the rituals performed in these temples remains uncertain, but the king's unique relationship with his god would have been symbolised in the rites performed by the king, perhaps attended by members of his family, when food, flowers and other offerings were presented to the Aten. These were placed on rows of small altars set out inside the temple courts. Although Akhetaten was undoubtedly the great centre of Aten's cult, and at one time histo-

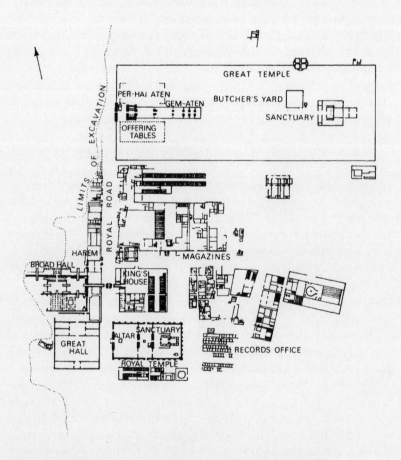

Figure 17 Plan of the Central City of Tell el Amarna (Akhetaten).

rians believed that the king devoted his attention only to this site, it is now known that, apart from the earlier temples built at Thebes, there were other centres, including that of Gem-Aten in Nubia. Indeed, the temples dedicated to this cult may have been much more widespread than present evidence indicates.

The city was supplied with food grown on the opposite bank of the river. In the cliffs to the east of the city, rock-cut tombs were prepared for the royal burials and also for those nobles who now paid lip-service to the Aten cult. These men, doubtless anxious for self-advancement, were mostly new courtiers whom the king had elevated in return for their professed devotion to the Aten. The depth of their devotion to the new cult is suspect, but in these tombs the wall decoration and inscriptions, now badly damaged, provide valuable information regarding many aspects of the cult. It is obvious that there was a break with the traditions of tomb art, and here scenes showing gods of the dead and the underworld are replaced by those depicting the king in his divine role. The reliefs also provide information relating to the layout of the Aten temples at Akhetaten, and to royal activities at the city, while the inscriptions are our main source of knowledge of the tenets of Atenism.

The site has been partially excavated by several archaeologists of different nationalities, but recent work has again been undertaken by a British team. The modern name of 'Tell el-Amarna' is often used for the site, which combines the name of a local tribe, the Beni Amran, with that of the nearby modern village of El-Till; sometimes, the term 'El-Amarna' is also used, and the whole period of occupation, including its distinctive religious beliefs, art, and literature, is frequently referred to as the 'Amarna Period'.

The cult of the Aten seems to have had little appeal to the ordinary people; the lack of a cult-statue which could be paraded at festivals, and of a mythology with human interest prevented the mass of people from identifying with the Aten. They continued to worship their time-honoured deities, as the discovery of traditional gods such as Bes in the workmen's village at El-Amarna has shown. The new faith was probably taken up only by the royal family and their courtiers. However, the move to Amarna cannot be regarded as a breakdown in the relationship between members of the royal family, for tomb scenes at Amarna indicate that Tiye, and possibly her husband, visited the younger couple at Amarna, and Tiye may have taken up residence there after she was widowed.

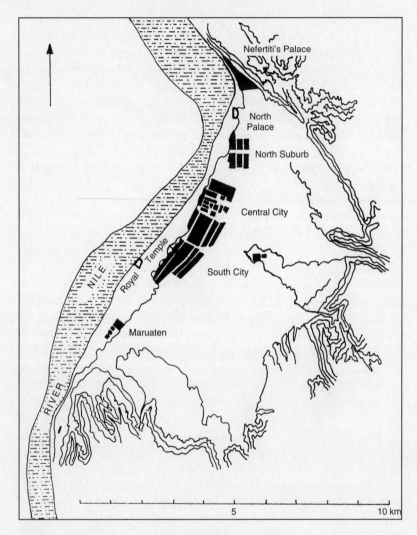

Map 3　Map of Tell el Amarna (Akhetaten) (after W. M. F. Petrie).

THE ROYAL FAMILY AT AKHETATEN

Six daughters were born to Akhenaten and Nefertiti, and the second
one, Maketaten, died shortly after the twelfth year of her father's
reign. She was buried in a subsidiary set of chambers in the royal

tomb at Amarna, where the wall scenes depict the family's grief at the loss of the young princess. Soon after this, Nefertiti is no longer mentioned in events at Amarna, and it has been suggested either that she died following her daughter's death, or that she and her husband separated, perhaps as the result of a disagreement over the development and future of their religious revolution, and that she went into exile. Between Years 13 and 15 of Akhenaten's reign, Meritaten, the eldest daughter, replaced Nefertiti as her own father's consort, and she appears to have borne him a daughter who lived only briefly. It was perhaps in an attempt to beget a male heir that Akhenaten married his daughter. However, he now took as his co-regent a young man named Smenkhkare, who was almost certainly a younger son of Amenophis III; the royal heiress, Meritaten, was given to Smenkhkare as his wife. Akhenaten now seems to have married his third daughter, Ankhesenpaaten, who also gave birth to a daughter who died immediately. During or after Year 17 of his reign, Akhenaten died, and was succeeded for a few months by Smenkhkare. However, this young ruler met an untimely death, and as there was no direct heir, the throne passed to his younger brother, Tutankhaten. He was only a boy of nine at his accession, but he was married to Akhenaten's widow, Ankesenpaaten, presumably because the elder daughter, Meritaten, had also died.

An intensive study has been made of the relationship of Smenkhkare and Tutankhaten to each other and to other members of the family. Although most of the bodies of the Amarna royal family have never been discovered, the art of this period is distinguished by certain physical abnormalities which are evident in the statues and representations of Akhenaten. These were then extended to the representations not only of members of his family, but also to those of courtiers and other personnel who were not related to him. Although there is some attempt at realism in the art which dates to the reign of Amenophis III, it was only after the court moved to Akhenaten that this new art form developed. The conventional artists were still employed at Thebes, and so Akhenaten employed new artists at Amarna and instructed them to explore fresh possibilities. He encouraged them, in line with his religious beliefs, to emphasise naturalism and to depict his own physical abnormalities. These distinctive works of art provide the only known major break with traditional forms throughout Egypt's history, and for the first time, the king's imperfections are not only shown but are emphasised. His peculiarities – the long, narrow face, slanting eyes, elongated head and malformed body with its excessively thin neck, broad hips and thighs and pronounced breasts – were exaggerated almost to the point of caricature. This soon became the accepted way of depicting the figure not only of the king but also of his subjects, who would have had normal physiques. Nevertheless, at its best, Amarna art, freed from the traditional religious conventions imposed on earlier generations of artists, expressed a joy in life. It showed informal scenes of the royal couple and their children, and emphasised the beauty of the plants and animals which reflected the creative power of the Aten.

The physical abnormalities which characterise the figure of Akhenaten in the art in the middle and later years of his reign have been the subject of much discussion. Since the mummies of the king and of members of his family have never been found, these theories remain speculative, but it has been suggested that he may have suffered from a disorder of the endocrine glands.

Akhenaten's supposed physical abnormality is of particular significance when it is considered in relation to a body found many years ago in Tomb 55 (sometimes referred to as the 'tomb of Tiye') in the Valley of the Kings. The tomb was unfinished, and the burial had been hastily prepared; some of the funerary equipment bore the name of Queen Tiye, and this originally led to the conclusion that the body in the tomb was that of a woman, most probably of the queen herself. However, a later examination of the body led to the suggestion that it was that of a young man, aged between twenty-three and twenty-five years. It was argued that this was the body of Akhenaten, brought back to Thebes for burial after the failure of the Amarna revolution. Further studies, however, showed that the skull, although an unusual shape, provided no evidence of hydrocephalus (a feature of Akhenaten's presumed abnormality), and it was maintained that the mummy was not that of Akhenaten but of his young co-regent, Smenkhkare.

The controversy has continued, but the most recent study (in the 1960's) has included the examination of this body, and of the mummies of Tutankhamun and of various other members of the royal family. Using a range of modern scientific techniques, including radiology and serology, this study concluded that the body in Tomb 55 should be identified as Smenkhkare, and that he and Tutankhamun were almost certainly full brothers. Smenkhkare died at about the age of twenty, while Tutankhamun was about nineteen. The parentage of these young men has also been considered, and although the palaeopathological evidence suggests that Amenophis III was almost certainly their father, the identity of their mother remains uncertain. It is possible that Tiye bore Amenophis III these sons, but she would have been advanced in years at the estimated time of Tutankhamun's birth, and it is more probable that Sitamun was their mother. She was the daughter of Amenophis III and Tiye, who married her father and became his queen. However, it is then perhaps strange that in Tutankhamun's tomb there were personal objects bearing the names of Amenophis III and Tiye, but nothing attributable to Sitamun. It is also possible that these sons were born to any of the minor queens or concubines in Amenophis III's extensive harem. Since Akhenaten had produced no direct heir, it was necessary to bring these young princes forward, and to consolidate their claims to the throne by marrying them to Akhenaten's daughters.

The premature death of Smenkhkare and the lack of an heir brought Tutankhaten to the throne. His tomb was discovered in AD 1922, and contained a virtually intact burial – the only example of an almost complete royal burial to have been found at Thebes. This has ensured his fame in recent times, but his short reign is primarily of interest because it reversed the religious and political policies of Akhenaten.

Aspects of Atenism

Akhetaten had remained hidden since its brief occupation until its discovery and excavation in recent years. Evidence from the site has encouraged scholars to ponder the development of Akhenaten's religious revolution and the motives which lay behind this break with tradition. In particular, they have tried to assess the character of the man. Preliminary studies of the material persuaded historians to describe him as a 'failed Messiah', and they acclaimed him as a far-sighted ruler whose solar monotheism was a revealed truth and whose reforms were curtailed by his untimely death. This assessment of Akhenaten tended to view him in terms of Western, Christian belief, instead of examining him as a king set against the background of Egyptian religion. More recently this concept of a visionary ruler has been replaced by the view that Akhenaten was a

political opportunist who introduced a new supreme deity in order
to destroy the power of Amen-Re' and his priesthood. By this action,
he restored the supremacy of the king, and may simply have been
carrying to its final conclusion the conflict between the king and
Amen-Re' which was probably started by Tuthmosis IV.

The origin of Akhenaten's solar monotheism has also been much
disputed. At one time, it was suggested that Tiye was of foreign origin
and that she may have brought with her the Aten cult, and nurtured
her son in this faith. Alternatively, Mutemweya, Tuthmosis IV's
Mitannian queen, could have introduced a set of foreign beliefs to
the Egyptian court or, it has been suggested, the many foreign
princesses and their attendants who entered the harem of
Amenophis III could have influenced Akhenaten's beliefs as he
grew up at Malkata. However, it has since been shown that the Aten
occurred earlier in the New Kingdom, and that Akhenaten's contribution was not the introduction of a new god but his attempt to make
this deity the object of exclusive worship. The extent to which the
Aten was a direct development of the old solar god Re' has also been
considered, and the new cult may have been an attempt on the part
of Akhenaten to revive the absolute divinity of the king as it had
existed in the early years of the Old Kingdom. He may have sought,
above all else, to restore royal supremacy which the cults of other
great gods had eroded. The cult of the Aten may have symbolised a
revival of Re''s royal patronage, but with the addition of some
contemporary features – the king now removed the god's priesthood
which, even in the Old Kingdom, had undermined royal power, and
he ensured that the Aten acquired a universal role as befitted the
great god of a world power. This also made the Aten equal in status
to the deposed Amen-Re' who had gained widespread acclaim and
supremacy as the creator and sustainer of peoples who lived outside
Egypt. Any god who attempted to usurp Amen-Re''s position would
have had to emphasise his universal power. The Aten was probably
at first regarded as a special aspect of Re', but the full name of the
Aten was then changed, and reference to Re'-Harakhte was removed
from the Aten's prenomen (first name) and replaced with the title
'Ruler of the Horizon'.

The beliefs which the cult incorporated are not described in any
one source, but scenes and inscriptions found in the tombs and the
city at Amarna have provided an insight into some aspects. The most
famous single text is the Hymn to the Aten (quoted in Appendix A2)

which was inscribed on the walls of some of the tombs at El-Amarna. It stresses the power which the god exercised as the creator of all mankind, animals, birds and plants, and emphasises the unique nature of the Aten. However, although the language of the hymn is undeniably beautiful, and seems to express new and original concepts, an examination of earlier literature, particularly the sun hymns written on previous occasions in the New Kingdom and the hymns to Amen-Re' in which he is addressed as the 'Sole One', shows that the Aten Hymn contains little that was not formerly attributed to other gods. Another similarity which has been much discussed is the close resemblance between passages in this hymn and verses in Psalm CIV in the Bible.

The Aten was regarded as the symbol of the creative force which the sun provided. Beneficent and universal, this gave life to all creation both within and beyond Egypt's boundaries. The Aten was represented as a disc from which the rays descended, each ending in a hand which bestowed bounty on the king and his family in return for his devotion to the god. Apart from the sun, and its symbol, the disc, the third element was the king; an almost complete identification was achieved between the god and the king so that they appear to have been regarded as virtually interchangeable in both concept and titles. Thus, the king was once again a god, a position which he had lost in the Old Kingdom, when he became the 'son of Re'', and he now acted as the sole representative of the Aten on earth.

No priesthood now stood between the king and his god, and the cults and priesthoods of all the other deities had been dispersed, their temples closed, and their revenues diverted to the Aten. Even the role which the priests had played in connection with the funerary cult was now apparently altered and the wall-scenes in the nobles' tombs at El-Amarna stress the dependence of the dead on their god-king. Some differences can also be observed in the funerary preparations; large scarabs were still inserted inside the mummy wrappings but these were no longer inscribed with the traditional spell from the Book of the Dead which was so closely associated with the cult of Osiris and the Day of Judgment. By making the eternity of his followers dependent upon himself rather than upon the traditional gods of the dead and the underworld, Akhenaten removed the need for reliance upon a funerary priesthood and dispensed with yet another stranglehold which the priests had maintained for generations. A major reason for the failure of Atenism may have been the attempt to discontinue the traditional Osirian concept of the afterlife and the inability to offer a convincing and popular alternative. The new cult does not seem to have provided a moral philosophy, and in general, the revolution probably centred on an attempt to revive the original concept of divine kingship in which the king alone enjoyed an individual eternity while his subjects experienced survival after death only through the king's bounty.

Akhenaten was regarded as a heretic by later generations; his name was obliterated from the monuments and his buildings at Thebes and at Akhetaten were destroyed. The hostility shown to him and his family may have resulted partly from the later propaganda of the reinstated priesthoods and the counter-revolutionaries, but there were many reasons why his revolution was doomed to failure. Even in his lifetime, the cult had only a limited appeal for it had little to offer the masses; it was probably only followed at court and certain other centres, and once Akhenaten died, there was no priesthood to sustain it, and his family and courtiers restored the traditional beliefs. Again, the religious revolution would have directly affected the economy and prosperity of the country; closure of the temples would have deprived many people of menial work, and the building of the new city of Akhetaten would have provided a great additional drain on resources and would have burdened all classes. The extent of Akhenaten's neglect of foreign affairs remains speculative. At one time he was regarded as a pacifist who allowed Egypt's Near Eastern empire to slip out of Egyptian control while he pursued his religious policies at Amarna, oblivious to all other claims on his time. However, this picture is now viewed with caution. Contemporary scenes show soldiers prominently represented at the royal court, and some reliefs depict the king as a warrior. Also there has been some revision of Akhenaten's 'pacifist' role in the Near East. Neither he nor his father pursued full-scale military expeditions there, perhaps because they realised that Egypt's best interests were served by diplomacy and subsidies of gold rather than by military force. However, the Amarna Letters (the correspondence found in the archives of the Record Office at Amarna), which were sent to the Egyptian king by the rulers of foreign and vassal states, indicate that Egypt's military aid to her vassals was now less reliable and prompt than in former years, providing the vassal states with many problems. However, there is no evidence that either economic burdens or the possible loss of prestige abroad prompted any popular uprising in Egypt, and the counter-revolution appears to have been masterminded by the king's own relatives and courtiers.

The counter-revolution

Akhenaten's death, closely followed by the death of Smenkhkare, left Egypt with no direct heir. If Akhenaten had left a son who had been instructed in his beliefs and who had lived to reach maturity on accession, it is possible that Atenism would have survived. However, Smenkhkare was succeeded by his younger brother, Tutankhaten, who was then aged about nine years. Marriage to Ankhesenpaaten, the eldest surviving daughter and also the widow of Akhenaten, consolidated the child's claim to the throne, but his immaturity made it impossible for him to continue Akhenaten's revolution, even if he had wished to do so. His advisers found it necessary to reinstate the traditional deities and to reverse the policies of the past fifteen years.

The men who now held the reins of power at court included the vizier Ay, a courtier of long-standing loyalty to the king at Amarna, and Horemheb, the army general under Akhenaten who had outwardly supported the revolution. Now, however, they acted together to restore the old values and traditions, perhaps realising that the revolution was no longer acceptable to the Egyptians, or perhaps now taking the opportunity to reverse policies with which they had always privately disagreed.

The court returned to Thebes, leaving forever the city of Akhetaten which had been inhabited for less than twenty years and was never completed. Later, at Horemheb's command, the city was destroyed and the stone removed for building projects elsewhere. The tombs were desecrated, the king's name was erased from the inscriptions, the Great Temple to the Aten was razed to the ground and its sacred contents were smashed and destroyed. The Theban temples to the Aten were similarly dismantled, and every effort was made to expunge all trace of the Aten cult and its hated royal patron. The remains of Akhetaten were soon covered by drifting sand, and its existence was only discovered by chance thousands of years later.

At Thebes, Tutankhaten and his wife emphasised their return to the worship of traditional deities by changing their names to Tutankhamun and Ankhesenamun. The young king undertook the

restoration of old temples and erected new monuments to the reinstated deities. The temples and their priesthoods which Akhenaten
had disbanded were now restored. However, Tutankhamun's
untimely death in his late teens again highlighted the problem of the
succession. He was buried in a tomb in the Valley of the Kings at
Thebes which had been prepared for another member of the royal
family. He left no living heir, although two mummified foetuses of
females were discovered in his tomb. These may have been the
offspring of his marriage to Ankhesenamun, although this remains
unconfirmed by the recent medical investigation of one of the
foetuses.

An internal conflict now arose concerning the succession. This is
apparent from a letter written by the widowed queen
Ankhesenamun to the king of the Hittites, who at that period were
Egypt's main enemy and rival. In this, she asks the king to send his
son to become her husband. Such an alliance with the royal heiress
would have conferred on the Hittite prince the right to rule Egypt,
and although the king sent his son, the prince was murdered on the
way, presumably by agents of those who were anxious to prevent
this marriage. Ankhesenamun was then married to Ay, the elderly
courtier of proven loyalty, and although he was not royal, this
alliance gave him the throne. He ruled for four years, continuing to
restore the traditionalist policies and, although a tomb had been
prepared for him at Amarna, he was buried as a king at Thebes. In
his Theban tomb, the inscriptions refer to Tey, his first wife, and not
to his queen, Ankhesenamun, whose name never appears again. The
queen's fate and that of her younger sisters is not known, but they
played no further part in the succession.

Ay was succeeded by Horemheb who became the last king of
Dynasty 18. Although of humble origin, Horemheb had been a
major figure in royal affairs throughout the Amarna period and had
risen to power through his professed allegiance to Akhenaten. It is
possible that he married Nefertiti's sister, since both his wife and the
queen's sister were named Mudnodjme. Whether he was simply an
opportunist who used the Amarna heresy to gain his own advancement, or whether he at first genuinely supported the revolution, only
later to become disillusioned, it is impossible now to determine.
However, he was the man eventually responsible for the systematic
destruction of all traces of the Aten cult, and for the restoration of a
strong, aggressive army, and a powerful priesthood who supported

a multitude of deities and owed their appointment to him. A copy of his restoration decree was inscribed on a stela in the Temple of Karnak, and it indicates that he undertook a widespread rehabilitation of the temples, restoring their priesthoods and their properties.

In the King Lists which give the legitimate rulers of Egypt, Horemheb's name appears immediately after that of Amenophis III, indicating that the traditionalists regarded Akhenaten and his immediate successors as kings who did not rule subject to the approval of Ma'at. Horemheb ruled Egypt for twenty-seven years, finally being buried at Thebes. The kingdom now passed to Pa-Ramesses, an old comrade and soldier who, as Ramesses I, inaugurated Dynasty 19. He inherited a country which was superficially stable, with a restored priesthood and reorganised army and law-courts. The kings of this dynasty reasserted their loyalty to the traditional gods and condemned Akhenaten to oblivion; they built great temples, and restored Egypt's prestige in the Near East by military force. However, the problems which may have prompted Akhenaten's revolution were still present, and by Dynasty 21, the power of Amen-Re''s priesthood led to a division of the country with the kings ruling from the capital of Tanis in the Delta, while a family of high-priests ruled from Thebes.

5

Some Contributions Made by Egyptian Religion to Other Religions

---

During the long period of Egypt's decline, the country was conquered and ruled by the Assyrians, the Persians, the Macedonian Greeks and, eventually, the Romans, and also spent periods of time under the kings of foreign origin such as the Libyan and 'Ethiopian' rulers. However, only the Greeks and the Romans fully attempted to adopt the national structure so that they could use it for their own purposes, and they alone took measures to institute or transform cults which would support the interests of the state by uniting the Egyptians and the Greeks who now lived in Egypt. Egypt had established contact with Greece and particularly with Crete since at least as early as the Middle Kingdom, but from Dynasty 26, when the kings had brought large numbers of Greek mercenaries into Egypt and settled them in colonies, Greek influence within the country developed markedly. After the conquest of Egypt by Alexander the Great in 332 BC, and the subsequent appointment of his Macedonian general Ptolemy as ruler of the country, the opportunity arose for numerous Greeks to enter and settle in Egypt. A bilingual society evolved, and separate legislature, law-courts, and political, economic and social privileges developed for the Greeks and the Egyptians, who now found themselves second-class citizens. In order to establish their rule with maximum benefit to themselves, the Ptolemies kept alive the national cult of the Pharaoh and adopted the privileges which theoretically belonged to the Egyptian king – the absolute ownership of the land, its resources and people. They also restored, enlarged and built Egyptian temples on a widespread scale, retaining all the basic architectural and cultic features of the earlier temples. They associated themselves with the royal and local gods, and many deities of the Greek and Egyptian pantheons underwent a process of syncretism. Thus, according to the Greek writer Herodotus, the Egyptian god Amun had the same form as Zeus, and Ptah, Egyptian god of crafts, became identified with Haephaistos; similarly, the Greeks equated Imhotep with their own god of medicine, and Anubis acquired some of the characteristics of Aiakos, the Greek judge of the dead.

However, the Ptolemies needed a deity who could be accepted and worshipped by both Greeks and Egyptians as a national god, and they attempted to achieve this aim by creating the god Sarapis who combined both Greek and Egyptian features. His name was probably a derivation of 'Osiris-Apis', and he embraced characteristics of the Apis bull-cult which had flourished for centuries at Memphis where, at the Serapeum, the bulls were interred when they died. However, Sarapis was given a Graecized human form. But, despite their ambition to provide a national deity whose status would equal that of Amun or Horus in earlier times, the rulers failed. Sarapis never gained the widespread acceptance by the native Egyptians which the old gods had enjoyed, and they retained their centuries-old loyalty to the Osirian deities. Nevertheless, Sarapis was widely acknowledged and worshipped throughout the Mediterranean region, and continued to be an important god in Roman times.

Their inability to inspire allegiance to an official cult did not mean that the rulers suppressed other gods. The Egyptians continued to worship a wide variety of deities and it seems that, although the structure of the state religion began to crumble, greater emphasis was placed on personal piety by the Egyptians. Regarded as the 'lord of fate', an individual deity exerted great influence over the lifestyle and standards of his worshipper, and although mortuary beliefs and customs were losing religious significance and, in many instances, reflecting commercial interests, nevertheless, the Greeks adopted the practice of mummification. They added their own distinctive features, such as the painted panel portraits which were now placed over the face of the mummy, and, as in the tomb of Petosiris at Tuna el-Gebel, contributed Greek styles to Egyptian concepts in tomb-art.

One Egyptian deity, Isis, came to receive worship and acclaim throughout the Graeco-Roman world, with the dissemination of her cult throughout the Roman Empire. The Isis-Osiris Mysteries were celebrated at Rome and Corinth, and her cult reached the Danube region, Germania, and Hadrian's Wall in Britain. She was entirely Egyptian in origin, and played a sympathetic role as the devoted wife of Osiris who helped to restore him to life, but as she now adopted new forms and characteristics to suit Greek tastes, and acquired additional powers as the director of fate and as 'lady of seafaring', Isis was assured of international acceptance.

While the religion was undergoing profound changes within Egypt, many elements of pharaonic culture were being preserved at Meroë, a city situated between the 5th and 6th cataracts of the Nile. At this site, now in modern Sudan, a line of kings ruled from sometime in the 6th century BC until the 4th century AD, when Meroë was destroyed by Aeizanes of Axum. These rulers were successors to the kings of Napata (another southern city) who had conquered and briefly ruled Egypt during the 8th century BC, before the invading Assyrians drove them back from Thebes to Nubia. These southerners, often referred to as the 'Ethiopians', ruled Egypt for part of Dynasty 25, and their religion, probably acquired originally from Egyptian priests who fled to Nubia, centred around the worship of Amen-Re'. When Napata declined, they established a new political and religious capital at Meroë. All direct contact between Egypt and the southern kingdom had now ceased, but from the Napatan rulers, the kings of Meroë inherited an Egyptianizing culture which preserved many of the old pharaonic beliefs and traditions. Although Napata and Meroë, the earliest African kingdoms known to history, were essentially African in character, the Meroitic civilisation was strongly influenced by Egyptian religious beliefs, gods, temple architecture and art, and funerary customs. The temples were decorated with reliefs showing local gods as members of the Egyptian pantheon, and the royal tombs were built as pyramids. Although Graeco-Roman art forms later affected this culture to a lesser degree, it was nevertheless the process of Egyptian-meroitic syncretism which remained the central feature, and at Meroë were to be found the last remnants of pharaonic civilisation.

It has been stated that 'The influence of Egyptian religion on posterity is mainly felt through Christianity and its antecedents' (S. Morenz, *Egyptian Religion*, p. 251), and links have been traced between both the Old and New Testaments and Egyptian religion. Essentially, Christianity and Judaism differed fundamentally from

Egyptian religion in that they are regarded as scriptural religions, revealed to mankind by God, whereas Egyptian religion was centred around ritual and cultic practices. Nevertheless, it has been shown that a number of elements were most probably derived from the Egyptian traditions. There have been many studies of Egypt's links with the Old Testament, and particularly of the associations through the Wisdom Literature. It is thought that this found its way from Egypt to Palestine. In particular, similarities have been noted and discussed between the Egyptian 'Instruction of Amenemope' and the Biblical Book of Proverbs, although the Instruction of Amenemope may be only a secondary source for the Book of Proverbs, since passages in Amenomope may have derived from original compositions in Hebrew or Aramaic. Other similarities have been noticed between the Amarna Hymn to the Aten and Psalm CIV in the Bible, and other Biblical passages and Egyptian texts. Also, the Judaic and Christian doctrine of creation through the word was probably influenced by the Egyptian creation myths, where such a concept is prominently figured.

Some of the Egyptian ideas and images were transmitted from the Old Testament to the New Testament and thus became part of early Christianity, but it has also been claimed that Egyptian religion had a more direct effect upon Christianity through the influence of Egypt upon the Hellenistic world. Some Christian concepts can thus be traced back to Egypto-Hellenistic forms, and ultimately to the religious beliefs of pharaonic Egypt.

The concept of the Trinity was particularly significant for early Christianity, and it has been claimed that, although this was essentially Biblical in tradition, the understanding of the 'three-in-one' in which God was expressed in three forms but was regarded as a single Deity, could reasonably have been transmitted from the principle behind the Egyptian triads which date from the New Kingdom. Other associations may exist between the Osiris-Isis myth, with its emphasis upon death, rebirth and resurrection and upon the Day of Judgment, and the later traditions; between the doctrine concerning Christ's pre-existence before the creation and the earlier Egyptian theologies concerning creation and the creator gods; and between the Isis cult and Mariolatry. The intermediary between the Egyptian religious tradition and Christianity was almost certainly provided by the great cultural centre of Alexandria and the general background of the Hellenistic world.

Although Egypt's contribution to Christianity is of the greatest significance in terms of world religions, some interesting survivals of ancient Egyptian festivals and customs can be seen in modern Egypt. Here, more than in any other part of the Muslim Empire, the culture of the new rulers was affected and determined by earlier, local traditions, and even today some of the ancient ceremonies have survived in a recognisable form. Two festivals are particularly noteworthy. The festival of Sham el-Nessim, when the families go out-of-doors to celebrate the coming of spring, and mark the occasion with gifts of coloured eggs, echoes the ancient festival held to rejoice at the rebirth of the vegetation and the renewal of life. Awru el-Nil commemorates the annual inundation of the Nile and today is the occasion of a national holiday, when flowers are thrown into the river, but this again is an ancient tradition recalling the yearly festival of the inundation, when prayers were offered to the god to request an adequate flood and prosperity for the land.

Two funerary occasions also have their origins in antiquity. The family of the deceased take food to his grave after a period of forty days have elapsed since death, and this is presented to the poor who gather at the grave or tomb. Although in Egypt burial is now completed shortly after death, in ancient times, a period of forty days passed between death and burial while the process of mummification was carried out. Nowadays, this occasion of el-Arbeiyin recalls the ancient Egyptian mortuary service which was performed at the time of burial, when relatives gathered at the tomb and, at the completion of the ceremonies, partook of a funerary meal. It is interesting to note that, although the ancient author Herodotus quotes a period of not more than seventy days for preparation of the dead before burial, both this survival, and experimental mummification carried out on dead rats as part of a research project at the University of Manchester, when the mummified bodies were shown to be dehydrated and stabilised after only forty days, would tend to indicate that the forty-day period was the accepted norm. Another surviving custom – the annual visit to the family grave, carrying food, including special white bread for the occasion, which is then presented to the poor – probably also recalls an ancient Egyptian tradition.

Ancient Egypt has contributed to the civilisation of mankind in many branches of learning and, in some instances, has laid the foundations for concepts, ideas and institutions which are still part of the fabric of society. Their religious beliefs hold value and interest for us as the guidelines and stimuli of an inventive and brilliant people but also, since the traces of these ancient traditions are still apparent in Judaism, Christianity and Islam, a study of the religion of the ancient Egyptians is relevant to an understanding of these three great faiths.

Part II

Primary Sources for the Study of Egyptian Religion

Primary Sources: Introduction

Our present knowledge of ancient Egyptian religious beliefs and customs is based on two main sources of evidence. First, the excavation of archaeological sites throughout Egypt has provided information derived from the architectural features and art decoration of pyramids, tombs and temples, and from the more humble cemeteries and town sites. The published excavation reports make this knowledge available to the general reader, and the bibliography given below (Appendix Al) provides a basic although not exhaustive list of these reports. In addition, a list of major archaeological sites is provided in Appendix B. Apart from the buildings, the excavations have revealed groups of antiquities, usually of a funerary nature, including coffins, furniture, models, statuary, ushabtis, jewellery and amulets. These are usually published either as part of the excavation report of the site, or in monographs dealing with specific classes of objects which frequently illustrate the collections held by a museum. The series of publications by Sir W. Flinders Petrie which concentrate on the Edwards collection at University College London (reprinted by Aris & Phillips, Warminster, England), forms a basis for study of such material. Finally, the mummified remains of the Egyptians, and particularly the Royal Mummies in the Cairo Museum, have afforded scholars the opportunity to expand their knowledge not only of the religious and funerary beliefs and customs and the living conditions of the Egyptians, but, as the result of palaeopathological investigations, to study the incidence of disease in the population.

The second primary source is the body of textual evidence. The ancient Egyptian writings, preserved on papyri, stelae, ostraca, and in tomb and temple inscriptions, have revealed a wealth of information regarding all aspects of the religion. Also, the Classical authors who wrote about Egypt have included much of interest concerning the religion. The basic religious texts are listed below, with reference to publications of modern translations. A short selection is also given (Appendix A2) of key passages from some of these texts. Most references are to publications in English, but sources in French and German are given where no English version is available.

Appendix A1

Primary sources: religious texts and archaeological bibliography

Primary sources, archaeological

1 TOMBS: GENERAL

W. B. EMERY, *Great Tombs of the First Dynasty*, vol. I (Cairo 1949); vol. 2 (Oxford 1954).

W. M. F. PETRIE, *Royal Tombs of the Earliest Dynasties*, 2 vols (London 1900–1).

W. M. F. PETRIE, *The Royal Tombs of the First Dynasty* (London 1900).

B. PORTER and R. L. B. MOSS, *Topographical Bibliography of Ancient Egyptian Hieroglyphic Texts, Reliefs and Paintings*, 7 vols (Oxford 1927–51).

G. A. REISNER, *The Development of the Egyptian Tomb down to the Accession of Cheops* (Cambridge, Oxford, London 1936).

2 TOMBS AND SITE EXCAVATIONS: ALPHABETICAL

Abukir

A-Q. MUHAMMED, 'An Ibis Catacomb at Abu-kir' in *ASAÉ* 66 (1987), 121–3.

Abusir

L. BAREŠ and M. VERNER, 'Excavations at Abusir 1990–1991 – Preliminary Report' in *ZÄS* 119 (1992), 108–16.

M. VERNER, 'Excavations at Abusir, Preliminary Reports, Season 1980/81' in *ZÄS* 109 (1982), 157–66; 'Season 1982' in *ZÄS* 111 (1984), 70–8; 'Season 1984/85' in *ZÄS* 113 (1986), 154–60; 'Season 1985/86' and 'Season 1987' in *ZÄS* 115 (1988), 77–84 and 163–71.

M. VERNER, 'A Late Dynasty 5 Cemetery at Abusir' in *ZÄS* 117 (1990), 72–8.

M. VERNER, 'An early Old Kingdom Cemetery at Abusir' in *ZÄS* 122 (1995), 78–90.

Abydos

E. NAVILLE, 'The Excavations at Abydos' in *Ancient Egypt* III (1914), 103–5.

D. RANDALL-MACIVER and A. C. MACE, *El Amrah and Abydos* (London 1902).

Akhmim

Y. S. S. AL-MASRI, 'Preliminary report on the excavations in Akhmim of the Egyptian Antiquities Organisation' in *ASAÉ* 69 (1983), 7–14.

F. W. F. VON BISSING, 'Tombeaux d'époque romaine à Akhmim' in *ASAÉ* 50 (1950), 547–84.

el-Amarna

N. DE G. DAVIES, *The Rock Tombs of El-Amarna*, 6 vols (London 1903–8).

H. W. FAIRMAN, 'Topographical Notes on the Central City, Tell el-Amarnah' in *JEA* 21 (1935), 136–9.

H. FRANKFORT and J. D. S. PENDLEBURY, *The City of Akhenaten* (London 1933).

J. D. S. PENDLEBURY, 'Excavations at Tell el-Amarna' in *JEA* 19 (1933), 129–36; 20 (1934), 113–18; 22 (1936), 194–8.

Aswan

F. W. F. von BISSING, 'Les tombeaux d'Assouan' in *ASAÉ* 15 (1915), 1–14.

Badari

G. BRUNTON and G. CATON-THOMPSON, The Badarian Civilisation (London 1928).

Beni Hasan

J. GARSTANG, 'Excavations at Beni Hasan (1902–4)' in *ASAÉ* 5 (1904), 215–28.

P. E. NEWBERRY, *Beni Hasan*, 4 parts (London 1893–1900).

Dahshur

A. FAKHRY, 'The Excavation of Snefru's Monuments at Dahshur: Second Preliminary Report' in *ASAÉ* 52 (1952–4), 563. See also A. FAKHRY, 'The Southern Pyramid of Sneferu' in *ASAÉ* 51 (1951), 509–22.

Deir el-Gebrawi

N. DE G. DAVIES, *The Rock Tombs of Deir el-Gebrawi* (London 1902).

Deir el-Medina
C. BONNET and D. VALBELLE, 'Le village de Deir el-Médineh; Étude archéologique' in *BIFAO* 76 (1976), 317–42; 75 (1975), 429–46.
B. BRUYÈRE, 'Deir el Médineh' in *Rev.d'Ég.* 2 (1929), 254–8.
B. BRUYÈRE, *Rapport sur les fouilles de Deir el Médineh*, 3 parts (Cairo 1933–9).
B. BRUYERÈ, 'La nécropole de Deir el Médineh' in *Chr.d'Ég.* 11 (1936), 329–40.
B. BRUYÈRE, 'Une tombe gréco-romaine de Deir el-Médineh' in *BIFAO* 36 (1936–7), 145–74; 38 (1939), 73–107.
J. J. CLÈRE, 'Monuments inédits des serviteurs dans la Place de Vérite' in *BIFAO* 28 (1929), 173–201.

Giza
Y. M. HARPUR, 'Two Old Kingdom Tombs at Giza' in *JEA* 67 (1981), 21–23.
W. M. F. PETRIE, *Gizeh and Rifeh* (London 1907).
G. A. REISNER, *A History of the Giza Necropolis*, 2 vols (Cambridge 1942, 1955).
G. A. REISNER, *Mycerinus* (Cambridge, Mass. 1931).
G. A. REISNER and C. S. FISHER, 'Preliminary Report on the Work of the Harvard-Boston Expedition in 1911–13' in *ASAÉ* 13 (1914), 227–52.

Helwan
W. WOOD, 'The Archaic Stone Tombs at Helwan' in *JEA* 73 (1987), 59–70.

Hermopolis (Tuna el-Gebel)
E. BARAIZE, 'L'Agora d'Hermoupolis' in *ASAÉ* 40 (1940–1), 741–60.
S. GABRA, 'Rapport préliminaire sur les fouilles de l'Université Égyptienne à Touna (Hermopolis Ouest)' in *ASAÉ* 32 (1932), 56–77; also *ASAÉ* 39 (1939), 483–527.

Hieraconpolis
H. CASE and J. C. PAYNE, 'Tomb 100: The Decorated Tomb at Hierakonpolis' in *JEA* 48 (1962), 5–18.
J. E. QUIBELL and F. W. GREEN, *Hierakonpolis*, 2 vols (London 1900–2).

Kahun
W. M. F. PETRIE, *Kahun, Gurob and Hawara* (London 1890).

Lahun
G. BRUNTON, *Lahun 1: The Treasure* (London 1920).
H. E. WINLOCK, *The Treasure of Lahun* (New York 1934)

Medum
W. M. F. PETRIE, *Medum* (London 1892).

Meir

A. M. BLACKMAN, *The Rock Tombs of Meir* (London 1914–53).

Memphis
M. JONES and A. M. JONES, 'The Apis House project at Mit Rahineh. First Season, 1982' in *JARCE* 19 (1982), 51–8.
H. S. SMITH ET AL., 'The Survey of Memphis, 1981' and 'The Survey of Memphis, 1982' in *JEA* 69 (1983), 30–42 and *JEA* 70 (1984), 23–32.

Mostagedda
G. BRUNTON, *Mostagedda and the Tasian Culture* (London 1937).

Naga-ed-Der
G. A. REISNER, 'Work of the Expedition of the University of California at Naga-ed-Der' in *ASAÉ* 5 (1904), 105–9.

Naqada
W. M. F. PETRIE and J. E. QUIBELL, *Naqada and Ballas* (London 1896).

Qau
G. BRUNTON, *Qau and Badari*, 3 vols (London 1927–30).

Saqqara
A. ABDALLA, 'The Cenotaph of the Sekwaskhet Family from Saqqara' in *JEA* 78 (1992), 93–112.
R. M. AWAD, 'The Causeway of the Ounas Pyramid' in *ASAÉ* 61 (1973), 151.
J. CAPART, 'The Memphite Tomb of King Harmhab' in *JEA* 7 (1921), 31–5.
N. DE G. DAVIES, *The Mastabah of Ptah-hetep and Akhet-hetep at Saqqara* (London 1900).
S. GOHARY, 'The Tomb-chapel of the Royal Scribe Amenemone at Saqqara' in *BIFAO* 91 (1991), 195–206.
M. Z. GONEIM, *Excavations at Saqqara, Horus Sekhem-khet, the Unfinished Pyramid at Saqqara* (Cairo 1957).
Z. HAWASS, 'A Fragmentary Monument of Djoser from Saqqara' in *JEA* 80 (1994), 45–56.
D. G. JEFFREYS and E. STROUHAL, 'North Saqqara 1978–1979: The Coptic Cemetery site at the Sacred Animal Necropolis, Preliminary Report' in *JEA* 66 (1980), 28–35 and *JEA* 82 (1996), 8–11.
G. T. MARTIN, 'The Tomb of Tia and Tia: Preliminary Report on the Saqqara Excavations, 1982' and 'Preliminary Report, 1983' in *JEA* 69 (1983), 25–9 and *JEA* 70 (1984), 5–12.

G. T. MARTIN ET AL., 'The Tomb Chambers of Iurudej: Preliminary Report on the Saqqara excavations, 1985' in *JEA* 72 (1986), 15–22.

G. T. MARTIN, 'The Saqqara New Kingdom Necropolis excavations, 1986' in *JEA* 73 (1987), 1–10.

G. T. MARTIN, 'The Tomb of Maya and Meryt: Preliminary report on the Saqqara excavations, 1987–88' in *JEA* 74 (1988), 1–14.

G. T. MARTIN, 'The EES-Leiden Saqqara Expedition, 1996' in *JEA* 82 (1996), 4–8.

I. J. MATHIESON and A. TAVARES, 'Preliminary Report of the National Museums of Scotland Saqqara Survey Project, 1990–91' in *JEA* 79 (1993), 17–32.

M. MOUSSA, 'A limestone lintel of 'Imn-m-ipt from Saqqara' in *ASAÉ* 70 (1984–5), 35.

P. T. NICHOLSON, 'Preliminary Report on work at the Sacred Animal Necropolis, North Saqqara, 1992' in *JEA* 80 (1994), 1–10.

A. PIANKOFF, *The Pyramid of Unas* (Princeton 1968)

J. PH. LAUER, 'Rapport sur les restaurations effectuées au cours de l'année 1929–30 dans les monuments de Zoser à Saqqara' in *ASAÉ* 27 (1927), 112–33; 28 (1928) 89–113; 29 (1929), 97–129; 30 (1930), 129–36; 31 (1931), 49–64; also in *ASAÉ* 32 (1932) – 62 (1977).

J. PH. LAUER, 'Les monuments de Zoser à Saqqarah (IIIe dynastie)' in *Rev. d'Ég.* 3 (1931), 11–19.

J. PH. LAUER, *Saqqara. The Royal Cemetery of Memphis. Excavations and Discoveries since 1850* (London 1976).

Z. Y. SAAD, 'Preliminary Report on the Royal Excavations at Saqqara (1941–2)' in *ASAÉ* 41 (1942), 381–403. Also Supplement in *ASAÉ* 46 (1947).

H. D. SCHNEIDER ET AL., 'The Tomb of Maya and Meryt: Preliminary Report on the Saqqara Excavations, 1990–1' in *JEA* 77 (1991), 7–22.

H. D. SCHNEIDER ET AL., 'The Tomb of Iniuia: Preliminary report on the Saqqara excavations, 1993' in *JEA* 79 (1993), 1–10.

Sudan

D. DUNHAM, *El Kurru* (Cambridge, Mass. 1950).

D. DUNHAM, *Nuri. Royal Cemeteries of Kush* (Boston 1955).

D. DUNHAM, *Royal Tombs at Meroë and Barkal* (Boston 1957).

D. N. EDWARDS, 'Post-Meroitic ('X-Group') and Christian burials at Sesebi, Sudanese Nubia. The excavations of 1937' in *JEA* 80 (1994), 159–78.

Tanis

A. DODSON, 'Some notes concerning the Royal Tombs at Tanis' in *Chr.d'Ég.* 63 (1988), 221–33.

P. MONTET, *La Nécropole royale de Tanis*, 2 vols (Paris 1947, 1952). Also in *ASAÉ* 39 (1939), 529–39; 46 (1947), 311–22.

Tebtunis

C. C. WALTERS, 'Christian paintings from Tebtunis' in *JEA* 75 (1989), 91–208.

Tell Basta

S. FARID, 'Preliminary Report on the Excavations of the Antiquities Department at Tell Basta (Season 1961)' in *ASAÉ* 58 (1964), 85.

Thebes

H. CARTER, *The Tomb of Tutankhamun*, 3 vols. (London 1923–33).

H. CARTER and A. H. GARDINER, 'The Tomb of Ramesses IV and the Turin Plan of a Royal Tomb' in *JEA* 4 (1917), 130–58.

N. DE G. DAVIES, *The Tomb of Ramose* (London 1941).

N. DE G. DAVIES, *Paintings from the Tomb of Rekh-mi-Re at Thebes* (New York, 1935, 1943).

N. DE G. DAVIES, with A. H. GARDINER, *Seven Private Tombs at Kurneh* (London 1948).

TH. M. DAVIS, *The Tombs of Harmhabi and Touatankhamanu* (London 1912).

TH. M. DAVIS, *The Tomb of Iouya and Touiyou* (London 1907).

A. FAKHRY, 'The Tomb of Nebamun, Captain of Troops (No. 145 at Thebes)' in *ASAÉ* 43 (1943), 369–87; also 'The Tomb of Paser (No. 367 at Thebes' in *ASAÉ* 43 (1943), 389–437.

A. H. GARDINER, *The Tomb of Huy, Viceroy of Nubia* (London 1926).

D. B. LARKIN and C. VAN SICLEN III, 'Theban Tomb 293 and the Tomb of the Scribe Huy' in *JNES* 34 (1975), 125.

R. MOND, 'Report on Work done in the Gebel esh-Sheikh Abd-el-Kurneh at Thebes' in *ASAÉ* 5 (1904), 97–104.

R. MOND, 'Report of work in the Necropolis of Thebes during the Winter of 1903–4' in *ASAÉ* 6 (1905), 65–96.

A. PIANKOFF, 'Vallée des Rois à Thebes-Ouest: La tombe no. 1. (Ramses VII)' in *ASAÉ* 55 (1958), 145.

A. PIANKOFF, 'La tombe de Ramses Ier' in *BIFAO* 56 (1957), 189–202.

J. E. QUIBELL, *Tomb of Yuaa and Thuiu* (Cairo 1908).

C. N. REEVES, 'A Reappraisal of Tomb 55 in the Valley of the Kings' in *JEA* 67 (1981), 48–55.

T. SÄVE-SÖDERBERGH, *Four Eighteenth Dynasty Tombs at Thebes* (Oxford 1957).

G. THAUSING and H. GOEDICKE, *Nofretari: A Documentation of her Tomb and its Decoration* (Graz, 1971).

A. E. P. WEIGALL, 'A Report on the Tombs of Sheikh Abd-el-Gurneh and el Assasîf' in *ASAÉ* 9 (1908), 118–36.

J. A. WILSON, 'The Theban Tomb (no. 409) of Si-Mut, called Kiki' in *JNES* 29 (1970), 187.

H. E. WINLOCK, 'The Tombs of the Kings of the 17th Dynasty at Thebes' in *JEA* (1924), 217–77.

H. E. WINLOCK, 'The Museum's Excavations at Thebes' in *Bull. MMA* 27 (1932), March, sect. 11, 4–37.

3 TEMPLES: GENERAL

F. DAUMAS, *Les Mammisis des temples égyptiens* (Paris 1958).
H. H. NELSON, 'The Significance of the Temple in the Ancient Near East: I. The Egyptian Temple with Particular Reference to the Theban Temples of the Empire Period' in *Biblical Archaeologist* 7 (1944) (The American Schools of Oriental Research).

4 TEMPLES: ALPHABETICAL

Abu Simbel
R. M. AWAD, 'Complementary Study to the Abu-Simbel Temples Research Project' in *ASAÉ* 61 (1973), 145.

Abusir
H. RICKE, 'Dritter Grabungsbericht über das Sonnenheiligtum des Königs Userkaf bei Abusir' in *ASAÉ* 55 (1958), 73.

Abydos
J. BAINES, 'Abydos, Temple of Sethos I: Preliminary Report' in *JEA* 70 (1984), 13–22.
A. EL-SAWI, 'A Nineteenth Dynasty representation of the winged Djed-pillar at Abydos' in *BIFAO* 87 (1987), 167–70.
A. H. ZAYED, 'The archives and treasury of the temple of Sety I at Abydos' in *ASAÉ* 65 (1983), 19–71.
A. H. ZAYED, 'The inscriptions on the exterior of the southern wall of the Temple of Ramesses II at Abydos' in *ASAÉ* 67 (1988), 79–114.
A. M. CALVERLEY and M. F. BROOME, *The Temple of King Sethos I at Abydos*, 4 vols (London and Chicago 1933–58).
W. K. SIMPSON, *The Terrace of the Great God at Abydos: The Offering Chapels of Dynasties 12 and 13* (Pennsylvania 1974).
H. FRANKFORT, *The Cenotaph of Seti I at Abydos* (London 1933).
M. A. MURRAY, *The Osireion at Abydos* (London 1904).
M. A. MURRAY, 'The Temple of Ramesses II at Abydos' in *Ancient Egypt* (1916), III, 121–38.

Assiut
S. GABRA, 'Une temple d'Amenophis IV à Assiout' in *Chr.d'Ég.* 6, 237.

Bubastis
E. NAVILLE, *The Festival Hall of Osorkon II in the Great Temple of Bubastis* (London 1892).

Deir el-Bahri

L. DABROWSKI 'Preliminary Report on the Reconstruction Work of the Hatshepsut Temple at Deir el-Bahri during 1961–2 Season' in *ASAÉ* 58 (1964), 37; also *ASAÉ* 60 (1968), 131–7, 139–52 (with J. Lipinska).

E. NAVILLE, *The Dynasty XIth Temple at Deir el-Bahri*, 3 vols (London 1907–13).

H. E. WINLOCK, 'Neb-hepet-Re' Mentu-hotpe of the Eleventh Dynasty' in *JEA* 26 (1940), 116–19.

H. E. WINLOCK, *Excavations at Deir el-Bahri* (New York 1942).

Denderah

E. CHASSINAT and F. DAUMAS, *Le Temple de Dendara* (Cairo 1934–65).

Elephantine

M. R. JENKINS, 'The Stela of Neferhotep from the sanctuary of Heqaib on Elephantine Island' in *JEA* 82 (1996), 199–202.

Edfu

E. CHASSINAT, *La Temple d Edfou* (Cairo 1897–1960).

Esna

S. SAUNERON, *Esna V: Les fêtes réligieuses d'Esna aux derniers siècles du paganisme* (Cairo 1962).

Giza

J. PH. LAUER, 'Le temple funéraire de Khéops à la grande pyramide de Gizeh' in *ASAÉ* 46 (1947), 245–61.

Hibis

E. CRUZ-URIBE, 'The Hibis Temple Project, 1984–85 Field Season, Preliminary Report' in *JARCE* 23 (1986), 157–66.

Gurneh/Qurneh

A. E. P. WEIGALL, 'A Report on the Excavation of the Funeral Temple of Thoutmosis III at Gurneh' in *ASAÉ* 7 (1906), 121–41.

el-Kab

S. CLARKE, 'El-Kab and its temples' in *JEA* 8 (1922), 16–40.

Karnak

H. CHEVRIER, 'Rapport sur les Travaux de Karnak (1933–4)' in *ASAÉ* 34 (1934), 159–75

Chicago University, Oriental Institute, *Reliefs and Inscriptions at Karnak*, 2 vols (Chicago 1936).

R. A. FAZZINI, 'Report on the 1983 season of excavation at the Precinct of the Goddess Mut' in *ASAÉ* 70 (1984–85), 287–310.

N. PILLET, 'Le Naos de Senousert I' in *ASAÉ* 23 (1923), 143–58.

D. B. REDFORD, 'An Interim Report of the Second Season of Work at the Temple of Osiris, Ruler of Eternity, Karnak' in *JEA* 59 (1973), 16–30.

D. B. REDFORD, 'Preliminary Report of the First Season of Excavation in East Karnak, 1975–6' in *JARCE* 14 (1977), 5–8. Also, 'Studies on Akhenaten at Thebes: I. A Report on the Work of the Akhenaten Temple Project of the University Museum, University of Pennsylvania' in *JARCE* 10 (1973), 77–94; 12 (1975), 9–14.

R. W. SMITH and D. B. REDFORD, *The Akhenaten Temple Project*, 2 vols (Warminster, England, 1976, 1980).

C. C. VAN SICLEN, 'Amenhotep II's Bark Chapel for Amun at North Karnak' in *BIFAO* 86 (1986), 353–60.

Khargeh

S. SAUNERON, 'Les temples gréco-romains de l'oasis de Khargeh' in *BIFAO* 55 (1955), 23–32.

Kom Ombo

A. BADAWY, *Kom Ombo Sanctuaries* (Cairo 1941)

Medamud

C. ROBINSON and A. VARILLE, *Description sommaire du temple primitif de Medamoud* (Cairo 1940).

Medinet Habu

Chicago University, Oriental Institute, *Medinet Habu*, 4 vols (Chicago 1932–40).

Memphis

M. JONES, 'The Temple of Apis in Memphis' in *JEA* 76 (1990), 141–8.

Philae

G. BÉNÉDITE, *Le Temple de Philae* (Paris 1893–5).

The Ramesseum

J. E. QUIBELL, *The Ramesseum* (London 1896).

Saqqara

M. MOUSSA, 'Excavations in the Valley Temple of King Unas at Saqqara' in *ASAÉ* 64 (1981), 75–7, and in *ASAÉ* 70 (1984–85), 33–4.

A. M. MOUSSA, 'Three recent finds in the Valley Temple of Unas' in *JEA* 70 (1984), 50–3.

H. S. SMITH and D. G. JEFFREYS, 'The Anubieion, North Saqqara,

Preliminary Report, 1978–79' and 'Preliminary Report, 1979–80' in *JEA* 66 (1980), 17–27, and *JEA* 67 (1981), 5–20.

Thebes

H. H. NELSON, *Key Plans showing Locations of Theban Temple Decorations* (Chicago 1941).

U. HÖLSCHER and R. ANTHES, *The Temples of the Eighteenth Dynasty* (Chicago 1939).

W. M. F. PETRIE, *Six Temples at Thebes* (London 1867).

H. E. WINLOCK, 'A Restoration of the Reliefs from the Mortuary Temple of Amenhotep I' in *JEA* 4 (1917), 11–15.

5 SMALL OBJECTS

Selected bibliography, but see also the series of Catalogues produced by the British Museum and the Cairo Museum, as well as Petrie's series on the Edwards' collection, University College London.

A. M. BLACKMAN, 'The Ka-House and the Serdab' in *JEA* 3 (1916), 250–4.

P. A. CLAYTON, 'Bronze Shawabti Figures' in *JEA* 58 (1972), 167–75.

J. D. COONEY, *Amarna Reliefs from Hermopolis in American Collections* (The Brooklyn Museum, New York 1965).

E. DABROWSKA SMEKTALA, 'Coffins found in the Area of the Temple of Tuthmosis III at Deir el-Bahri' in *BIFAO* 66 (1968), 171–82.

G. DARESSY, 'Les cercueils des prêtres d'Ammon' in *ASAÉ* 8 (1907), 3–38

G. DARESSY, *Cercueils des cachettes royales* (Cairo 1909).

M. C. C. EDGAR, 'The Sarcophagus of an Unknown Queen' in *ASAÉ* 8 (1907), 276–81.

I. E. S. EDWARDS, *The Treasures of Tutankhamun* (New York 1973).

W. C. HAYES, *Royal Sarcophagi of the XVIIIth Dynasty* (Princeton 1955).

W. C. HAYES, 'The Sarcophagus of Sennemut' in *JEA* 36 (1950), 19–23.

G. MASPERO, *Les Momies royales de Deir el-Bahari* (Cairo 1889).

G. MASPERO and H. GAUTHIER, *Sarcophages des époques persane et ptolémaïque* (Cairo 1939).

P. E. NEWBERRY, *Funerary Statuettes and Model Sarcophagi* (Cat. Gén. du Musée du Caire, Cairo 1930).

W. M. F. PETRIE, Funeral Figures in Egypt in *Ancient Egypt* (1916), IV, 151–61.

W. M. F. PETRIE, *Prehistoric Egypt Corpus* (London 1921).

W. M. F. PETRIE, *Funeral Furniture and Stone Vases* (London 1937).

W. M. F. PETRIE, *Ceremonial Slate Palettes* (London 1953).

J. SAMSON, *Amarna, City of Akhenaten and Nefertiti: Key Pieces from the Petrie Collection* (Warminster, England 1972).

A. W. SHORTER, 'The Study of Egyptian Funerary Amulets' in *Chr. d'Ég.* 6, 312.

G. E. SMITH, *The Royal Mummies* (Cairo 1912).

W. S. SMITH, *Ancient Egypt as Represented in the Museum of Fine Arts, Boston* (Boston 1960).

H. E. WINLOCK, *The Treasure of Three Egyptian Princesses* (New York 1948).

Primary sources, textual

1   CLASSICAL AUTHORS

Original texts with English translations of Herodotus, Diodorus Siculus, Strabo, Pliny the Elder, and Plutarch in the Loeb Classical Library series (London and Cambridge, Mass.) Also, Manetho (trans. by W. G. Waddell, Loeb (London 1940)).

J. G. GRIFFITHS, *Plutarch, De Iside et Osiride* (edited with introduction, translation and commentary, University of Wales Press, Cardiff, 1970).

2   ANCIENT EGYPTIAN TEXTS – GENERAL

J. H. BREASTED, *Ancient Records of Egypt*, 5 vols (Chicago 1906–7).

A. ERMAN, *The Ancient Egyptians: A Sourcebook of their Writings* (trans. by A. M. Blackman, with Introduction by W. K. Simpson, New York 1966).

A. H. GARDINER, *Hieratic Papyri in the British Museum* (3rd series), 2 vols (London 1935).

G. LEFÉBURE, *Romans et contes égyptiens de l'époque pharaonique* (Paris 1949).

S. G. J. QUIRKE and W. J. TAIT, 'Egyptian manuscripts in the Wellcome Collection' in *JEA* 80 (1994), 145–58.

A. W. SHORTER, *Catalogue of Egyptian Religious Papyri in the British Museum* (London 1938).

J. A. WILSON in J. B. PRITCHARD, *Ancient Near Eastern Texts relating to the Old Testament* (Princeton 1950).

3   BIBLIOGRAPHY FOR SPECIFIC TEXTS

The Pyramid Texts
On the walls of the pyramids of the late Old Kingdom and First Intermediate Period.

T. C. ALLEN, *Occurrences of Pyramid Texts, with Cross Indexes of these and other Egyptian mortuary texts* (Chicago 1950).

ERMAN, *The Ancient Egyptian*, 2–13.

R. O. FAULKNER, 'The "Cannibal Hymn" from the Pyramid Texts' in *JEA* 10 (1924), 97–103.

S. A. B. MERCER, *The Pyramid Texts in Translation and Commentary* (New York, London, Toronto 1952); *Literary Criticism of the Pyramid Texts* (London 1956).

The Coffin Texts
On coffins of the Middle Kingdom; briefly revived in Dynasty 26.
A. DE BUCK and A. H. GARDINER (eds), *The Egyptian Coffin Texts*, (Chicago, 1935–61).
R. O. FAULKNER, *The Ancient Egyptian Coffin Texts*, 3 vols (Warminster, England, 1973–8).

New Kingdom 'Books'
T. G. ALLEN, 'Additions to the Book of the Dead' in *JNES* 11 (1952), 177. Also, *The Egyptian Book of the Dead. Documents in the Oriental Institute Museum at the University of Chicago* (Chicago 1960).
T. ANDRZEJEWSKI, 'Le Livre des Portes dans la salle du sarcophage du tombeau de Ramesès III' in *ASAÉ* 57 (1962), 1.
P. BUCHER, 'Les textes à la fin des première, deuxième, et troisième heures du livre "de ce qu'il y a dans la Douat". Textes compares des tombes de Thoutmosis III, Aménophis II et Séti Ier' in *BIFAO* 30 (1931), 229–47.
E. A. BUDGE, *The Book of the Dead*, 3 vols (London 1898).
E. A. BUDGE, *The Book of Opening the Mouth* (Books of Egypt and Chaldea, vols. 26–7) (London 1909).
W. R. DAWSON, 'A Rare Vignette from the Book of the Dead' in *JEA* 10 (1924), 40.
R. O. FAULKNER, *An Ancient Egyptian Book of Hours* (Oxford 1958); also, 'An Ancient Egyptian "Book of Hours"' in *JEA* 40 (1954), 34–9.
CH. MAYSTRE, 'Le Livre de la Vache du Ciel dans les tombeaux de la Vallée des Rois' in *BIFAO* 40 (1941), 53–115.
CH. MAYSTRE and A. PIANKOFF, *Le Livre des Ports* (Cairo 1939).
A. PIANKOFF, 'Les differents "livres" dans les tombes royales du Nouvel Empire' in *ASAÉ* 40 (1940), 283–9.
A. PIANKOFF, 'Le livre du jour dans la tombe (no. 132) de Ramose' in *ASAÉ* 41 (1942), 151–8. Also, 'Quelques passages du Livre du Jour et de la Nuit dans le temple funéraire de Ramsès III à Medinet Habu' in *ASAÉ* 43 (1942), 351–3.
A. PIANKOFF, 'Le Tableau d'Osiris et les divisions V, VI et VII du Livre des Ports' in *ASAÉ* 56 (1959), 229.
Especially, *Hymns to the Sun*. These were two songs found in tombs of the New Kingdom, either in the form of an inscription, or written in the Book of the Dead placed in the tomb. One greeted the sun in the morning (*Book of the Dead*, ch. XV, A 11) and the other was the evening hymn (ch. XV, B 11). A translation is given in ERMAN, *The Ancient Egyptian*, 138–9.

Wisdom Literature: Old Kingdom and Middle Kingdom
ERMAN, *The Ancient Egyptian,* 54–84.
A. H. GARDINER, 'New Literary Sources from Ancient Egypt' in *JEA* I (1914), 20–35
A. H. GARDINER, 'The Instruction addressed to Kagemni and his Brethren' in *JEA* 32 (1946), 71–4.
B. GUNN, *The Instruction of Ptah-hotep and the Instruction of Ke'gemni* (London 1918).
Also, WILSON, *ANET,* 414 ff.
The Instruction for Amenemmes I: ERMAN, *The Ancient Egyptian,* 72–4; WILSON, *ANET,* 418 ff.

Wisdom Literature: New Kingdom
Text of Amenemope: Preserved completely in Pap. Anastasi 1 (London) and also a fragment on a Turin papyrus and excerpts on eight ostraca. Translated A. H. Gardiner, *Hieratic Texts,* I (Leipzig 1911); see also ERMAN, *The Ancient Egyptian,* 214 ff.
Wisdom of Ani: A late imitation of the old Wisdom Instructions. From a Dynasty 22 papyrus in Cairo. See ERMAN, *The Ancient Egyptian,* 234 ff.

Meditations and pessimistic literature
R. O. FAULKNER, 'The Man who was Tired of Life' in *JEA* 42 (1956), 21–40.
A. H. GARDINER, *The Admonitions of an Egyptian Sage* (Leipzig 1909); also WILSON, *ANET,* 441 ff.; ERMAN, *The Ancient Egyptian,* 92 ff.
A. H. GARDINER, 'New Literary Works from Ancient Egypt' in *JEA* I (1914), 100 ff.; also WILSON, *ANET,* 444 ff.; ERMAN, *The Ancient Egyptian,* 86 ff., 110 ff.
R. J. WILLIAMS, 'Reflections on the Lebensmude' in *JEA* 48 (1962), 49–56.

Songs at banquets (in the tombs)
A. H. GARDINER, *Proceedings of the Society of Biblical Archaeology* 35, p. 165 ff.; ERMAN, *The Ancient Egyptian,* 132, 251–3.
M. LICHTHEIM, 'Songs of the Harpers' in *JNES* 4 (1945), 178 ff.

Hymns to deities and the king
Great Hymn to Amun: a papyrus in Cairo written in the reign of Amenophis III, see ERMAN, *The Ancient Egyptian,* 283 ff. Prayer to Amun as the righteous judge: Pap. Anastasi 2, 6, 5 ff.. and Pap. Bologna 1094, 2.3 ff. see ERMAN, *The Ancient Egyptian,* 308; Prayer to Amun in the Court of Law: Pap. Anastasi 2, 8.5 ff. See ERMAN, *op. cit.,*308.
Hymn to the Sun from el Amarnah: in a tomb at Amarna as a prayer of the deceased who later became King Ay; see Davies, *The Rock Tombs of el-Amarnah,* 6, p. 29 ff. and ERMAN, *The Ancient Egyptian,* 288 ff.
Hymns to King Sesostris: a papyrus of Dynasty 12 found in the ruins of the

town of Kahun, see F. LL. GRIFFITH, *Hieratic Papyri from Kahun and Gurob* (London 1898), 1 ff. See ERMAN, *The Ancient Egyptian,* 1 ff.
Prayer for the King in el-Amarnah: see DAVIES, *The Rock Tombs of el-Amarnah,* 3, Pl. XXIX, and trans. p. 31 ff.; also ERMAN, *op. cit.,* 292.

Narratives
King Cheops and the Magicians: see ERMAN, 33 ff.

Historical inscriptions with religious significance
W. F. ALBRIGHT, *The Amarna Letters from Palestine* (Cambridge Ancient History, vol. II, ch. XX); see also WINCKLER, *The Tell el-Amarna Letters* (transl. J. M. P. METCALF. Berlin 1896).
J. BENNETT, 'The Restoration Inscription of Tutankhamun' in *JEA* 25 (1939), 8–15
J. J. ČERNY, *Catalogue des ostraca hiératiques non littéraires de Deir el Médineh* (Cairo 1937).
H. W. FAIRMAN and B. GRDSELOFF, 'Texts of Hatshepsut and Sethos I inside Speos Artemidos' in *JEA* 33 (1947), 12–33.
G. GRAINDOR, 'Inscriptions de la nécropole de Touna el-Ghebel' in *BIFAO* 32 (1932), 97–119. For texts from the tomb of Petosiris, see G. LEFÉBURE in *ASAÉ* 20 (1920) – 22 (1922).
W. C. HAYES, 'Inscriptions from the Palace of Amenhotep III' in *JNES* 10 (1951), 35, 82, 156, 231.
S. A. B. MERCER, *The Tell el-Amarna Tablets* (Toronto 1939).
T. E. PEET, *The Great Tomb Robberies of the Twentieth Egyptian Dynasty,* 2 vols (Oxford 1930); also, 'The Great Tomb Robberies of the Ramesside Age: Papyri Mayer A and B' in *JEA* 2 (1915), 173–7; 204–6.
M. SANDMAN, *Texts from the Time of Akhenaten* (Brussels 1938).

Important inscriptions of myths
E. DRIOTON, *Le Texte dramatique d'Edfou* (Cairo 1948).
H. W. FAIRMAN, 'The Myth of Horus at Edfu: I' in *JEA* 21 (1935), 26–36; 'II' in *JEA* 28 (1942), 32–8; 29 (1943), 2–36; 30 (1944), 5–22.
J. G. GRIFFITHS, *The Conflict of Horus and Seth* (Liverpool 1961).

Astronomical and medical texts
R. A. PARKER, *The Calendars of Ancient Egypt* (Chicago 1950).
O. NEUGEBAUER and R. A. PARKER, *Egyptian Astronomical Texts,* 3 vols (Providence, 1969).
J. H. BREASTED, *The Edwin Smith Surgical Papyrus* (Chicago 1930).
Chester Beatty VI Medical Papyrus: A. H. GARDINER, *Hieratic Papyri,* No. 53–4 (London 1935).
B. EBBELL, *The Papyrus Ebers* (Copenhagen 1937).
F. JONCKHEERE, *Le Papyrus médical Chester Beatty* (Brussels 1947).
G. A. REISNER, *The Hearst Medical Papyrus* (Leipzig 1905).

Appendix A2

Selected passages from Egyptian religious literature

King Cheops and the Magicians

(King Cheops is being entertained by his sons who relate the wonderful deeds performed by magicians of the past. Finally, Prince Hardedef comes before his father.)

Then Prince Hardedef stood up to speak and said: 'Hitherto you have heard only examples of what they knew that have gone before (us), and one does not know the truth from falsehood. But even in your own time there is a magician.' Then said his majesty: 'Who is that, Har(dedef), my son?' And Hardedef said: 'There is a townsman of 110 years, and he eats 500 loaves of bread, a haunch of beef in the way of meat, and drinks 100 jugs of beer, unto this very day. He knows how to put on again a head that has been cut off, and he knows how to make a lion follow him, with its leash trailing upon the ground. He knows the number of the locks(?) of the sanctuary of Thoth, to make the like thereof for his Horizon (i.e. pyramid).'

Then his majesty said: 'You yourself, Hardedef, my son, will bring him to me.'

(Hardedef then makes the voyage by river to Dedi's house, and brings him back to the royal Court.)

Now when he reached the Residence, Prince Hardedef entered in to make report to the majesty of King Cheops. And Prince Hardedef said: 'O king, my lord, I have brought Dedi.' His majesty said: 'Go, bring him to me.' Then his majesty proceeded to the pillared hall of the palace, and Dedi was brought in unto him. And his majesty said: 'How is it, Dedi, that I have never seen you before?' And Dedi said: 'It is he who is summoned that comes. The sovereign summoned me, and lo, I am come' And his majesty said: 'Is it true, what is said, that you can put on again a head that has been cut off?' And Dedi said: 'Yes, that I can, O king, my lord.' And his majesty said: 'Have brought unto me a prisoner that is in prison, that his punishment may be inflicted.' And Dedi said: 'But not on a man, O king, my lord! Lo, is not such a thing rather commanded to be done to the august cattle?'

And a goose was brought unto him, and its head was cut off; and the goose was placed on the western side of the hall, and its head on the eastern side of the hall. And Dedi said his say of magic, and thereupon the goose stood up and waddled, and its head likewise. Now when one part had reached the other, the goose stood up and cackled. And he had a duck brought unto him, and there was done unto it the like. And his majesty had an ox brought to him, and its head was made to tumble to the ground. And Dedi said his say of magic, and the ox stood up behind him, while its leash fell to the ground.

And King Cheops said: 'It has been said that you know the number of the locks(?) of the sanctuary of Thoth.' And Dedi said: 'So it pleases you, I do not know the number thereof, O king, my lord, but I know the place where they are.' And his majesty said: 'Where is that?' And Dedi said: 'There is a chest of flint in the chamber named 'The Inventory' in Heliopolis. (Lo, they are) in the chest.' And Dedi said: 'O king, my lord, lo, it is not I that bring them to you.' And his majesty said: 'Who then will bring it to me?' And Dedi said: 'It is the eldest of the three children who are in the belly of Red-dedet that will bring it to you.' And his majesty said: 'But I desire that you say who she is, this Red-dedet.' And Dedi said: 'It is the wife of a priest of Re' of Sakhebu, that has conceived three children of Re', lord of Sakhebu. He has told her that they will exercise this excellent office (i.e. the kingship) in this entire land, and that the eldest of them will be high priest in Heliopolis.' Then his majesty's heart grew sad thereat. And Dedi said: 'Pray, what is this mood, O king, my lord? Is it because of the three children? Then I say to you: your son, his son, and then one of them.' And his majesty said: 'When will she give birth, pray, (this) Red-dedet?' (And Dedi said): 'She will give birth on the fifteenth day of the first winter month.'

(The king orders Dedi to be given a home with Prince Hardedef and a food allowance. The story then continues.)

Now on one of these days it came to pass that Red-dedet suffered the pangs of childbirth. Then said the majesty of Re' of Sakhebu to Isis, Nephthys, Mesekhent, Hekat and Khnum: 'Up go you and deliver Red-dedet of the three children that are in her womb, they will exercise this excellent office in this entire land. They will build your temples, they will furnish your altars with victuals, they will replenish your libation-tables, and they will make great your offerings.' Then these deities went, when they had taken on the forms of dancing-girls, and Khnum was with them and bore their carrying-chair.

And they came to the house of Rewoser (i.e. Red-dedet's husband) and found him standing with his loin-cloth hanging down. Then they presented to him their necklaces and rattles. Then he said unto them: 'My mistresses, behold there is a lady here who is in travail.' And they said: 'Let us see her; lo, we understand midwifery.' And he said unto them: 'Come.' then they entered in before Red-dedet, and shut (the door of) the room upon them and her. And Isis placed herself in front of her, and Nephthys behind her, and Hekat hastened the birth. And Isis said: 'Be not lusty in her womb as truly as you are named User-ref' (i.e. Userkaf, first king of Dynasty 5). This child slipped forth on to her hands, a child of one cubit with strong bones; the royal titulary of his limbs was of gold, and his head-cloth of true lapis-lazuli. They washed him, cut his navel-string, and laid him on a sheet upon a brick. And Mesekhent drew near to him and she said: 'A king that will exercise the kingship in the entire land.' And Khnum gave health to his body.

(The births of the other two children are then described in the same manner.)

And these divinities went forth, after that they had delivered Red-dedet of the three children. And they said: 'Let your heart be glad, Rewoser! Behold, three children are born to you.'

Wisdom literature (Selected passages from the 'Instructions')

THE INSTRUCTION OF PTAHHOTEP

The instruction of the superintendent of the capital, the vizier Ptahhotep, under the majesty of King Isesi, who lives for ever and ever. . . .
(*You can learn something from every one.*)
Do not be arrogant because of your knowledge, and have no confidence in that you are a learned man. Take counsel with the ignorant as with the wise, for the limits of excellence cannot be reached, and no artist fully possesses his skill. A good discourse is more hidden than the precious green stone, and yet it is found with slave-girls over the mill-stones.
(*You will get on best in life with the aid of right and truth.*)
If you are a leader and give command to the multitude, strive after every excellence, until there is no fault in your nature. Truth is good and its worth is lasting, and it has not been disturbed since the day of its creator, whereas he that transgresses its ordinance is punished. It lies as a (right) path in front of him that knows nothing. Wrong-doing(?) has never yet brought its venture to port. Evil indeed wins wealth, but the strength of truth is that it endures, and the (upright) man says: 'It is the property of my father.'
(*Concerning behaviour as a guest.*)
If you are one that sits where stands the table of one who is greater than you, take, when he gives, that which is set before you. Look not at that which lies before him, but look at that which lies before you; do not shoot many

glances at him, for it is an abhorrence to the ka if one offends it. Cast down your countenance until he greets you, and speak only when he has greeted you. Laugh when he laughs – that will be well-pleasing in his heart, and what you do will be acceptable.

(*Do not slight those who have risen in the world.*)

If you are a humble person and in the train of a man of repute, one that stands well with the god, know nothing of his former insignificance. Do not raise your heart against him on account of what you know about him aforetime. Reverence him in accordance with what has happened to him, for wealth does not come of itself . . . it is God that creates repute. . . .

(*Behaviour towards petitioners.*)

If you are one to whom petition is made, be kind when you hear the speech of a petitioner. Do not deal roughly with him . . . a petitioner is well pleased if one nods to his addresses until he has made an end of that about which he came . . .

(*Warning against covetousness.*)

If you desire your conduct to be good, to set yourself free from all that is evil, then beware of covetousness, which is a malady, diseaseful, incurable. Intimacy with it is impossible; it makes the sweet friend bitter, it alienates the trusted one from the master, it makes bad both father and mother, and it divorces a man's wife. . . .

(*The advantage of marriage.*)

If you are a man of note, found for yourself a household, and love your wife at home as is fitting. Fill her belly, clothe her back; unguent is the remedy for her limbs. Make glad her heart as long as she lives; she is a goodly field for her lord.

THE INSTRUCTION FOR KAGEMNI

(*On behaviour at a meal.*)

If you sit with a greedy person, eat only when his meal is over, and if you sit with a drunkard, take only when his desire is satisfied. . .

(*Do not be boastful.*)

Do not be boastful of your strength in the midst of those of your own age. Be on guard against any withstanding you. . . .

THE INSTRUCTION OF DUAUF

Instruction which a man named Duauf, the son of Khety, composed for his son, named Pepi, when he voyaged up to the Residence, in order to put him in the School of Books, among the children of the magistrates. . . .

He said unto him: 'I have seen him that is beaten, him that is beaten; you are to set your heart on books. I have seen him that is set free from forced labour: behold, nothing surpasses books. . . .

'Would that I might make you love books more than thy mother, would that I might bring their beauty before your face. It is greater than any calling.

... If he has begun to succeed, and is yet a child, men greet him. . . .I have never seen a sculptor on an errand, nor a goldsmith as he was being sent forth, but I have seen the smith at his task at the mouth of his furnace. His fingers were like stuff from crocodiles, he stank more than the offal (?) of fishes.

'. . . . the small bricklayer with the Nile mud, he spends his life among the cattle . . . his clothes are stiff . . . he works with his feet, he pounds. . . .

'Behold, there is no calling that is without a director except (that of) the scribe, and he is the director.'

The Pyramid Texts (A selection of passages)

UTTERANCE 467 – THE DECEASED'S JOURNEY TO THE SKY

He that flies flies! He flies away from you, you men. He is no longer on earth, he is in the sky. You his city-god, his ka is at your side. He rushes at the sky as a heron, he has kissed the sky as a hawk, he has leapt skyward as a grasshopper.

UTTERANCE 267 – THE DECEASED'S JOURNEY TO THE SKY

You have your heart, Osiris; you have your feet, Osiris; you have your arm, Osiris. He has his own heart; he has his own feet; he has his own arm. A ramp to the sky is built for him, that he may go up to the sky thereon. He goes up on the smoke of the great exhalation. He flies as a bird, and he settles as a beetle on an empty seat that is in the ship of Reʿ: 'Stand up, get forth, you without. . . that he may sit in your seat.' He rows in the sky in your ship, O Reʿ, and he comes to land in your ship, O Reʿ. When you ascend out of the horizon, he is there with his staff in his hand, the navigator of your ship, O Reʿ. You mount up to the sky and are far from earth . . .

UTTERANCE 273–274 – THE DECEASED DEVOURS THE GODS

He has broken up the backbones and the spinal marrow, he has taken away the hearts of the gods. He has eaten the Red Crown, he has swallowed the Green One. He feeds on the lungs of the Wise Ones; he is satisfied with the living on hearts and their magic; he rejoices when he devours the . . . which are in the Red Crown. He flourishes and their magic is in his belly, his dignities are not taken from him. He has swallowed the understanding of every god. . . . Lo, their soul is in his belly, their lordliness is with him. His superfluity of food is more than that of the gods, and what is burnt for him is their bones. Their souls are with him, and their shadows are with their companions. . . .

UTTERANCE 508 – THE GODDESSES SUCKLE THE DECEASED

He that ascends ascends! He ascends. The mistress of Buto rejoices, and the heart of her that dwells in el-Kab is dilated, on that day when he ascends at the place of Re'. He has trampled for himself these your rays into a ramp beneath his feet, that he may go up thereon to his mother, the living snake that is upon Re'. She has compassion on him, she gives him her breast, that he may suck it: 'My son, O king, take to thee this my breast and suck it, O king.'

FROM UTTERANCE 524 – THE FATE OF THE DECEASED'S ENEMIES

He is stronger than they, when he appears upon his riverbank. Their hearts fall to (?) his fingers. They of the sky have their entrails, they of the earth their red blood. Poverty has their inheritances, the past their dwellings, a high Nile their gates. (But) he is glad of heart, glad of heart, he, the Sole One, the Bull of the Sky. He has put them to flight that did this to him, he has destroyed their survivors.

The Hymn to the Sun from el-Amarna

Beautiful is your appearing in the horizon of heaven, you living sun, the first who lived! You rise in the eastern horizon and fill every land with your beauty. You are beautiful and great, and shine, and are high above every land. Your rays, they encompass the lands so far as all that you have created. You are Re', and you reach unto their end and subdue them for your dear son. You are far off, yet your rays are upon earth. You are before their face . . . your going.

When you go down in the western horizon, the earth is in darkness as if it were dead. They sleep in the chamber, their heads wrapped up, and no eye perceives the other. Though all their things were taken, while they were under their heads, yet they would not know it. Every lion comes forth from his den, and all worms that bite. Darkness. . . the earth is silent, for he who created it rests in his horizon.

When it is dawn and you rise in the horizon and shine as the sun in the day, you dispel the darkness and shed your beams. The Two Lands are in festival, awake, and stand on their feet, for you have raised them up. They wash their bodies, they take their garments, and their hands praise your arising. The whole land, it goes about its work.

All creatures are content with their pasture, the trees and herbs are verdant. The birds fly out of their nests and their wings praise your ka. All wild beasts dance on their feet, all that fly and flutter – they live when you arise for them. The ships voyage down and upstream likewise, and every way is open because you arise. The fishes in the river leap up before your face. Your rays are in the sea. You who create (male children) in women, and make seed in men! You who maintain the son in the womb of his mother and soothe him so that he does not weep, you nurse in the womb. Who gives breath in order to keep alive all that he has made. When he comes forth from the womb into the world(?) on the day wherein he is born, you open his mouth (so that it might speak) and supply what is needed.

The chick in the egg (already) chirps in the shell, for you give it breath therein to sustain its life. You make for it its strength (?) in the egg in order to break it. It comes forth from the egg to chirp. . .; it walks upon its feet when it comes forth therefrom.

How much is there that you have made, and that is hidden from (me), oh sole god, to whom none is to be likened! You have fashioned the earth according to your desire, you alone, with men, cattle and all wild beasts, all that is upon the earth and goes on foot, and all that soars above and flies with its wings.

The lands of Syria and Nubia, and the land of Egypt – you put every man in his place and you supply their needs. Each one has his provisions, and his lifetime is reckoned. Their tongues are diverse in speech, and their form likewise. Their skins are distinguished, (for?) you distinguish the peoples. You make the Nile in the underworld, and bring it whither you wish, in order to sustain mankind, even as you have made them. You are lord of them all, who wearies himself on their behalf, the lord of every land, who arises for them, the sun of the day, greatly reverenced. All far-off peoples, you make that on which they live. You have (also) put the Nile in the sky that it may come down for them, and may make the waves upon the hills like a sea, in order to moisten their fields in their townships. How excellent are all your designs, O Lord of Eternity! The Nile in heaven, you appoint it for the foreign peoples and all the beasts of the wilderness that walk on feet; and the (real) Nile, it comes forth from the underworld for Timuris.

Your rays suckle every field, and, when you arise, they live and thrive for you. You make the seasons in order to sustain all that you have created, the winter to cool them, and the heat (that they may taste you(?)). You have made the sky afar off in order to rise therein, in order to behold all that you have made. You are unique, arising in your forms as the living sun, appearing, shining, withdrawing, returning(?). You make millions of forms of yourself alone. Cities, townships, fields, road and river – all eyes behold you over against them, as the sun of the day above the earth.

You are in my heart, and there is none other that knows you except your son, Neferkheprure-Sole-One-of-Re', whom you make to comprehend your design and might. The earth came into being at the beckoning of your hand, for you created them. When you rise, they live, when you set, they die. You yourself are lifetime, and men live in you. The eyes look on your beauty until you set. All work is laid aside when you set on the right. When you rise, (you) cause (the) . . . to thrive for the king. . . since you founded the earth. You raise them up for your son, the king of Upper and Lower Egypt, who lives in Truth, lord of the Two Lands, Neferkheprure-Sole-One-of-Re', son of Re', who lives in truth, lord of diadems, Akhenaten, great in his duration, and for the great royal wife whom he loves, Mistress of the Two Lands, Nefernefrure-Nefertiti, that lives and is young for ever and ever.

The Dispute with his Soul of One who is Tired of Life (Selected passages)

Then my soul opened its mouth to me, to answer what I had said: 'If you call burial to mind, it is sadness, it is the bringing of tears, it is making a man sorrowful, it is haling a man from his house and casting him upon the hill (i.e. where the tombs were situated). Never again will you go forth to behold the sun. They who built in granite and fashioned a hall (?) in the pyramid, who achieved what is goodly in this goodly work – when the builders are become gods (i.e. as soon as the kings are dead and buried), then their offering-tables are empty (and they are) even as the weary ones which die upon the dyke without a survivor (i.e. to bury them); the flood has taken its end of them and likewise the heat of the sun, and the fish of the riverbank hold converse with them (i.e. nibble the corpses).

(The man then relates to his soul the disillusionment and discomforts which he must at present endure in life.)

Lo, my name is abhorred,
Lo, more than the odour of carrion,
On days in summer, when the sky is hot.

Lo, my name is abhorred,
Lo, more than catching fish
On the day of the catch, when the sky is hot.

Lo, my name is abhorred,
Lo, more than the odour of birds,
More than the hill of willows with the geese.

Lo, my name is abhorred,
Lo, more than the odour of fishermen,
More than the shores of the swamps, when they have fished. . . .

(In the second poem, further evils of life are described by the man.)

To whom do I speak to-day?
Brothers are evil,
Friends of today, they are not lovable.

To whom do I speak today?
Men are covetous,
Every one seizes his neighbour's goods.

To whom do I speak today?
Gentleness has perished,

Insolence has come to all men.

To whom do I speak today?
The sick man is the trusty friend,
The brother that is with him has become the enemy.

To whom do I speak today?
None remembers the past,
None at this moment does good to him that has done it.

To whom do I speak today?
I am laden with misery,
And lack a trusty friend

To whom do I speak today?
The sin that smites the land,
It has no end.

(In the third poem, the man then compares the delights of death with the turmoil of life.)

Death is before me today,
As when a sick man becomes whole,
As when one walks abroad after sickness

Death is before me today,
As the odour of myrrh,
As when one sits under the sail on a windy day.

Death is before me today,
As the odour of lotus flowers,
As when one sits on the shore of drunkenness.

Death is before me today
As a well-trodden path
As when a man returns from the war to his house.

Death is before me today
As when a man longs to see his house again
After he has spent many years in captivity.

(The man and his soul have each given their argument; the man, weary of the tribulations of life, seeks to end his existence on earth, but his soul, fearing that it will then be deprived of the comforts of a tomb and food provisions, has described the uncertainty of funerary arrangements, and urges the man: 'Listen to me, lo, it is good for a man when he - listens. Follow the glad day and forget care.' Finally, the man and his soul agree to continue life together until the natural lifespan is completed.)

This is what my soul said to me: 'Cast aside lamentation, my comrade, my brother . . . . I will abide here, if you reject the west (i.e. death). But when you reach the west and your body is united with the earth, then I will alight after you are at rest. Let us have an abode together.'

The Admonitions of a Prophet (A selection of passages)

(The *First Poem* – this describes the general state of the country, probably at the end of the Old Kingdom.)
Nay, but poor men now possess fine things. He who once made for himself no sandals now possesses riches. . . .
Nay, but many dead men are buried in the river. The stream is a sepulchre, and the Pure Place (i.e. House of Embalming) is become a stream.
Nay, but the high-born are full of lamentations, and the poor are full of joy. Every town says: 'Let us drive out the powerful from our midst. . . .'
Nay, but the gates, columns and walls are consumed with fire; (and yet) the chamber(?) of the king's palace (still) endures and stands fast. . . .
Nay, but gold and lapis lazuli, silver and turquoise, carnelian and bronze, marble and . . . are hung about the necks of slave-girls. But noble ladies walk through the land, and mistresses of house say: 'Would that we had something we could eat.'. . .
Nay, but the great and small say: 'I wish I were dead.' Little children say: 'He ought never to have caused me to live.'. . .
Nay, but the laws of the judgment-hall are placed in the vestibule. Yea, men walk upon them in the streets, and the poor tear them up in the alleys. . . .

(In the *Second Poem*, the narrator describes the complete upheaval of the society; the kingship is now destroyed, and the role of the classes is reversed.)
Behold, a thing has been done that did not happen aforetime; it is come to this that the king has been taken away by poor men. . . Behold, it is come to this, that the land is despoiled of the kingship by a few senseless people. . . .
Behold, the poor of the land have become rich; he that possesses something is now one who has nothing. . . .
Behold, the bald head that used no oil now possesses jars of pleasant myrrh.
Behold, she that had no box now possesses a coffer. She that looked at her face in the water now possesses a mirror . . . .

(The text continues to list the appalling conditions to be found throughout Egypt, but in the *Sixth Poem*, there is mention of the good times which will return when peace is restored.)

It is good, however, when the hands of men build pyramids and dig ponds, and make for the gods plantations with trees.

It is good, however, when rejoicing is in (men's) mouths, and the magnates of districts stand and look on at the jubilation in their houses(?), clad in fine raiment. . . .

(Thus, the sage Ipuwer describes the political and social disintegration to the aged king (probably Pepy II) at his court, and urges the ruler, who is apparently ignorant of the dangers in his land, to take firm action. However, even the kingship is swept away, and only the hope that peace will return can support the Egyptians in these times of chaos.)

Appendix B

A selective list of major religious sites in Egypt

The sites are listed under the names by which they are best known, but the alternative ancient Egyptian, Greek or modern versions are included where relevant.

Abu Gurob

The solar temple of Niuserre (Dynasty 5) is situated here, probably erected on the occasion of his jubilee festival. It was excavated in AD 1898–1901 on behalf of the Berlin Museum, and although little remains of the valley temple or the causeway, it is possible to see part of the solar obelisk and the altar in the court. The solar temple of Userkaf (Dynasty 5), now very poorly preserved, lies to the south.

Abu Roash

The ruins of the pyramids and cemeteries of the Old Kingdom. The most interesting is the limestone pyramid of Djedefre', son of Cheops.

Abu Simbel

Rock temples built by Ramesses II (Dynasty 19) in years 26 to 34 of his reign, to impress the Nubians with Egypt's might. The Great Temple is dedicated to Amen-Re' and Re'-Harakhte, as well as to other principal deities. The four large statues of Ptah, Amen-Re', Ramesses II and Re'-Harakhte in the sanctuary are so positioned that, with the exception of the non-solar Ptah, the rays of the sun strike them directly during the solstices. North of this temple, Ramesses II built a smaller sanctuary, hewn from the mountain, which was dedicated to Hathor and to his queen, Nefertari. In recent years, these temples were removed from their original site to a higher situation, to protect them from the rising waters of the reservoir lake, created by the construction of the High Dam at Aswan. This project was undertaken by an international team.

Abu Sir

A group of pyramids belonging to Sahure, Niuserre, Neferirkare, and Neferefre (Dynasty 5), excavated in AD 1902–8 by the German Oriental Institute. There are also some mastabas (Dynasty 5), the most notable being that of Ptahshepses, excavated by De Morgan in AD 1893.

Abydos (Eg. Ebot)

One of the most ancient and important religious sites, Abydos was originally devoted to the cult of Khentiamentiu, but it soon became the great centre of Osiris.

THE NECROPOLIS

Situated in the desert, the four main sections are: south (el-Araba) where the tombs of the New Kingdom, the temples of Sethos I and Ramesses II, and the Osireion are situated; north of this, the graves of the Old Kingdom; further north, the tombs of the Middle Kingdom and graves of Dynasties 18–20; to the west, in the hill of Umm el-Ga'ab, tombs of the kings of the earliest dynasties.

THE TEMPLE OF SETHOS I

Built by Sethos I and completed by Ramesses II (Dynasty 19), this was the mortuary temple of Sethos I, with provision for the worship of the chief deities – Amen-Re', Ptah, Re'-Harakhte, Osiris, Isis and Horus – as well as a special set of chambers where the annual resurrection of Osiris was enacted. The ground plan differs from those of other temples in that it is L-shaped; the temple is also unique in possessing seven shrines in the sanctuary, and the Osiris Complex. The temple was almost completely excavated in AD 1859 by Mariette, and has some of the finest carvings yet discovered. The wall reliefs, illustrating an extensive series of rites, have formed the basis for research into the rituals performed in Egyptian temples.

THE OSIREION (CENOTAPH OF SETHOS)

Built on the same axis, and situated at the rear of the Sethos Temple, the purpose of this building remains obscure, although it was probably connected in some way with the Osiris rituals and may have been regarded as the cenotaph of Sethos as an Osiris. It was orignally hidden by an artificial mound, and has heen dated tentatively to the reign of Sethos, although the style of its construction in limestone and granite is reminiscent of Chephren's Valley Temple at Gizeh. It was discovered in AD 1903 by Margaret Murray and excavated in 1911–26 by the Egypt Exploration Society.

TEMPLE OF RAMESSES II

This temple, built by Ramesses II, was dedicated to Osiris and to the king's own mortuary cult; it is now in a ruinous state, although the remaining wall reliefs indicate its original magnificence.

Akhmim (Eg. Epu or Khente-Min; Gk. Chemmis or Panopolis)

Named after its deity, Min, the once great temples of this town are now much destroyed. Nearby are the nobles' rock-cut tombs of Dynasty 6.

Amarna (el-Amarna, Eg. Akhetaten)

Capital city of the 'heretic' pharaoh Amenophis IV (Akhenaten), built towards the end of Dynasty 18. The site, 280 miles from Thebes and some 155 miles from the Delta, included the Great Temple to the Aten in the centre of the city, another nearby temple, the king's palace, the north palace, and two southern palaces. There were also offices, magazines, houses and villas for the officials and workers, but little remains of any of these buildings.

To the north and south of the city, the necropolises were situated, but most of the tombs remained unfinished. Of the southern tombs, those of Tutu, Mahu and Ay are important, while in the northern group, those of note include Huya, Merire I, Panehesy, and the royal tomb of Akhenaten and his family.

Assiut (Gk. Lycopolis)

The modern city stands on the site of the ancient capital of the 15th nome of Upper Egypt, the cult centre of the god Wepwawet. It was especially important during the First Intermediate Period and the Middle Kingdom, and the tombs of the local nomarchs are cut in the nearby mountainside.

Aswan (Eg. Yebu)

In antiquity named 'Elephant Land', this title was later restricted to the island and town of Elephantine. The quarries at Aswan provided excellent granite for Egypt from the Old Kingdom onwards, and the site commanded the cataracts and the main trading route to Nubia. To the north of Elephantine, on the west bank, are the tombs of the nobles of Elephantine, dating to the end of the Old Kingdom and to the Middle Kingdom. They are similar in design to the rock-cut tombs at Beni Hasan.

Avaris

It has been suggested (but without conclusive evidence) that this capital city of the Hyksos rulers can be identified as the Delta site of Tanis (San el-Hagar).

Beni Hasan

The nomarchs of the 16th or Antelope nome, with its provincial centre at Monet-Khufu, were buried in rock tombs quarried out in the nearby hillside. These date to the First Intermediate Period and the Middle Kingdom.

Of these thirty-nine tombs, twelve are decorated with brightly painted scenes of daily life. There is also a rock-cut temple to Pakhet (the Speos Artemidos) south of the tombs, built by Tuthmosis III and Hatshepsut (Dynasty 18).

Bubastis (modern Tell Basta; Eg. Per-Bast)
This was the capital of the Bubastite nome, and the centre of Bastet the cat-goddess, whose temple was discovered here. Started by Cheops and Chephren in Dynasty 4, it was completed in its final form by the kings of Dynasty 22 who made Bubastis their residence. There is a large necropolis, and a huge cat cemetery where many bronze statuettes of the goddess and of cats have been discovered.

Busiris (Eg. Djedu)
The ancient Delta town which was one of Osiris' major cult centres.

Buto (modern Tell el-Fara'in; Eg. Pe)
The capital of Lower Egypt in the predynastic period, and cult centre of the cobra-goddess Edjo. Little remains of the ancient town.

Coptos (modern Quft; Eg. Kebtoyew)
This town was dedicated to Min, the god of fertility and also of travellers, since this was the commercial centre for the caravans which set out to the Red Sea *en route* for Punt, the land which supplied incense for temple rituals.

Dahshur
Five pyramids can still be seen here: the North Brick Pyramid of Sesostris III (Dynasty 12); that of Amenemmes II (Dynasty 12); the South Brick Pyramid of Amenemmes III (Dynasty 12); the Bent or Rhomboidal Pyramid, probably built by Sneferu (Dynasty 4); and the Northern Stone Pyramid constructed for Sneferu (Dynasty 4).

Denderah (Eg. Enet; Gk. Tentyra)
A well-preserved temple (Graeco-Roman period), dedicated to Hathor, whose husband, Horus, and son, Ihy, also received worship here. This was a cult centre from as early as the Old Kingdom.

Edfu (Eg. Dbot; Gk. Apollonopolis Magna)
Edfu was the capital of the 2nd nome of Upper Egypt and was a centre from the Old Kingdom, but only the fine Ptolemaic temple remains, dedicated to Horus the Behdetite, accompanied by his wife, Hathor of Denderah, and his son, Harsomtus.

Esna (Eg. Te-swet; Gk. Latopolis)
Of the temple of Khnum, built in the Roman period, only the vestibule now

remains. The inscriptions here are some of the last ancient texts to be written in hieroglyphs.

The Fayoum

A fertile oasis which lies a short distance to the west of the Nile Valley; it is linked to the river and to the valley by a natural channel, the Bahr Yusuf. The area was particularly favoured by the kings of the Middle Kingdom, and was sacred to the crocodile god Sobek. These rulers inaugurated the scheme of land reclamation around the great natural expanse of water of Lake Qarun (Lake Moeris). The most important religious sites here include:

HAWARA

Amenemmes III built one of his pyramids here, on the south side of which stood the 'Labyrinth', containing the king's mortuary temple. It was a great tourist attraction in antiquity and was described by Strabo who visited the site. To the north was the necropolis used from the Middle Kingdom by the wealthier inhabitants of the town of Shedet (Gk. Crocodilopolis). In this area, several hundred mummy portraits, dating to the Graeco-Roman period, came to light.

EL-LAHUN (ILLAHUN)

Sesostris II build his pyramid here, together with shaft tombs for his family. About 1¼ miles to the north lies the site of Hetep-Sesostris, which Sir Flinders Petrie excavated in the late 1880s. He called this workmen's village by the name of Kahun. It was built by Sesostris II to house the men and their families who were engaged in building his pyramid, but it was deserted about 100 years later.

EL-LISHT (EG. IT-TOWE)

This was the capital city of the kings of Dynasty 12, where Amenemmes I and Sesostris I built their pyramid complexes, surrounded by nobles' tombs; these were examined and excavated by the Metropolitan Museum of New York.

Gizeh

One of the most famous religious sites in the world, Gizeh was primarily the necropolis area of the kings of Dynasty 4. The most notable monuments include: the Great Pyramid of Cheops with its solar barques; the pyramid of Chephren with its associated Valley Temple which is a well-preserved example of the splendid and simple architecture of this period; the Great Sphinx, a couchant lion with a human head (probably representing Chephren), hewn from a natural outcrop of rock; and the pyramid of Mycerinus and its associated small pyramids.

Heliopolis (Eg. Iwnw; later known as On)
The ancient centre of the solar cult, where Re' usurped power from Atum, and where the first solar temple, with the Benben (the solar cult symbol), was erected. In the Old Kingdom, it became the centre where the Heliopolitan cosmogony, claiming the city as the site of creation, was developed. Only an obelisk of Sesostris I now remains of the great Middle Kingdom solar temple, and little survives to testify to its past glory, although the site still awaits extensive excavation.

Heracleopolis Magna (modern Ihnasya; Eg. Hat-nen-nesut)
The nome capital and cult centre of the ram god Herishef (identified by the Greeks with Heracles). The poorly preserved ruins stretch over a mile, and the necropolis, excavated by Petrie in AD 1920–1, lies on the left bank of the Bahr Yusuf, near Sedment.

Hermopolis Magna (modern el-Ashumunein; Eg. Khnumu)
The capital of the 15th (Hare) nome of Upper Egypt, the city's patron was Thoth, the ibis-headed god of wisdom and learning, and it was the centre of Hermopolitan theology. The Greeks later identified Thoth with Hermes. The site is now very ruined, but columns belonging to the Greek agora are still standing, and the Temple of Thoth, founded by Amenophis III, is remarkable for the remaining colossal granite statutes of Thoth in the form of a crouching baboon. The ruins of a New Kingdom temple to Amun and of a Middle Kingdom temple have also been discovered, and excavations have revealed decorated blocks, re-used for later building, from a temple built by Akhenaten. About six miles to the west is Tuna el-Gebel, the site of the city's necropolis, and also the cemetery of ibises and baboons. Here, there are subterranean galleries where the mummified birds and animals were placed in wall niches, and an embalmer's workshop, where the necessary preparations were carried out. The most famous tomb in the area is that built for the family of Petosiris, High Priest of Thoth *c.*300 BC; it is remarkable because the wall reliefs, while copying the Egyptian themes of earlier periods, also display a strong Greek influence in terms of style and composition.

Hieraconpolis (Eg. Nekhen) and el-Kab (Gk. Eileithyiaspolis)
Hieraconpolis and el-Kab formed the ancient capital of Upper Egypt, sacred to the vulture-goddess Nekhbet. Hieraconpolis became the centre of the worship of Horus, the falcon god, who was the first royal patron. The temple was excavated by J. E. Quibell in AD 1897–8. Tombs dating to the Old and Middle Kingdoms were found nearby at Kom el-Ahmar, and New Kingdom tombs were discovered in the vicinity. El-Kab was excavated by Quibell in 1897, and, although the ruins of the town are badly preserved, the remains of several New Kingdom temples were uncovered. About a mile away are rock tombs dating to the end of the Middle Kingdom and the

beginning of the New Kingdom; these thirty-one tombs belonged to the local nobles and are similar to those found at Kom el-Ahmar.

Kom Ombo

A double temple (Graeco-Roman period) dedicated to both Sobek (the right-hand side of the building) and Haroeris (left-hand side).

Medum

Sneferu's unfinished pyramid, with its mortuary temple and surrounding nobles' tombs, was built here.

Memphis (Eg. 'White Walls')

Once the great capital of Egypt, founded by Menes, Memphis was the cult centre of Ptah and of the Memphite cosmogony. Its strategic position ensured that it never ceased to be a city of great importance in antiquity, even when the capital was moved elsewhere, but today only a vast field of debris remains, apart from a colossal statue of Ramesses II which once stood in front of a temple, an alabaster sphinx (probably Dynasty 18), and the ruins of the great Temple of Ptah.

Naqada

The site of one of the earliest Predynastic settlements (together with Badari). A damaged mastaba of brick, dating from the time of Menes (Narmer), was discovered near here by De Morgan in AD 1897. Nearby are the ruins of Ombos (excavated by Petrie in AD 1895), the predynastic capital and centre of Seth's cult. Extensive cemeteries of this date lie in the vicinity.

Philae (Eg. Pi-lak)

An island in the Nile at Aswan, once threatened with complete submersion by the rising waters of Lake Nasser, as a result of the construction of the High Dam. The ancient monuments built on the island have been dismantled and re-erected on a nearby island, so that there is access to them throughout the year. The most famous is the Temple of Isis, whose worship continued here even after the rest of Egypt had been Christianised. Other deities who received cults included Osiris, Harpocrates, Nephthys, Hathor, Khnum and Satet.

Sais

An ancient Delta city, dedicated to Neith, the goddess of hunting and weaving, Sais became the capital of Egypt in Dynasty 26, when local princes seized power and introduced a brief resurgence of brilliance.

Saqqara

This famous site, recalling the name of Sokar, the Memphite god of the dead, was the necropolis of Memphis, and contains funerary monuments of almost every period of Egypt's history. It was perhaps most important during the Old Kingdom, and the most famous buildings include: the Step Pyramid and its complex built for Zoser (Dynasty 3) by Imhotep; shaft tombs of important persons of Dynasty 27 when Egypt was under Persian domination; the Pyramid of Unas (Dynasty 5) with the first inscribed Pyramid Texts; the Pyramid of Sekhemkhet (the 'Unfinished Pyramid'); the mastaba-tombs of Ptah-hotep and Ti (Dynasty 5), Mereruka, Kagemni and Ankhmahor (Dynasty 6); and the Serapeum, the subterranean galleries discovered by Mariette in AD 1850–1, where the sacred Apis bulls were buried in sarcophagi. Apis, with a cult at Memphis, was the sacred animal of Ptah and was associated with Osiris. Great attention was lavished on the bull's funeral and the animal was mummified, while the priests selected its successor.

Travelling south from Saqqara, the ruined pyramids of Pepy I, Merenre, and Isesi are situated to the west, and those of Ibi and Pepy II lie close by; also nearby is the Mastabat Faraun, built by King Shepseskaf of Dynasty 4 but resembling the tombs of the earlier dynasties.

Tanis (modern San el-Hagar; Eg. Djanet)
A confused heap of ruins, this site has been tentatively identified with the Hyksos capital Avaris and also with the site of the Residence of Pi-Ramesses, founded and built by Ramesses II, although Qantir may in fact be Pi-Ramesses. Tanis (the name given to the city from Dynasty 21 onwards) was still important in Roman times, but is most famous for the discovery here of the royal burials of Dynasty 21.

Thebes (Eg. Weset; Gk. Thebai)
The ancient site of the great New Kingdom capital; the monuments of Thebes stretch along both the east and west banks of the river. From Dynasty 12 onwards, it became the religious centre of Amun and by the New Kingdom, it held an unrivalled position as the capital of Egypt's empire. The main areas and monuments are:

ON THE EAST BANK

The Temple of Luxor (The 'Southern Harem')
Built by Amenophis III (Dynasty 18) and dedicated to Amun, Mut and Khonsu, this temple came to be regarded as the residence of Amun's consort, Mut. It was further embellished by Tutankhamun and Ramesses II.

The Temple of Amun at Karnak
Started at the beginning of Dynasty 12, this complex came to include the sanctuaries of Ptah, Montu and Mut, as well as that of Amun. It was constantly undergoing extension and alteration, but the buildings date mainly to the reigns of kings ruling in Dynasties 18, 19, 20, 22, 25 and the

Ptolemaic period. In the main Amun temple there are various famous features, including the avenues of ram-headed sphinxes, the Great Hypostyle Hall, the Great Festival Hall of Tuthmosis III and the Sacred Lake.

ON THE WEST BANK

On this side of the river the tombs and funerary monuments of the New Kingdom were built.

Royal mortuary temples
These include the Temple of Sethos I at Qurneh; the Colossi of Memnon (the famous statues which are all that remains of Amenophis III's temple); the Ramesseum (mortuary temple of Ramesses II), dedicated to Amun and also a temple school; the mortuary temple of Ramesses III at Medinet Habu, dedicated to Amun, which incorporated the king's residence and an administrative centre; the nearby temple begun by Hatshepsut and Tuthmosis III; Hatshepsut's temple at Deir el-Bahri, and the adjacent funerary tomb-temple of Mentuhotep.

Royal tombs of the New Kingdom
The tombs of the kings were situated in the Valley of the Kings (Biban el-Moluk); amongst the finest and most famous are those of Tutankhamun, Amenophis II, Sethos I, Ramesses VI, and Ramesses IX. Some of the queens and the princes and princesses were buried in the Valley of the Queens (Biban el-Harem); the tomb of Queen Nefertari is the most beautiful.

Private or non-royal tombs of the New Kingdom
There are more than 500 tombs, mostly belonging to the nobles of the New Kingdom. They are found in five different areas: Dra Abu el-Naga (the northernmost group), Asasif, Sheikh Abd el-Qurna, Deir el-Medina and Qurnet Marai. The most notable tombs in the area of Asasif belonged to Nebamun and Kheruef (both Dynasty 18), while in the area of Sheikh Abd el-Qurna, the tombs of the following are justifiably famous: Nakht (royal scribe of Tuthmosis IV), Userhet (prophet of Tuthmosis I, Neferhotep (reign of Horemheb), Ramose (vizier under Amenophis III and Amenophis IV), whose tomb is decorated in both traditional and Amarnan styles, Menna (surveyor under Tuthmosis IV), Horemheb, Ineni (inspector of Amun's granaries), and Rekhmire (governor of Thebes and vizier under Tuthmosis III and Amenophis II). At Deir el-Medina, there is the village of the necropolis workmen, and nearby are their tombs, the most notable built for Ipuy, Pashedu, and Sennedjem.

This (modern el-Birba)
The early dynastic capital of Egypt. Cemeteries here and at the neighbouring village of Mahasna have been discovered and excavated.

Part III

Secondary Sources for the Study of
Egyptian Religion

Appendix C

Secondary sources and additional bibliography dealing with specific aspects and controversies

Modern literary sources on the subject of Ancient Egypt are extensive and a number of specialised journals are devoted to the study of Egyptology, while others deal with the wider field of Near Eastern archaeology, literature and religion. This bibliography, while not comprehensive, attempts to include the major sources for the study of Egyptian religion, as well as references to special aspects and controversies. In some cases, where difficulty may be experienced in obtaining access to a particular publication, reference is given to a review of the book in one of the specialist journals.

In this second, revised edition of the book, a select bibliography of recently published books is included for the general reader.

1   Select Bibliography for the General Reader

R. DAVID, *Discovering Ancient Egypt* (London 1993).

R. DAVID, *The Pyramid Builders of Ancient Egypt* (London 1996).

R. DAVID and A. DAVID, *A Biographical Dictionary of Ancient Egypt* (London 1992).

A. DODSON, *After the Pyramids: The Valley of the Kings and beyond* (Warminster 1997).

R. B. PARTRIDGE, *Faces of Pharaohs* (Warminster 1996).

G. PINCH, *Magic in ancient Egypt* (London 1994).

S. QUIRKE, *Ancient Egyptian Religion* (London 1992).

C. N. REEVES, *Valley of the Kings: the decline of a royal necropolis* (London 1990).

M. RICE, *Egypt's Legacy* (London 1997).

R. K. RITTNER, *The Mechanics of Ancient Egyptian Magical Practice* (*Studies in Oriental Civilization* 54) (Chicago 1993).

G. E. SMITH and W.R.DAWSON, *Egyptian Mummies* (London 1924; 2nd ed., London 1991).
J. A. TYLDESLEY, *Daughters of Isis: women of ancient Egypt* (London 1994).

2   General Sources

J. H. BREASTED, *Development of Religion and Thought in Ancient Egypt* (London 1912).
Cambridge Ancient History (revised edition: various authors) (Cambridge 1962–).
J. ČERNY, *Ancient Egyptian Religion* (London 1952) (out of print but very useful if a second-hand copy can be obtained).
J. P. A. ERMAN, *A Handbook of Egyptian Religion* (London 1907).
H. FRANKFORT, *Ancient Egyptian Religion* (New York 1948).
H. FRANKFORT, *Kingship and the Gods* (Chicago 1948).
H. FRANKFORT, H. A. FRANKFORT, J. A. WILSON and T. JACOBSEN, *Before Philosophy* (Harmondsworth 1949).
C. J. GADD, *Ideas of Divine Rule in the Ancient Near East* (The Schweich Lectures of the British Academy 1945) (London 1948).
A. H. GARDINER, *Ancient Egyptian Onomastica*, 3 vols (Oxford 1947).
A. H. GARDINER, *Egypt of the Pharaohs* (Oxford 1961).
W. C. HAYES, *The Scepter of Egypt*, 2 vols (New York, 1953, 1959).
V. IONS, *Egyptian Mythology*, (London 1968).
J. M. A. JANSSEN, *Annual Egyptological Bibliography*, 9 vols (Leiden 1948–56).
H. KEES, *A Cultural Topography* (London 1961).
A. LUCAS, *Ancient Egyptian Materials and Industries* (Rev., J. R. HARRIS, London 1962).
S. A. B. MERCER, *The Religion of Ancient Egypt* (London 1949).
S. MORENZ, *Egyptian Religion* (London 1973).
I. A. PRATT, *Ancient Egypt* (New York Public Library 1925; supplement, 1925–41.)
A. W. SHORTER, *An Introduction to Egyptian Religion* (London 1931).
J. A. WILSON, *The Burden of Egypt* (Chicago 1951).
H. E. WINLOCK, *The Rise and Fall of the Middle Kingdom in Thebes* (New York 1947).

3   Texts

CLASSICAL

T. W. AFRICA, 'Herodotus and Diodorus on Egypt' in *JNES* 22 (1963), 254.
R. ENGELBACH and D. E. DERRY, 'Introduction: Herodotus with notes on his Text' in *ASAÉ* 41 (1942), 235–69.

J. G. GRIFFITHS, 'Human Sacrifices in Egypt: the Classical Evidence' in *ASAÉ* 48 (1948), 409–23.

M. MILLER, 'Herodotus as a Chronographer' in *Klio* (1965), 109–28.

L. V. ŽABKAR, 'Herodotus and the Egyptian Idea of Immortality' in *JNES* 22 (1963), 57.

EGYPTIAN TEXTS

General

For a selected bibliography, see ERMAN, *Ancient Egyptians,* pp. xxxix–xl.

A. M. BLACKMAN in Simpson, *The Psalmists* (Oxford 1926), for the influence of Egyptian literature on the Hebrew sources.

H. G. FISCHER, 'A Didactic Text of the Late Middle Kingdom' in *JEA* 68 (1982), 45–50.

D. MUELLER, 'An Early Egyptian Guide to the Hereafter' in *JEA* 58 (1972), 99–125.

R. K. RITTNER, 'O.Gardiner 363: A Spell against Night Terrors' in *JARCE* 27 (1990), 25–42.

W. K. SIMPSON ET AL., *The Literature of Ancient Egypt. An Anthology of Stories, Instructions and Poetry* (London 1972).

L. V. ŽABKAR, 'A Hymn to Osiris Pantocrator at Philae. A study of the main functions of the *sdm.f* form in Egyptian religious hymns' in *ZÄS* 108 (1981), 141–71.

The Pyramid Texts

J. P. ALLEN, 'The Pyramid Texts of Queens Ipwt and *Wdbt-n.(j)*' in *JARCE* 23 (1986), 1–26.

DIA'ABOU-GHAZI, 'Bewailing the King in the Pyramid Texts' in *BIFAO* 66 (1968), 157–64.

DIA'ABOU-GHAZI, 'The First Appearance of Re and his Continuous Being as Depicted in the Pyramid Texts' in *BIFAO* 68 (1969), 47–52.

W. M. DAVIS, 'The Ascension-Myth in the Pyramid Texts' in *JNES* 36 (1977), 161.

R. O. FAULKNER, 'The King and the Star-religion in the Pyramid Texts' in *JNES* 25 (1966), 153.

S. E. THOMPSON, 'The origin of the Pyramid Texts found on Middle Kingdom Saqqara coffins' in *JEA* 76 (1990), 17–26.

V. A. TOBIN, 'Divine conflict in the Pyramid Texts' in *JARCE* 30 (1993), 93–110.

R. WEILL, 'L'incantation anti-osirienne insérée dans la composition du chapitre Pyramides 1264–1279' in *BIFAO* 46 (1947), 159–97.

The Coffin Texts

R. O. FAULKNER, 'A Coffin Text Miscellany' in *JEA* 68 (1982), 27–30.

W. FEDERN, 'The "Transformations" in the Coffin Texts: a New Approach' in *JNES* 19 (1960), 241.

L. H. LESKO, 'The Field of Hetep in the Egyptian Coffin Texts' in *JARCE* 9 (1971–2), 89–102.

R. H. O'CONNELL, 'The emergence of Horus: an analysis of Coffin Text Spell 148' in *JEA* 69 (1983), 66–87.

The Book of the Dead

T. G. ALLEN, *The Book of the Dead or Going Forth by Day* (Chicago 1974); also L. V. ŽABKAR, 'Some Observations on T. G. Allen's edition of the Book of the Dead' in *JNES* 24 (1965), 75.

A. DE BUCK, 'The Earliest Version of the Book of the Dead' in *JEA* 35 (1949), 87–97.

M. MOSHER, JR. 'Theban and Memphite Book of the Dead traditions in the Late Period' in *JARCE* 29 (1992), 143–72.

S. UCHIDA, 'A fragment of the Book of the Dead in Waseda University Library, Tokyo' in *JEA* 82 (1996), 202–6.

A. A-H. YOUSSEF, 'The Cairo Imduat Papyri (JE 96638 a,b,c)' in *BIFAO* 82 (1982), 213–36.

King Cheops and the Magicians

A. H. GARDINER, 'The Secret Chambers of the Sanctuary of Thoth' in *JEA* 11 (1925), 2–5.

H. GOEDICKE, 'Thoughts about the Papyrus Westcar' in *ZÄS* 120 (1993), 23–36.

On Hardedef, see W. STEVENSON SMITH, *The Old Kingdom in Egypt* (Cambridge Ancient History, vol. 1, ch. XIV).

The Wisdom Literature

Ptahhotep: WILSON, *ANET*, 412–44.

Kagemni: W. FEDERN in *JEA* 36 (1950), 48–50.

Duauf: WILSON, *ANET*, 432–4

Merikare: Additional fragments in R. CAMINOS, *Literary Fragments in the Hieratic Script* (Oxford 1956), 26–7.

Sehetibre: CH. KUENTZ, in *Studies presented to F. LL. Griffith.* Ed. S. R. K. Glanville (London 1932), 97–110.

Amenemmes: R. ANTHES, 'The Legal Aspect of the Instruction of Amenemhet' in *JNES* 16 (1957), 176; 17 (1958), 208–9.

H. GOEDICKE, 'The Beginning of the Instruction of King Amenemhet' in *JARCE* 7 (1968), 15–22.

A. DE BUCK, in Institut Français d'Archeologie Orientale, Memoires, Tome 66, 67, *Mélanges Maspero* (Cairo 1934–8),1, 847–52.

Additional ostraca with portions of text in H. GOEDICKE and E. F. WENTE, *Ostraka Michaelides* (Wiesbaden 1962) and J. ČERNY and A. H. GARDINER, *Hieratic Ostraca* I (Oxford 1957).

Ani: WILSON, *ANET* 420–1; A. H. GARDINER in *JEA* 45 (1959), 12–15.

Amenemope: A. M. BLACKMAN 'The Psalms in the Light of Egyptian Research' in D. C. SIMPSON, *The Psalmists* (London 1926); F. LL. GRIF-FITH in *JEA* 12 (1926), 191–231; R. O. KEVIN, *The Wisdom of Amen-em-apt and its Possible Dependence upon the Hebrew Books of Proverbs* (Philadelphia, 1931); K. LUDWIG, 'The Wisdom of Amen-em-ope and the Proverbs of Solomon' in *AJSL* 43 (1926–7), 8; D. C. SIMPSON, 'The Hebrew Book of Proverbs and the Teaching of Amenophis' in *JEA* 12 (1926), 232–9; R. J. WILLIAMS, 'The Alleged Semitic Origins of the Wisdom of Amen-em-ope' in *JEA* 47 (1961), 100–6; WILSON, *ANET*, 421–4.

The Contendings of Horus and Seth
A. H. GARDINER, *The Library of A. Chester Beatty: Description of Hieratic Papyrus with a Mythological Story, Love-songs and other Miscellaneous Texts* (London 1931); *Hieratic Papyri in the British Museum*, 3rd series (London 1935); H. GOEDICKE, 'Seth as a Fool' in *JEA* 47 (1961), 154; WILSON, *ANET*, 431–2.

Admonitions of a Prophet
A. M. BLACKMAN in *JEA* 11 (1925), 213 ff.; R. O. FAULKNER in *JEA* 50 (1964), 24–36; J. van SETERS in *JEA* 50, 13–23.

Songs at Banquets
WILSON, *ANET*, 469; E. F. WENTE, 'Egyptian "Make Merry" Songs Reconsidered' in *JNES* 21 (1962), 118–28.

Great Hymn to Amun
WILSON, *ANET*, 365–7.

Hymn to the Sun at el-Amarnah
WILSON, *ANET*, 369–71. Several shorter hymns are given in translation in WILSON, *ANET* and R. CAMINOS, *Late-Egyptian Miscellanies* (London 1956), 60–3.

4 Historical

ASPECTS OF PREDYNASTIC AND ARCHAIC EGYPT

B. ADAMS, *Ancient Hierakonpolis* (Warminster 1974).

J. BAILLET, 'L'anthropophagie dans l'Égypte primitive' in *BIFAO* 30 (1931), 65–72.

K. BARD, 'A quantitative analysis of the predynastic burials in Armant cemetery 1400–1500' in *JEA* 74 (1988), 39–56.

E. J. BAUMGARTEL, *The Cultures of Predynastic Egypt* (Oxford 1947).

R. P. CHARLES, 'Essai sur la chronologie des civilisations prédynastiques d'Égypte' in *JNES* 16 (1957), 240.

LE COMTE DU MESNIL DU BUISSON, 'Le décor asiatique du couteau de Gebel el-Arak' in *BIFAO* 68 (1969), 63–84.

J. C. PAYNE, 'Tomb 100: The Decorated Tomb at Hierakonpolis Confirmed' in *JEA* 59 (1973), 31–5. Also B. J. KEMP, 'Photographs of the Decorated Tomb at Hierakonpolis' in *JEA* 59, 36–43.

I. E. S. EDWARDS, 'Some Early Dynastic Contributions to Egyptian Architecture' in *JEA* 35 (1949), 123–8.

W. B. EMERY, *Archaic Egypt* (Harmondsworth 1961).

R. ENGELBACH, 'A Fountain Scene of the Second Dynasty' in *JEA* 20 (1934), 185–8.

D. R. ENGLES, 'An Early Dynastic cemetery at Kafr Ghattati' in *JARCE* 27 (1990), 71–88.

G. GODRON, 'Études sur l'époque archaïque' in *BIFAO* 57 (1958), 143–56.

S. HENDRICKX, 'Two protodynastic objects in Brussels and the origin of the Bilobate cult-sign of Neith' in *JEA* 82 (1990), 23–42.

G. D. HORNBLOWER, 'Predynastic Figures of Women and their Successors' in *JEA* 15 (1939), 29–47.

G. D. HORNBLOWER, 'Funerary Designs of Predynastic Jars' in *JEA* 16 (1930), 1–18.

W. C. HAYES, 'Most Ancient Egypt' in *JNES* 23 (1964), 74–273.

E. O. JAMES, *Prehistoric Religion. A Study in Prehistoric Archaeology* (London 1957).

G. JÉQUIER, 'Les temples primitifs et la persistence des types archaïques dans l'architecture religieuse' in *BIFAO* 6 (1908), 25–41.

F. JESI, 'Rapport sur les recherches relatives à quelques figurations du sacrifice human dans l'Égypt pharaonique' in *JNES* 17 (1958), 194.

H. J. KANTOR, 'The Final Phase of Predynastic Culture: Gerzean or Semainean?' in *JNES* 3 (1944), 110.

B. J. KEMP, 'Abydos and the Royal Tombs of the First Dynasty' in *JEA* 52 (1966), 13–22.

B. J. KEMP, 'Merimda and the Theory of House Burial in Prehistoric Egypt' in *Chr.d'Ég.* 43 (1968), 313–24.

J. LEIBOVITCH, 'Une scène de sacrifice ritual chez les anciens égyptiens' in *JNES* 12 (1953), 59.

M. A. MURRAY, 'Burial Customs and Beliefs in the Hereafter in Predynastic Egypt' in *JEA* 42 (1956), 86–96.

P. E. NEWBERRY, 'The Set Rebellion of the 2nd Dynasty' in *Ancient Egypt* (1922), II 40–6.

D. O'CONNOR, 'New funerary enclosures (Talbezirke) of the Early Dynastic Period at Abydos' in *JARCE* 26 (1989), 51–86.

W. M. F. PETRIE, *The Making of Egypt* (London 1939).

R. WEILL, 'Notes sur l'histoire primitive des grandes religions égyptiennes' in *BIFAO* 47 (1948), 59–150.

B. WILLIAMS and T. J. LOGAN, 'The Metropolitan knife handle and aspects of Pharaonic imagery before Narmer' in *AJSL* 46 (1987), 245–85.

B. WILLIAMS, 'Narmer and the Coptos colossi' in *JARCE* 25 (1988), 35–60.

J. A. WILSON, 'Buto and Hierakonpolis in the Geography of Egypt' in *JNES* 14 (1955), 209.

The Dynastic Race and contact with Mesopotamia

D. E. DERRY, 'The Dynastic Race in Egypt' in *JEA* 42 (1956), 80–5.

R. ENGELBACH, 'An Essay on the Advent of the Dynastic Race in Egypt and its Consequences' in *ASAÉ* 42 (1943), 193–221.

P. GILBERT, 'Fauves au long cou commune à l'art égyptien et à l'art sumerien archaïques' in *Chr.d'Ég.* 22 (1947), 38–41.

P. GILBERT, 'Synchronismes artistiques entre Égypte et Mesopotamie de la période thinite à la fin de l'Ancien Empire égyptien' in *Chr.d'Ég.* 26 (1951), 225–36.

H. KANTOR, 'The Early Relations of Egypt with Asia' in *JNES* 1 (1942), 174.

H. KANTOR, 'Further Evidence for Early Mesopotamian Relations with Egypt' in *JNES* 11 (1952), 239.

E. von ROSEN, *Did Prehistoric Egyptian Culture Spring from a Marsh-dwelling People?* (Stockholm, 1929). Reviewed in *Chr.d'Ég.* 5 (1930), 104.

THE MIDDLE KINGDOM

A. DODSON, 'The tombs of the kings of the Thirteenth Dynasty in the Memphite necropolis' in *ZÄS* 114 (1987), 36–45.

A. LEAHY, 'A protective measure at Abydos in the XIII Dynasty' in *JEA* 75 (1989), 41–60.

S. A. NAGUIB, 'A Middle Kingdom stela in Oslo' in *Chr.d'Ég.* 55 (1980), 17–22.

W. K. SIMPSON, 'Studies in the Twelfth Egyptian Dynasty: 1. The Residence of It-towy 2. The Sed Festival in Dynasty 12' in *JARCE* 2 (1963), 53–64.

H. E. WINLOCK. *The Rise and Fall of the Middle Kingdom in Thebes* (New York 1947).

The Hyksos

R. M. ENGELBACH, *The Hyksos Reconsidered* (Chicago 1939).

T. SÄVE-SÖDERBERGH, 'The Hyksos Rule in Egypt' in *JEA* 37 (1951), 53–71.

CL. F. A. SCHAEFFER, 'A propos de la chronologie de la XIIe dynastie égyptienne et des Hyksos' in *Chr.d'Ég.* 22 (1947), 225–9.

J. VAN SETERS, 'The Hyksos Burials in Palestine: a Review of the Evidence' in *JNES* 30 (1971), 110.

THE NEW KINGDOM

L. BRADBURY, 'Nefer's inscription on the death date of Queen Ahmose-Nefertary and the Deed found pleasing to the King' in *JARCE* 22 (1985), 73–96.

W. E. EDGERTON, *The Thutmosid Succession* (Chicago 1933).

O. J. SCHADEN, 'Clearance of the Tomb of King Ay' in *JARCE* 21 (1984), 39–64.

Amarna

C. ALDRED, 'The End of the Amarna Period' in *JEA* 43 (1957), 30–41.

C. ALDRED, 'Year Twelve at el-Amarna' in *JEA* 43 (1957), Brief Comms. p. 114.

C. ALDRED, 'The Beginning of the el-Amarna Period' in *JEA* 45 (1959), 19–33.

C. ALDRED, *Akhenaten and Nefertiti* (New York 1973).

N. DE G. DAVIES, 'Akhenaten at Thebes' in *JEA* 9 (1923), 132–52.

R. ENGELBACH, 'Material for a Revision of the History of the Heresy Period of the XVIIIth Dynasty' in *ASAÉ* 40 (1940–1), 133–83.

H. W. FAIRMAN, 'The Supposed Year 21 of Akhenaten' in *JEA* 46 (1960), Brief. Comms., p. 108.

P. GILBERT, 'Les corégences d'Amenophis IV et l'art thébain durant la période amarnienne' in *Chr. d'Ég.* 39 (1964), 15–24. For the coregency, see also H. W. FAIRMAN in *City of Akhenaten*, ed. J. D. S. Pendlebury (London 1951), vol. 3, 152–7.

D. B. REDFORD, 'Some Observations on Amarna Chronology' in *JEA* 45 (1959), 34–7.

K. C. SEELE, *The Co-regency of Ramesses II with Sethos I and the Date of the Great Hypostyle Hall at Karnak* (Chicago 1940).

K. C. SEELE, 'King Ay and the Close of the Amarna Age' in *JNES* 14 (1955), 168.

THE HAREM CONSPIRACY

The Turin Papyrus: see BREASTED, *Ancient Records* 4, para. 416 ff. Lee and Rollin Papyrus: see A. de BUCK, 'The Judicial Papyrus of Turin' in *JEA* 23 (1937), 152 ff. Also, Comment in *JEA* 42, 8–9. See also Goedicke in *JEA* 49 (given under *Magic* references.)

THE TOMB ROBBERIES AND SOCIAL UNREST

J. CAPART, A. H. GARDINER and B. van de WALLE, 'New Light on the Ramesside Tomb Robberies' in *JEA* 22 (1936), 169–93.

W. F. EDGERTON, 'The Strikes in Ramesses III's Twenty-ninth Year' in *JNES* 10 (1951), 137.

T. E. PEET, 'Fresh Light on the Tomb Robberies of the 20th Dynasty at Thebes' in *JEA* 11 (1925), 162–4.

EGYPT'S RELATIONS WITH OTHER COUNTRIES AND PEOPLES

P. GILBERT, 'L'adaptation de l'architecture religieuse de l'Égypte aux sites de Basse Nubie' in *Chr. d'Ég.* 35 (1960), 47–64.

H. R. HALL, 'Egypt and the External World in the Time of Akhenaten' in *JEA* 7 (1921), 39–53.

I. M. KAMEL, 'Foreign deities in the eastern Delta' in *ASAÉ* 65 (1983), 83–89.

P. MONTET, 'L'art syrien vu par les Égyptiens du Nouvel Empire' in *BIFAO* 30 (1931), 765–85.

A. L. OPPENHEIM, 'The Archives of the Palace of Mari' in *JNES* 11 (1952), 129; 13 (1954), 141.

J VERCOUTTER , *Essai sur les relations entre Égyptiens et Préhellènes* (Paris 1954)

S. YEIVIN, 'Canaanite Ritual Vessels in Egyptian Cultic Practices' in *JEA* 62 (1976), 110–14.

J. ČERNY, 'Greek Etymology of the Name Moses' in *ASAÉ* 41 (1942), 349–54.

E. CHIERA, 'Habiru and Hebrews' in *AJSL* 49 (1933), 115.

R. DE VAUX, 'Le problème des Hapiru après quinze années' in *JNES* 27 (1968), 221.

S. FREUD, *Moses and Monotheism* (reviewed in *Chr. d'Ég.* 15 (1940), 83–5).

A. H. GARDINER 'The Geography of the Exodus: an Answer to Professor Naville and Others' in *JEA* 10 (1924), 87–96.

J. E. GRIFFITHS, 'The Egyptian Derivation of the Name Moses' in *JNES* 12 (1953), 225.

U. G. KRAELING, 'The Origin of the Name "Hebrews"' in *AJSL* 58 (1941), 237.

P. MONTET, *Le Drame d'Avaris. Essai sur la pénétration des Sémites en Égypte* (Paris 1940).

E. NAVILLE, 'The Geography of the Exodus' in *JEA* 10 (1924), 18–39.

T. E. PEET, *Egypt and the Old Testament* (Liverpool 1922).

D. B. REDFORD, *A Study of the Biblical Story of Joseph (Genesis 37–50)* (Leiden 1970). Reviewed in *Oriens Antiquus* 12 (1973), 233–42.

H. E. ROWLEY, 'Early Levite History and the Question of the Exodus' in *JNES* 3 (1944), 73.

H. H. ROWLEY, *From Joseph to Joshua* (London 1950).

T. SÄVE-SÖDERBERGH, *The 'prw Vintagers in Egypt* (Uppsala 1952).

J. SCHWARTZ, 'Le "Cycle de Petoubastis" et les commentaires égyptiens de l'Exode' in *BIFAO* 49 (1950), 67–83.

J. VERGOTE, *Joseph en Égypte, Genese, Chp. 37–50, à la lumière des études égyptologiques récentes* (Louvain 1959).

H. M. WIENER, 'The Historical Character of the Exodus' in *Ancient Egypt* (1926), IV, 104–15. (See GARDINER in *JEA* 10 (1924)).

J. A. WILSON, 'The Éperu of the Egyptian Inscriptions' in *AJSL* 49 (1932–3), 275.

THE JEWISH COLONY AT ELEPHANTINE

C. E. GORDON, 'The Origin of the Jews in Elephantine' in *JNES* 14 (1955), 56.

S. S. HORN and L. L. H. WOOD, 'The 5th Century Jewish Calendar at Elephantine' in *JNES* 13 (1954), 1.

E. C. P. MACLAURIN, 'Date of the Foundation of the Jewish Colony at Elephantine' in *JNES* 27 (1968), 89.

B. PORTEN, 'The Religion of the Jews of Elephantine in the Light of the Hermopolis Papyri' in *JNES* 28 (1969), 116.

V. TSCHERIKOWER, *The Jews in Egypt in the Hellenistic-Roman Age in the Light of Papyri* (Jerusalem 1945).

A. VINCENT, *La Religion des Judeo-Araméens d'Eléphantine* (Paris 1937). (Reviewed in *Chr.d'Ég.* 15 (1940), 89–90.)

THE GRAECO-ROMAN PERIOD

H. K BELL, 'Hellenic Culture in Egypt' in *JEA* 8 (1922), 139–55.

H. I. BELL, *Egypt from Alexander the Great to the Arab Conquest* (Oxford 1918). (Review in *ASAÉ* 50 (1950), 601–4)

H. I. BELL, 'Roman Egypt from Augustus to Diocletian' in *Chr. d'Ég.* 13 (1938), 347–63.

P. M. FRAZER, *Ptolemaic Alexandria*, vol. I Text; Vol. 2 Notes (Oxford 1972).

J. GRAFTON MILNE 'Egyptian Nationalism under Greek and Roman Rule' in *JEA* 14 (1928), 226–34.

M. ROSTOVTZEFF, 'The Foundations of Social and Economic Life in Hellenistic Times' in *JEA* 6 (1920), 161–78.

ASPECTS OF ART AND ARCHITECTURE WITH REFERENCE TO RELIGIOUS USES

C. ALDRED, *Art in Ancient Egypt: Old Kingdom* (London, 1949); *Middle Kingdom* (1950); *New Kingdom* (1951).

A. BADAWY, *A History of Egyptian Architecture* (Giza 1954).

A. BADAWY, 'Special Problems of Egyptian Architecture' in *Oriens Antiquus* 1 (1962), 185–95.

A. BADAWY, 'The Architectural Symbolism of the Mammisi-chapels of Egypt' in *Chr.d'Ég.* 38 (1963), 78–90.

A. BADAWY, *Ancient Egyptian Architectural Design: a Study of the Harmonic Principle* (Los Angeles, 1965).

J. BAINES, 'Techniques of decoration in the Hall of Barques in the Temple of Sethos I at Abydos' in *JEA* 75 (1989), 13–30.

H. FRANKFORT, 'The Origins of Monumental Architecture in Egypt' in *AJSL* 58 (1941), 329.

H. FRANKFORT (ed.), *The Mural Painting of el-Amarnah* (London 1929).

N. DE G. DAVIES, 'Mural Paintings in the City of Akhenaten' in *JEA* 7 (1921), 1–7.

NINA M. DAVIES, *Ancient Egyptian Paintings*, 3 vols (Chicago 1936).

J. M. GALAN, 'Bullfight scenes in ancient Egyptian tombs' in *JEA* 80 (1994), 81–96.

G. GOYON, 'La technique de construction du Grand Temple d'Abou Simbel' in *Chr.d'Ég.* 42 (1967), 269–80.

Y. HARPUR, 'The identity and positions of relief fragments in museums and private collections: the reliefs of *R'-htp* and *Nfrt* from Meydum' in *JEA* 72 (1986), 23–40.

E. IVERSEN, *Canon and Proportions in Egyptian Art* (London 1955).

O. E. KAPER, 'The Astronomical Ceiling of Deir el-Haggor in the Dakhleh Oasis' in *JEA* 81 (1995), 175–96.

K. LANGE and M. HIRMER, *Egypt: Architecture, Sculpture and Painting in Three Thousand Years* (London 1956).

J. MALEK, 'The monuments recorded by Alice Lieder in the 'Temple of Vulcon' at Memphis in May, 1853' in *JEA* 72 (1986), 101–12.

L. MANNICHE, 'The Tomb of Nakht, the Gardener, at Thebes (No.161), as copied by Robert Hay' in *JEA* 72 (1986), 55–78.

I. NOSHY, *The Arts in Ptolemaic Egypt. A Study of Greek and Egyptian Influences in Ptolemaic Architecture and Sculpture* (Oxford 1937).

H. SCHÄFER, *Principles of Egyptian Art* (ed. with epilogue by E. Brunner-Traut; trans. and ed. J. R. BAINES) (Oxford 1974).

W. STEVENSON-SMITH, *A History of Egyptian Sculpture and Painting in the Old Kingdom* (Oxford 1946).

W. STEVENSON-SMITH, *The Art and Architecture of Ancient Egypt* (Harmondsworth 1958).

CL. VANDERSLEYEN, 'Les proportions relatives des personnages dans les statues-groupes' in *Chr.d'Ég.* 48 (1973), 13–25.

M. S. VENIT, 'The painted tomb from Wardion and the decoration of Alexandrian tombs' in *JARCE* 25 (1988), 71–92.

D. WHITE, '1987 Excavations on Bates's island, Marsa Matruh: Second Preliminary Report' in *JARCE* 26 (1989), 87–114.

R. H. WILKINSON, 'New Kingdom Astronomical Paintings and methods of finding and extending direction' in *JARCE* 28 (1991), 149–54.

J. A. WILSON, 'The Artist of the Egyptian Old Kingdom' in *JNES* 6 (1947), 231.

TOMBS: ADDITIONAL INFORMATION

A. BADAWY, 'The Ideology of the Superstructure of the Mastaba-tomb in Egypt' in *JNES* 15 (1956), 180.

M. R. BELL, 'An Armchair Excavation of KV55' in *JARCE* 27 (1990), 97–138.

J. BOURRIAU, 'Three monuments from Memphis in the Fitzwilliam Museum' in *JEA* 68 (1982), 51–59.

H. CARTER, 'A Tomb Prepared for Queen Hatshepsut and Other Recent Discoveries at Thebes' in *JEA* 4 (1917), 130–58.

W. J. CHERF, 'Some forked staves in the Tut'ankhamun Collection' in *ZÄS* 115 (1988), 107–10.

J. D. COONEY, 'A Relief from the Tomb of Haremhab' in *JEA* 30 (1944), 2–4.

NINA M. DAVIES, 'Some Representations of tombs from the Theban Necropolis' in *JEA* (1938), 25–40.

NINA and N. DE G. DAVIES, *The Theban Tomb Series* (published for the Egypt Exploration Society, London 1915–33).

N. DE G. DAVIES and A. H GARDINER, *The Tomb of Amenemhet* (London 1915).

A. M. DODSON, 'The tombs of the kings of the early 18th Dynasty at Thebes' and 'The tombs of the queens of the Middle Kingdom' in *ZÄS* 115 (1988), 110–36 and *ZÄS* 116 (1989), 181.

A. M. DODSON and J. JANSSEN, 'A Theban tomb and its tenants' in *JEA* 75 (1989), 125–38.

W. B. EMERY, *A Funerary Repast in an Egyptian Tomb of the Archaic Period* (London 1962).

A. FAKHRY, 'A Note on the Tomb of Kheruef at Thebes' in *ASAÉ* 43 (1942), 447–532.

G. GAILLARD, 'Identification de l'oiseau amâ figuré dans une tombe de Beni-Hassan' in *BIFAO* 33 (1933), 169–89.

A. H. GARDINER, 'The Memphite Tomb of the General Haremhab' in *JEA* 39 (1953), 3–12. See also Porter and Moss, 3, p. 195–7.

A. B. LLOYD, 'The Egyptian Labyrinth' in *JEA* 56 (1970), 81–100.

E. MACKAY, 'On the Use of Beeswax and Resin as Varnishes in Theban Tombs' in *Ancient Egypt* (1920), II, 35–8.

E. MACKAY, 'The Cutting and Preparation of Tomb-chapels in the Theban Necropolis' in *JEA* 7 (1921), 154–68.

J. MALEK, 'Two problems connected with New Kingdom tombs in the Memphite area' in *JEA* 67 (1981), 156–65.

J. MALEK, 'The Royal Butler Hori at Northern Saqqara' in *JEA* 74 (1988), 125–36.

P. D. MANUELIAN, 'Two fragments of relief and a new model for the Tomb of Montuemhet at Thebes' in *JEA* 71 (1985), 98–121.

K. MICHALOWSKI, 'The Labyrinth Enigma: Archaeological Suggestions' in *JEA* 54 (1968), 219–22.

P. MONTET, 'Les scènes de boucherie dans les tombes de l'Ancien Empire' in *BIFAO* 7 (1909), 41–65.

P. MONTET, 'Notes sur les tombeaux de Beni-Hassan' in *BIFAO* 9 (1911), 1–36.

A. PIANKOFF, *The Tomb of Ramesses VI* (New York 1954).

M. SALEH, 'The tomb of the Royal Scribe Qen-amun at Khokha (Theban Necropolis, No.412)' in *ASAÉ* 69 (1983), 15–28.

A. J. SPENCER, 'First and second owners of a Memphite tomb chapel' in *JEA* 68 (1982), 20–26.

N. STRUDWICK, 'Three monuments of Old Kingdom Treasury officials' in *JEA* 71 (1985), 43–51.

P. VENTURA, 'The largest project for a royal tomb in the Valley of the Kings' in *JEA* 74 (1988), 137–56.

W. von BISSING, 'A propos de Beni-Hassan' in *ASAÉ* 5 (1904), 110–12.

W. A. WARD, 'The date of the reused false door of *Njntm-m-s3.f* at Saqqara' in *JEA* 70 (1984), 87–91.

H. WILD, ' "L'adresse aux visiteurs" du tombeau de Ti' in *BIFAO* 58 (1959), 101–14.

A. WILKINSON, 'Jewellery for a procession in the bed-chamber in the tomb of Tut'ankhamun' in *BIFAO* 84 (1984), 335–46.

H. E WINLOCK, 'The Theban Necropolis in the Middle Kingdom' in *AJSL* 32 (1915–16), 1.

H. E. WINLOCK, 'Notes on the Reburial of Tuthmosis I' in *JEA* 15 (1929), 56–68. Also, A. H. Gardiner, 'The Benefit Conferred by Reburial' in *JEA* 37 (1951), Brief Comms., p. 112.

FUNERARY RITES AND EQUIPMENT

A. ABDALLA, 'A group of Osiris-cloths of the XXI Dynasty in the Cairo Museum' in *JEA* 74 (1988), 157–64.

A. O. A. ABDALLAH, 'An unusual private stela of the XXI Dynasty' in *JEA* 70 (1984), 65–72.

S. ABD EL AAL, 'Stela of Intef and his family' in *ASAÉ* 65 (1983), 173–4.

D. ARNOLD, 'Block statue of Ankh-Wennefer' in *Bull.MMA* 52 (1994–5), 10–11 (Recent Acquisitions).

J. BENNETT, 'The symbolism of a mummy-case' in *JEA* 53 (1967), Brief Comms., 165.

M. L. BIERBRIER, 'Two confusing coffins' in *JEA* 70 (1984), 82–86.

CAMPBELL BONNER, *Studies in Magical Amulets, chiefly Graeco-Egyptian* (London 1950)

NINA M. DAVIES, 'An Unusual Depiction of Ramesside Funerary Rites' in *JEA* 32 (1946), 69–70.

F. A.-M. GATTAS, 'Some selected amulets from Tell el-Balaman Abu-Galal (1978)' in *ASAÉ* 65 (1983), 149–56.

H. GAUTHIER, 'La nécropole de Thèbes et son personnel' in *BIFAO* 13 (1917), 153–68.

R. M. HALL and J. JANSSEN, 'Six inscribed objects in the National Museum of Archaeology, Malta' in *Chr.d'Ég.* 59 (1984), 14–26.

M. EATON-KRAUSS, 'The coffins of Queen Ahhotep, consort of Seqen-en-re and mother of Ahmose' in *Chr.d'Ég.* 65 (1990), 95–205.

C. LILYQUIST, 'Some Dynasty 18 Canopic Jars from royal burials in the Cairo Museum' in *JARCE* 30 (1993), 111–16.

R. MADDIN ET AL., 'Old Kingdom models from the Tomb of Impy: metallurgical studies' in *JEA* 70 (1984), 33–41.

P. D. MANUELIAN and C. E. LOEBEN, 'New light on the recarved sarcophagus of Hatshepsut and Thutmose I in the Museum of Fine Arts, Boston' in *JEA* 79 (1993), 121–56.

E. THOMAS, 'The Four Niches and Amuletic Figures in Theban Royal Tombs' in *JARCE* 3 (1964), 71–8.

B. VACHALA, 'Sarcophagi from rock tombs at Nag el-Fariq (Egyptian Nubia)' in *ZÄS* 114 (1987), 166–79.

W. A. WARD, 'The Origin of Egyptian Design-amulets' in *JEA* 56 (1970), 65–80.

H. E. WINLOCK, 'Notes on the jewels from Lahun' in *Ancient Egypt* (1920), III, 74–87.

MUMMIFIED REMAINS

A. BATRAWI, 'The Skeletal Remains from the Northern Pyramid of Sneferu' in *ASAÉ* 51 (1951), 435–40. Also, 'The Pyramid Studies: A Small Mummy from the Pyramid of Dahshur' in *ASAÉ* 48 (1948), 585–609.

E. A. W. BUDGE, *The Mummy* (Cambridge 1925).

R. A. CAMINOS, 'The Rendells Mummy bandages' in *JEA* 68 (1982), 145–55.

R. C. CONNOLLY, R. G. HARRISON and SOHEIR AHMED, 'Serological Evidence for the Parentage of Tutankhamun and Smenkhkare' in *JEA* 62 (1976), note on p. 184.

G. DARESSY, 'Planches de momies' in *ASAÉ* 19 (1920), 141–4.

G. DARESSY and G. E. SMITH, 'Ouverture des momies provenant de la seconde trouvaille de Deir el-Bahri: I. Procès-verbaux des 12 Mai et 16 Juin 1903; II. Report on the four mummies' in *ASAÉ* 4 (1903), 150–5, 156–60.

A. R. DAVID (ed.), *The Manchester Museum Mummy Project: Multidisciplinary Research on Ancient Egyptian Mummified Remains* (Manchester 1979).

W. R. DAWSON, 'A Mummy of the Persian Period' in *JEA* 11 (1923), 76–7.

W. R. DAWSON, 'On two Mummies Formerly Belonging to the Duke of Sutherland' in *JEA* 13 (1927), 155–61.

W. R. DAWSON, 'Making a Mummy' in *JEA* 13 (1927), 40–9.

W. R. DAWSON, 'A Note on the Egyptian Mummies in the Castle Museum, Norwich' in *JEA* 15 (1959), 186–90.

W. R. DAWSON and P. H. K. GRAY, *Catalogue of Egyptian Antiquities in the British Museum. I: Mummies and Human Remains* (London 1968).

D. E. DERRY, 'Note on the Skeleton hitherto believed to be that of King Akhenaten' in *ASAÉ* 31 (1931), 115–19.

D. E. DERRY, 'An X-ray Examination of the Mummy of King Amenophis 1' in *ASAÉ* 34 (1934), 47–8.

D. E. DERRY, 'Report on Human Remains from the Granite Sarcophagus Chamber in the Pyramid of Zoser' in *ASAÉ* 35 (1935), 28–30.

D. E. DERRY, 'The "Mummy" of Sit-Amun' in *ASAÉ* 39 (1939), 411–16.

D. E. DERRY, 'Note on the remains of Shashanq' in *ASAÉ* 39 (1939), 549–51.

D. E. DERRY, 'An Examination of the Bones of King Psusennes I' in *ASAÉ* 40 (1940), 969–70.

D. E. DERRY, 'Report on the Skeleton of King Amenemopet Har Nakht' in *ASAÉ* 41 (1942), 149–50.

L. DIENER, 'A Human-masked and Doll-shaped Hawk-mummy' in *Chr.d'Ég.* 48 (1973), 60–6.

I. E. S. EDWARDS, *The Pyramids of Egypt* (Harmondsworth 1985).

R. ENGELBACH, 'Notes on the Coffin and Mummy of Princess Sit-Amun' in *ASAÉ* 39 (1939), 405–9.

P. GHALIOUNGUI, 'A Medical Study of Akhenaten' in *ASAÉ* 47 (1947), 29–46.

P. H. K. GRAY, 'Embalmers' "restorations"' in *JEA* 52 (1966), 129–37.

P. H. K. GRAY, 'Two Mummies of Ancient Egyptians in the Hancock Museum, Newcastle' in *JEA* 53 (1967), 75–8.

P. H. K. GRAY, 'An Account of a Mummy in the County Museum and Art Gallery, Truro' in *JEA* 56 (1970), 132–4.

P. H. K. GRAY, 'Artificial Eyes in Mummies, in *JEA* 57 (1971), 125–6.

P. H. K. GRAY, 'Notes Concerning the Position of the Arms and Hands of Mummies with a View to Possible Dating of the Specimen' in *JEA* 58 (1972), 200–4.

E. M. GUEST, 'Pathology and Art at el-Amarna' in *Ancient Egypt* (1953), III, IV, 81–8.

E. M. GUEST, 'A Note on an Alleged Resemblance between Deformed Skulls of the Caucasus Region and the Heads of el-Amarna' in *Ancient Egypt* (1933), III, IV, 113–14.

J. E. HARRIS and K. R. WEEKS, *X-raying the Pharaohs* (New York 1975).

R. G. HARRISON, 'An Anatomical Examination of the Pharaonic Remains purported to be Akhenaten' in *JEA* 52 (1966), 95–119.

R. G. HARRISON ET AL. 'A Mummified Foetus from the Tomb of Tutankhamun' in *Antiquity* 53, no. 207 (1979), 21.

R. G. HARRISON, and R. C. CONNOLLY, 'Microdetermination of Blood Group Substances in Ancient Human tissue' in *Nature*, vol. 224 (1969), p. 326.

R. G. HARRISON, R. C. CONNOLLY and A. ABDALLA, 'The Kinship of Smenkhkare and Tutankhamun Demonstrated Serologically' in *Nature*, 224 (1969), pp. 325–6.

Z. ISKANDER and A. el-M. SHAHEEN, 'Temporary Stuffing Materials used in the Process of Mummification in Ancient Egypt' in *ASAÉ* 58 (1964), 197; 61 (1973), 65.

J. P. LAUER and D. E. DERRY, 'Découverte à Saqqarah d'une partie de la momie du roi Zoser' in *ASAÉ* 35 (1935), 25–7.

J. P. LAUER and Z. ISKANDER, 'Données nouvelles sur la momification dans l'Égypte ancienne' in *ASAÉ* 53 (1955–6), 167.

F. F. LEEK, 'The Problem of Brain Removal during Embalming by the Ancient Egyptians' in *JEA* 55 (1969), 112–16.

F. F. LEEK, 'A Technique for the Oral Examination of a Mummy' in *JEA* 57 (1971), 105–9.

F. F. LEEK, 'How Old was Tutankhamun?' in *JEA* 63 (1977), 112–15.

F. P. LEEK, *The Human Remains from the Tomb of Tutankhamun* (Tutankhamun's Tomb Series) (Oxford 1972).

A. LUCAS, 'The Use of Natron by the Ancient Egyptians in Mummification' in *JEA* 1 (1914), 119–58.

A. LUCAS, 'The Use of Bitumen by the Ancient Egyptians in Mummification' in *JEA* 1 (1914), 241–5.

A. LUCAS, 'The Occurrence of Natron in Ancient Egypt' in *JEA* 18 (1932), 62–6.

A. LUCAS, 'The Use of Natron in Mummification' in *JEA* 18 (1932), 125–40.

A. LUCAS, 'Artificial Eyes in Ancient Egypt' in *Ancient Egypt* (1934), II, 84–99.

O. V. NIELSEN, 'Human Remains' in *The Scandinavian Joint Expedition to Sudanese Nubia*, vol. 9 (Stockholm 1970).

A. NIWINSKI, 'The Bab el-Gusus tomb and the royal cache in Deir el-Bahri' in *JEA* 70 (1984), 73–81.

D. RANDALL-MACIVER, *The Earliest Inhabitants of Abydos – a Craniological Study* (Oxford 1901).

'Recherches sur les momies d'animaux de l'ancienne Égypte: I. Sur les poissons momifies, par MM. Lortet et Hugounenc. II. Sur les oiseaux momifies, par MM. Lortet et Gaillard' in *ASAÉ* 3 (1902), 15–18; 18–21.

M. A. RUFFER, *Studies in the Palaeopathology of Egyptian Mummies* (Chicago 1921).

A. T. SANDISON, 'The Use of Natron in Mummification in Ancient Egypt' in *JNES* 22 (1963), 259.

S. SAUNERON, *Rituel de l'embaumement, Pap. Boulaq 111, Pap. Louvre 5* (Cairo 1952).

G. E. SMITH, 'Report on the unwrapping of the mummy of Menephtah' in *ASAÉ* 8 (1907), 108–12.

G. E. SMITH, 'The Antiquity of Mummification' in the *Cairo Scientific Journal* 2 (1908), 204–5.

G. E. SMITH, 'Egyptian Mummies' in *JEA* 1 (1914), 189–206.

P. E. SPIELMANN, 'To what Extent did the Ancient Egyptians employ Bitumen for Embalming?' in *JEA* 18 (1932), 177–80.

E. STEFANSKI 'Inscribed and Decorated Mummy-wrappings in Chicago' in *AJSL* 48 (1931–2), 45.

A. VARILLE, 'Toutankhamon est-il fils d'Amenophis III et de Satamon?' in *ASAÉ* 40 (1940), 651–7.

G. WAGNER, 'Étiquettes de momies grècques de l'IFAO' in *BIFAO* 74 (1974), 45–62.

A. WEIGALL, 'The Mummy of Akhenaten' in *JEA* 8 (1922), 193–200.

H. E. WINLOCK, 'A Late Dynastic Embalmer's Table' in *ASAÉ* 30 (1930), 102–4

H. E. WINLOCK, *Materials used at the Embalming of King Tutanthamun* (Metropolitan Museum of Art Papers, no. 10), (New York, 1941).

A. ZAKI and Z. ISKANDER, 'Materials and Method used for Mummifying the Body of Amentefnekht, Saqqara 1941' in *ASAÉ* 42 (1943), 223–5.

M. R. ZIMMERMAN, 'The Mummies of the Tomb of Nebwenenet: Palaeopathology and Archaeology' in *JARCE* 14 (1977), 33–6.

THE PYRAMIDS AND THE OLD KINGDOM SUN-CULT

T. G. ALLEN, 'Some Egyptian Sun Hymns' in *JNES* 8 (1949), 349.

R. ANTHES, 'Note Concerning the Great Corporation of Heliopolis' in *JNES* 13 (1954), 191.

A. BADAWY, 'The Periodic System of Building a Pyramid' in *JEA* 63 (1977), 52–8.

A. BATRAWI, 'The Pyramid Studies – Anatomical Reports' in *ASAÉ* 47 (1947), 97–111

J. CAPART, 'Ra, juge des morts' in *Chr.d'Ég.* 14 (1939), 233–6.

J. ČERNY, 'A Note on the Recently Discovered Boat of Cheops' in *JEA* 41 (1955), 75–9.

M. CHATELET, 'Le rôle des deux barques solaires' in *BIFAO* 15 (1918), 139–52.

G. DARESSY, 'Les formes du soleil aux differentes heures de la journée' in *ASAÉ* 17 (1917), 197–208.

G. I. DAVEY, 'The Structure of the Meidum Pyramid' in *JEA* 63 (1977), Brief Comms., p. 174.

I. E. S. EDWARDS, *The Pyramids of Egypt* (Harmondsworth 1985).

I. E. S. EDWARDS, 'The Collapse of the Meidum Pyramid' in *JEA* 60 (1974), note on p. 251.

G. GOYON, 'La chaussée monumentale et le temple de la vallée de la pyramide de Kheops' in *BIFAO* 67 (1969), 49–70.

G. GOYON, 'Quelques observations effectuées autour de la pyramide de Kheops' in *BIFAO* 67 (1969), 71–86.

J. E. G. HARRIS, 'A Suggestion Regarding the Construction of the Pyramids' in *JEA* 30 (1944), Brief Comms., p. 74.

J. K. HOFFMEIER, 'The use of basalt in floors of Old Kingdom pyramid temples' in *JARCE* 30 (1993), 117–24.

J. P. LAUER, 'Remarques sur la planification de la construction de la grande pyramide' in *BIFAO* 73 (1973), 127–42.

CH. MAYSTRE, 'Les Dates des Pyramids de Snefrou' in *BIFAO* 35 (1935), 89–98.

K. MENDELSSOHN, 'A Building Disaster at the Meidum Pyramid' in *JEA* 59 (1973), 60–71.

K. MESSIHA and HISHMET, 'A New Concept about Implements Found in the Excavations at Giza' in *ASAÉ* (1964), 209.

K. MESSIHA, 'The Valley Temple of Khufu (Cheops)' in *ASAÉ* 65 (1983), 9–18.

W. I. PERRY, 'The Cult of the Sun and the Cult of the Dead in Egypt' in *JEA* 11 (1925), 191–200.

A.PIANKOFF, 'The Sky-goddess Nut and the Night Journey of the Sun' in *JEA* 20 (1934), 57–61.

A. M. ROTH, 'Social change in the Fourth Dynasty: the spacial organisation of pyramids, tombs and cemeteries' in *JARCE* 30 (1993), 33–56.

H. EL-SAADY, 'Two Heliopolitan stelae of the New Kingdom' in *ZÄS* 122 (1995), 101–4.

ABDEL AZIZ SALEM, 'Some problems relating to the Punt Reliefs at Deir el-Bahri' in *JEA* 58 (1972), 150–8.

E. THOMAS, 'Air Channels in the Great Pyramid' in *JEA* 39 (1953), Brief Comms., p. 113.

TEMPLES: ARCHITECTURE AND DECORATION

P. BARGUET, 'La structure du temple Iper-Sout d'Amon à Karnak, du Moyen Empire à Amenophis II' in *BIFAO* 52 (1953), 145–55.

E. CHASSINAT, 'Le temple d'Horus Behoudti à Dendérah' in *Rev.d'Ég.* 1 (1925), 298–308

H. CHEVRIER, 'Note sur l'érection des obélisques' in *ASAÉ* 52 (19524), 309.

L. A. CHRISTOPHE, 'La Salle V du Temple de Séthi ler à Gournah' in *BIFAO* 49 (1950), 117–80.

L. DABROWSKI, 'The Main Hypostyle Hall of the Temple of Hatshepsut at Deir el-Bahri' in *JEA* (1970), 101–4.

G. DARESSY, 'Sur le naos de Senusert Ier trouve à Karnak' in *Rev. de l'Ég.* 1 (1925), 203–11.

NINA M. DAVIES, 'Two pictures of Temples' in *JEA* 41 (1955), 80–2.

R. ENGELBACH, Origin of the Great Hypostyle Hall at Karnak in *Ancient Egypt* (1924), III, 65–71.

A. GUTBUB, 'Les inscriptions dedicatoires du trésor dans le Temple d'Edfou' in *BIFAO* 50 (1952), 33–48.

J. LECLANT, 'Quelques données nouvelles sur l'edifice dit de Taharqa près du Lac Sacre à Karnak' in *BIFAO* 49 (1950), 181–92.

J. LECLANT, 'La colonnade éthiopienne à l'est de la grande enceinte d'Amon à Karnak' in *BIFAO* 53 (1953), 113–72.

C. LEGRAIN, 'Le logement et transport des barques sacrées et des statues des dieux dans quelques temples égyptiens' in *BIFAO* 13 (1917), 176.

J. MONNET-SALEH, 'Observations sur le temple de Dendour' in *BIFAO* 68 (1969), 1–14.

MAHMUD ABD EL-RAZIK, 'The Dedicatory and Building Texts of Ramesses II in Luxor Temple' in *JEA* 61 (1975), 125–36; also, the Texts in *JEA* 60 (1974), 142–60.

ABDEL AZIZ SALEM, 'Some Problems Relating to the Punt Reliefs at Deir el-Bahri' in *JEA* 58 (1972), 15–8.

S. SAUNERON, 'Les querelles impériales vues à travers les scènes du temple d'Esné' in *BIFAO* 51 (1952), 123–35.

K. C. SEELE, 'Ramesses VI and the Medinet Habu Procession of Princes' in *JNES* 19 (1960), 184.

A. J. SPALINGER, 'Historical observations on the military reliefs of Abu Simbel and other Ramesside temples in Nubia' in *JEA* 66 (1980), 83–99.

Z. WYSOCKI, 'The upper court colonnade of Hatshepsut's temple at Deir el-Bahri' in *JEA* 66 (1980), 54–69.

TEMPLES: RITES, FESTIVALS, KINGSHIP AND ASSOCIATED CEREMONIES, AND TEMPLE PERSONNEL

C. ALDRED, 'The "New Year" Gifts to Pharaoh' in *JEA* (1969), 73–81.

A. BADAWY, 'The Civic Sense of Pharaoh and Urban Development in Egypt' in *JARCE* 6 (1967), 103–13.

L. BELL, 'Luxor Temple and the cult of the Royal Ka' in *AJSL* 44 (1985), 251–93.

C. J. C. BENNETT, 'Growth of the *Htp-di-nsw* Formula in the Middle Kingdom' in *JEA* 27 (1941), 77–82.

A. M. BLACKMAN, 'The Significance of Incense and Libations' in *ZÄS* 50 (1912), 69–75.

A. M. BLACKMAN, 'Some Notes on the Ancient Egyptian Practice of Washing the Dead' in *JEA* 5 (1918), 117–24.

A. M. BLACKMAN, 'The House of the Morning' in *JEA* 5 (1918), 148–65.

A. M. BLACKMAN, 'The Sequence of the Episodes in the Egyptian Daily Temple Liturgy' in *JMEOS* (1918–19), 27–53.

A. M. BLACKMAN, 'The Rite of Opening the Mouth in Ancient Egypt and Babylonia' in *JEA* 10 (1924), 47–78.

A. M. BLACKMAN, 'Myth and Ritual in Ancient Egypt' in *Myth and Ritual* (ed. S. H. Hooke) (Oxford, 1953), 15–19.

A. M. BLACKMAN, 'The King of Egypt's Grace before Meat' in *JEA* 31 (1945), 57–73.

A. M. BLACKMAN and H. W. FAIRMAN, 'The Consecration of an Egyptian Temple according to the Use of Edfu' in *JEA* 32 (1946), 75–91.

A. M. BLACKMAN and H. W. FAIRMAN, 'The Significance of the Ceremony *Hwt Bhsw* in the Temple of Horus at Edfu' in *JEA* 35 (1949), 98–112; 36, (1950), 63–81.

C. J BLEEKER, *Egyptian Festivals, Enactments of Religious Renewal* (Leiden 1967).

J. H. BREASTED, 'The Philosophy of a Memphite priest' in *ZÄS* 39 (1901), 39–54.

B. M. BRYAN, 'The career and family of Minmose, High Priest of Osiris' in *Chr.d'Ég.* 61 (1986), 15–30.

J. ČERNY, 'Le culte d'Amenophis I chez les ouvriers de la nécropole thébaine' in *BIFAO* 27 (1927), 159–203.

A. R. DAVID, *Religious Ritual at Abydos, c. 1300 B.C.* (Warminster 1973). Also, revised 2nd ed., *A Guide to Religious Ritual at Abydos* (Warminster 1981).

E. DRIOTON, 'Le Texte Dramatique d'Edfou' in Supplément to *ASAÉ*, Cahier 11 (1948).

H. W. FAIRMAN, 'Worship and Festivals in an Egyptian Temple' in *BJRL* 37 (1954), 165–202.

H. W. FAIRMAN, 'The Kingship Rituals of Egypt' in *Myth, Ritual and Kingship* (ed. S. H. Hooke) (Oxford, 1958), 74–104.

G. FOUCART, 'La belle fête de la vallée' in *BIFAO* 24 (1924–30), 1–209.

G. A. GABALLA and K. A. KITCHEN, 'The Festival of Soker' in *Orientalis* 38 (1969), 4.

A. H. GARDINER, 'The Mansion of Life and the Master of the King's Largess' in *JEA* 24 (1938), 83–91.

A. H. GARDINER, 'The Baptism of Pharaoh' in *JEA* 36 (1950), 3–12. 'Addendum' in *JEA* 37 (1951), Brief. Comms., p. 111.

A. H. GARDINER, 'The Coronation of King Haremhab' in *JEA* (1953), 13–31.

H. GAUTHIER, *Les Fêtes du dieu Min* (Cairo 1931).

F. W. GREEN, 'The Secret Chambers of the Sanctuary of Thoth' in *JEA* 16 (1930), 33–4.

F. Ll. GRIFFITH, *Stories of the High Priests of Memphis* (Oxford 1900).

J. G. GRIFFITHS, 'The Costume and Insignia of the King in the Sed-festival' in *JEA* 41 (1955), Brief Comms., p. 127.

J. G. GRIFFITHS, 'The Interpretation of the Horus Myth of Edfu' in *JEA* 44 (1958), 75–85.

J. G. GRIFFITHS, 'Remarks on the Horian Elements in the Royal Titulary' in *ASAÉ* 56 (1959), 63.

S. GOHARY, 'A Lintel of Penherishef, Chief Agent of Amun's leading priests' in *BIFAO* 86 (1986), 183–86.

L. HABACHI, 'God's Fathers and the Role they played in the History of the First Intermediate Period' in *ASAÉ* 55 (1958), 167.

W. C. HAYES, 'Royal Decrees from the Temple of Min at Coptos' in *JEA* 32 (1946), 3–23.

G. D. HORNBLOWER, 'The Ancestor Cult in Ancient Egypt' in *Ancient Egypt* (1930), I, 20–2; 'Postscript to "Ancestor Cult in Ancient Egypt"' in *Ancient Egypt* (1930), II, 43–4.

M. E. A. E. IBRAHIM, 'Miscellaneous Passages about King and Kingship according to the Inscriptions of the Temple of Edfu' in *ASAÉ* 60 (1968), 297–300.

M. ISLER, 'An ancient method of finding and extending direction' in *JARCE* 26 (1989), 191–206.

J. JANSSEN, 'Requisitions from Upper Egyptian temples (P.BM.10401)' in *JEA* 77 (1991), 79–94.

CH. KUENTZ, 'Quelques monuments du culte de Sobek' in *BIFAO* 28 (1929), 113–72.

J. LECLANT, 'Le role du fait et de l'allaitement d'après les textes des pyramides' in *JNES* 10 (1951), 123.

G. LEFEBURE, *Histoire des grands pretres d'Amon de Karnak* (Paris 1929).

M. MATTHIEW, 'A Note on the Coronation rites in Ancient Egypt' in *JEA* 16 (1930), 31–2.

C. MAYSTRE, 'Sur les grands prêtres de Ptah' in *JNES* (1949), 84.

P. MONTET, 'Études sur quelques prêtres et fonctionnaires du dieu Min' in *JNES* 9 (1950), 18.

A. M. MOUSSA, 'Two blocks bearing a celebration of a jubilee festival and a part of a cornice with the cartouches of Sety I from Memphis' in *ASAÉ* 68 (1982), 115–18.

M. A. MURRAY, 'Costume of Early Kings' in *Ancient Egypt* (1926), II, 33–40.

M. A. MURRAY, 'An Early Sed-festival' in *Ancient Egypt* (1932), III, 70–2.

H. H. NELSON, 'The Rite of "Bringing the Foot" as Portrayed in Temple Reliefs' in *JEA* 35 (1949), 82–6.

H. H. NELSON, 'Certain Reliefs at Karnak and Medinet Habu and the Ritual of Amenophis 1' in *JNES* 8 (1949), 201, 310.

E. OTTO, 'An Ancient Egyptian Hunting Ritual' in *JNES* 9 (1950), 164.

T. E. PEET, 'The Supposed Revolution of the High Priest Amenhotep' in *JEA* 12 (1926), 24–5.

E. A. E. REYMOND, 'The Cult of the Spear in the Temple of Edfu' in *JEA* 51 (1965), 144–8.

L. REUTTER, 'Analyses des parfums egyptiens' in *ASAÉ* 13 (1914), 49–78.

A. M. ROTH, 'The *pss-kf* and the "Opening of the Mouth" ceremony: a ritual of birth and rebirth' in *JEA* 78 (1992), 113–48.

A. M. ROTH, 'Fingers, stars and the "Opening of the Mouth": the nature and function of the *ntrwj*-blades' in *JEA* 79 (1993), 57–80.

S. SAUNERON, 'Le "Chancelier du Dieu" dans son double role d'embaumeur et de prêtre d'Abydos' in *BIFAO* 51 (1952), 137–71.

A. R. SCHULMAN, 'A Cult of Ramesses III at Memphis' in *JNES* 22 (1963), 177.

A. R. SCHULMAN, 'Two unrecognised monuments of Shedsunefertem' in *AJSL* 39 (1980), 303–31.

A. R. SCHULMAN, 'The iconographic theme; "Opening of the Mouth" on stelae' in *JARCE* 21 (1984), 169–96.

P. J. SIJPESTEIJN, 'The Egyptian priests of 23413' in *Chr.d'Ég.* 59 (1984), 121.

A.W. SHORTER, 'Reliefs Showing the Coronation of Ramesses II' in *JEA* 20 (1934), 18–9.

A. SPALINGER, 'Some revisions of temple endowments of the New Kingdom' in *JARCE* 28 (1991), 21–40.

A. J. SPENCER, 'Two Enigmatic Hieroglyphs and their Relation to the Sed festival' in *JEA* 64 (1978), 52–5.

J. H. TAYLOR, 'A priestly family of the 25th Dynasty' in *Chr.d'Ég.* 59 (1984), 27–57.

S. E. THOMPSON, 'The anointing of officials in ancient Egypt' in *AJSL* 53 (1994), 15–25.

K. JANSEN-WINKELN, 'The career of the Egyptian High Priest Bakenkhons' in *AJSL* 52 (1993), 221–5.

E. P. UPHILL, 'A Joint Sed-festival of Thutmose III and Queen Hatshepsut' in *JNES* 20 (1961), 248.

B. VAN DE WALLE, 'L'érection du pilièr Djed' in *La Nouvelle Clio* 6 (1954), 283–97.

E. F. WENTE, 'Two Ramesside Stelas Pertaining to the Cult of Amenophis I' in *JNES* 22 (1963), 30.

E. F. WENTE, 'The Suppression of the High Priest Amenhotep' in *JNES* 25 (1966), 73.

J. YOYETTE, 'Prêtres et sanctuaires du nome héliopolite à la Basse Époque' in *BIFAO* 54 (1954), 83–116.

L. W. ŽABKAR, 'Adaption of ancient Egyptian texts to the temple ritual at Philae' in *JEA* 66 (1980), 127–36.

ASPECTS OF VARIOUS DEITIES

H. TE VELDE, 'Some remarks on the Structure of the Egyptian Divine Triads' in *JEA* 57 (1971), 80–6

A. H. GARDINER, 'The Gods of Thebes as Guarantors of Personal Property' in *JEA* 48 (1962), 57–69.

J. LEIBOVITCH, 'Gods of Agriculture and Welfare in *Ancient Egypt*' in *JNES* 12 (1953), 73.

M. L. BUHL, 'The Goddesses of the Egyptian Tree Cult' in *JNES* 6 (1947), 80.

G. A. WAINWRIGHT, 'The Origin of Storm-gods in Egypt' in *JEA* 49 (1963), 13–20.

G. GAILLARD, 'Les animaux consacrés à la divinité de l'ancienne Lycopolis' in *ASAÉ* 27 (1927), 33–42.

N. and B. LANGTON, 'The Cat in Ancient Egypt' in *ASAÉ* 40 (1940–1), 993–6.

O. HOMEY, *The Cat in the Mysteries of Religion and Magic* (Reviewed in *Chr.D'Ég.* 11 (1936), 430–2).

J. CAPART,'Chats sacrés' in *Chr.d'Ég.* 18 (1943), 35–7.

F. DAUMAS, 'L'origine d'Amon de Karnak' in *BIFAO* 65 (1967), 201–14.

J. H. GALAN, 'EA 164 and the god Amun' in *AJSL* 51 (1992), 287–91.

P. LACAU, 'L'érection du mât devant Amon-Min' in *Chr.d'Ég.* 28 (1953), 13–22.

H. H. NELSON, 'The Identity of Amon-Re of United-with-Eternity' in *JNES* 1 (1942), 127.

A. PIANKOFF, 'A Pantheistic Representation of Amon' in *Ancient Egypt* (1935), I, 49–51.

J. E. TOWERS, 'A Syrian god and Amen-Ra?' in *Ancient Egypt* (1931), III, 75–76.

G. A. WAINWRIGHT, 'Some aspects of Amun' in *JEA* 20 (1934), 139–53.

G. A. WAINWRIGHT, 'The origin of Amun' in *JEA* 49 (1963), 21–3.

D. MONTSERRAT, 'The kline of Anubis' in *JEA* 78 (1992), 301–7.

R. K. RITNER, 'Anubis and the lunar disc' in *JEA* 71 (1985), 149–55.

M. A. MURRAY, 'The god 'Ash' in *Ancient Egypt* 1934, II, 115–17.

E. J. SHERMAN, 'Djedhor the Saviour, statue base 01 10589' in *JEA* 67 (1981), 82–102.

L. B. ELLIS, 'The sistrum of Isis' in *Ancient Egypt* (1927), I, 19–25.

M. GALVIN, 'The hereditary status of the titles of the Hathor' in *JEA* 70 (1984), 42–49.

A. M. MOUSSA, 'A figure of Isis suckling her son Horus' in *ASAÉ* 65 (1983), 127–8.

D. P. SILVERMAN, 'The Priestess of Hathor, '*nh-hwt-Hr*' in *ZÄS* 110 (1983), 80–9.

V. A. TOBIN, 'Isis and Demeter: symbols of divine motherhood' in *JARCE* 28 (1991), 187–200.

B. GRDSELOFF, 'Le dieu *Dw3w*, patron des oculistes' in *ASAÉ* 41 (1942), 207–17.

A. H. GARDINER, 'Horus the Behdetite' in *JEA* 30 (1944), 23–60.

A. H. GARDINER, *Horus, Royal God of Egypt* (Grafton, Mass. 1942).

M. GILULA, 'An Egyptian etymology of the name of Horus?' In *JEA* 68 (1982), 259–65.

E. S. MELTZER, 'Horus *dn* "Cutter", "Severer (of Heads)"?' in *JNES* 3 1 (1972), 338.

P. A. PICCIONE, 'Mehen, mysteries, and resurrection from the coiled serpent' in *JARCE* 27 (1990), 43–52.

L. KAKOSY, 'A Memphite Triad' in *JEA* 66 (1980), 48–53.

L. KAKOSY, 'The Nile, Euthenia, and the Nymphs' in *JEA* 68 (1982), 290–8.

G. A. WAINWRIGHT, 'The Emblem of Min' in *JEA* 17 (1931), 185–95.

G. A. WAINWRIGHT, 'Some Celestial Associations of Min' in *JEA* 21 (1935), 152–70

W. SHORTER, 'The God Nebekau' in *JEA* 21 (1935), 41–8.

D. A. ASTON, 'Two Osiris figures of the Third Intermediate Period' in *JEA* 77 (1991), 95–108.

J. BAINES, 'R. T. Rundle Clark's Papers on the Iconography of Osiris' in *JEA* 58 (1972), 286–95.

A. M. BLACKMAN, 'Osiris and the Sun God? A Reply to Mr. Perry' in *JEA* 11 (1928), 201–9.

A. O. BOLSHAKOV, 'Princess *Hm.t-R'(w)*: the first mention of Osiris?' in *Chr.d'Ég.* 67 (1992), 203–10.

E. A. BUDGE, *Osiris and the Egyptian Resurrection*, 2 vols (London 1911).

D. DELIA, 'The refreshing water of Osiris' in *JARCE* 29 (1992), 181–90.

J. G. FRAZER, *The Golden Bough* part 4, vol. 2 – *Adonis, Attis, Osiris* (London 1914).

A. H. GARDINER, 'Was Osiris an ancient king subsequently deified?' in *JEA* 46 (1960), Brief Comms., p. 104.

J. S. F. GARNOT, 'A Hymn to Osiris in the Pyramid Texts' in *JNES* 8 (1949), 98.

J. G. GRIFFITHS, *The Origins of Osiris* (Münchner ägyptologische Studien, vol. 9) (Berlin 1966).

J. G. GRIFFITHS, 'Osiris and the Moon in Iconography' in *JEA* 62 (1976), 153–9.

G. D. HORNBLOWER, 'Osiris and his Rites' in *Man* 1937, nos 186, 200.

G. D. HORNBLOWER, 'Osiris and the Fertility Rites' in *Man* (1941), no. 71.

M. A. MURRAY, 'The Dying God' in *Ancient Egypt* (1928), 1, 8–11.

W. M. F. PETRIE, 'Osiris in the Tree and Pillar' in *Ancient Egypt* (1928), II, 40–4.

E. OTTO, *Egyptian Art and the Cults of Osiris and Amun* (London 1966).

S. SAUNERON, 'Plutarque: Isis et Osiris' in *BIFAO* 51 (1952), 49–51.

W. SPEIGELBERG, 'The Shepherd's Crook and the So-called "flail" or "Scourge" of Osiris' in *JEA* 15 (1939), 80–3.

A. M. J. TOOLEY, 'Osiris Bricks' in *JEA* 82 (1996), 167–80.

A. S. YAHUDA, 'The Osiris Cult and the Designation of Osiris Idols in the Bible' in *JNES* 3 (1944), 194.

M. WERBROUCK, 'L'Esprit de Pe' in *Chr.d'Ég.* 27 (1952), 43–50.

E. L. ERTMAN, 'The Earliest Known Three-dimensional Representation of the God Ptah' in *JNES* 31 (1972), 83.

S. HOLMBERG, *The God Ptah* (Lund 1946).

G. A. WAINWRIGHT, 'The Ram-headed God of Hermopolis' in *JEA* 19 (1953), 160–1.

G. A. WAINWRIGHT, 'Seshat and the Pharaoh' in *JEA* 26 (1940), 30–40.

G. DARESSY, 'Seth et son animal' in *BIFAO* 13 (1917), 77–92.

G. NAGEL, 'Set dans la barque solaire' in *BIFAO* 28 (1929), 33–9.

P. E. NEWBERRY, 'The Pig and the Cult-animal of Set' in *JEA* 14 (1928), 211–95.

H.TE. VELDE, 'The Egyptian God Seth as a Trickster' in *JARCE* 7 (1968), 37–40.

H. EL-SAADY, 'Reflections on the goddess Tayet' in *JEA* 80 (1994), 213–17.

T. BOYLAN, *Thoth, the Hermes of Egypt* (London 1922).

T. G. H. JAMES, 'A wooden figure of Wadjet with two painted representations of Amasis' in *JEA* 68 (1982), 156–65.

MAGIC, ASTRONOMY AND MEDICINE

A. M. BLACKMAN, 'Some Remarks on an Emblem upon the Head of an Ancient Egyptian Birth-goddess' in *JEA* 3 (1916), 199–206.

A. M. BLACKMAN, 'The Pharaoh's Placenta and the Moon-god Khonsu' in *JEA* 3 (1916), 235–49,

W. R. DAWSON, *Magician and Leech* (London 1929).

E. DRIOTON, 'Religion et magie. L'opinion d'un sorcier égyptien' in *Rev.d'Ég.* 1 (1925), 153–7.

O. EL-AGURY, 'Dwarfs and pygmies in ancient Egypt' in *ASAÉ* 71 (1987), 53–60.

E. DRIOTON, 'Religion et magie: un avertissement aux chercheurs de formules' in *Rev.d'Ég.* 2 (1929), 52–4.

A. H. GARDINER, 'Magic (Egyptian)' in Hastings (Ed.), *Encyclopaedia of Religion and Ethics* (Edinburgh 1925), 8, p. 268, no. 10.

P. GHALIOUNGUI, *Magic and Medical Science in Ancient Egypt* (London 1963).

P. GHALIOUNGUI, 'The liver and bile in ancient Egyptian lore and medicine' in *ASAÉ* 64 (1981), 15–24.

H. GOEDICKE, 'Was Magic used in the Harem Conspiracy against Ramesses III?' in *JEA* 49 (1963), 71–92.

F. LEXA, *La Magie dans l'Égypte antique depuis l'Ancien Empire jusqu'à l'époque copte* (Paris 1975).

A. M. MOUSSA, 'The Tomb of the Physician at Giza' in *ASAÉ* 71 (1987), 195–8.

W. M. F. PETRIE, 'The Royal Magician' in *Ancient Egypt* (1925), III, 65–70.

G. P. G. SOBHY, 'Customs and Superstitions of the Egyptians connected with Pregnancy and Childbirth' in *Ancient Egypt* (1923), I, 9–16.

W. E. CRUM, 'Bricks as Birth-stool' in *JEA* 28 (1942), Brief Comms., p. 69.

W. R. DAWSON, 'The Mouse in Egyptian and Later Medicine' in *JEA* 10 (1974), 83–6.

W. R. DAWSON, 'Studies in the Egyptian Medical Texts, I' in *JEA* I8 (1932), 150–4; II in *JEA* 19 (1933), 133–7 and 20 (1934), 41–6; IV in *JEA* 20 (1934), 185–8; V in *JEA* 21 (1935), 37–40.

R. ENGELBACH, 'Some remarks on Ka-statues of abnormal men in the Old Kingdom' in *ASAÉ* 38 (1938), 285–96.

P. GHALIOUNGUI, 'La notion de maladie dans les texts égyptiens et ses rapports avec la théorie humorale' in *BIFAO* 66 (1968), 37–48.

P. GHALIOUNGUI, 'Les plus anciennes femmes-médecin de l'histoire' in *BIFAO* 75 (1975), 159–64.

P. GHALIOUNGUI, 'The Persistance and Spread of Some Obstetric Concepts held in Ancient Egypt' in *ASAÉ* 62 (1977), 141–54.

W. GOLÉNISCHEFF, 'Racial Types at Abu Simbel' in *Ancient Egypt* (1917), II, 57–61.

CL. GORTEMAN, *Médecins de cour dans l'Égypte du IIIe siècle avant J.C.* Reviewed in *Chr.d'Ég.*, 32 (1957), 313–36.

Z. ISKANDER and J. F. HARRIS, 'A skull with silver bridge to replace in central incisor' in *ASAÉ* 62 (1977), 85–90.

F. JONCKHEERE, 'Coup d'oeil sur la médecine égyptienne. L'intérêt des documents non médicaux' in *Chr.d'Ég.* 20 (1945), 24–32; also, 'Le monde des malades dans les textes non médicaux' in 25 (1950), 213–32; 'Le cadre professional et administratif des médecins égyptiens' in 26, (1951), 237–68; 'Médecins de Cour et médecine palatine sous les Pharaons' in 27 (1952), 51–87; 'Considérations sur l'Auxiliaire médical pharaonique' in 28 (1953), 46–61; 'Prescription médicales sur ostraca hiératiques' in 29 (1954), 46–61.

F. F. LEEK 'The Practice of Dentistry in Ancient Egypt' in *JEA* 53 (1967), 51–8.

F. F. LEEK, 'Teeth and Bread in Ancient Egypt' in *JEA* 58 (1972), 126–32.

J. GRAFTON MILNE, 'The Sanatorium of Der el-Bahri' in *JEA* 1 (1914),96–8.

F. DAUMAS, 'Le sanatorium de Dendera' in *BIFAO* 56 (1957), 35–58.

M. PILLET, 'Les scènes de naissance et de circoncision dans le temple nord-est de Mout, à Karnak' in *ASAÉ* 52 (1952–4), 77.

H. E. SIGERIST, *A History of Medicine*, vol. I, *Primitive and Archaic Medicine* (New York 1951).

E. S. THOMAS, 'Deformation of the Head' in *Ancient Egypt* (1925), I, 3.

J. A.WILSON, 'A Note on the Edwin Smith Surgical Papyrus' in *JNES* (1952), 76.

W. R. DAWSON, 'Some observations of the Egyptian Calendar of Lucky and Unlucky Days' in *JEA* 12 (1926), 260–4.

J. DELPECH-LABORIE, 'Est-il possible de determiner les étoiles des tableaux astronomiques égyptiens?' in *Chr.d'Ég.*, 16 (1941) 251–2.

A. EL-MOHSEN BAKIR, 'The Cairo Calendar of Lucky and Unlucky Days' in *ASAÉ* 48 (1948), 425–33.

E. BARAIZE, 'Rapport sur la mise en place d'un moulage du zodiaque de Dendérah' in *ASAÉ* 20 (1920), 1–2

H. CHATLEY, 'Egyptian Astronomy' in *JEA* 26 (1940), 120–6; 'Egyptian Astronomy: Letters from Dr Eisher and Dr Chatley' in *JEA* 27 (1941) 149–52.

O. NEUGEBAUER, 'The Origin of the Egyptian Calendar' in *JNES* 1 (1942), 396.

O. NEUGEBAUER, 'The History of Ancient Astronomy: Problems and Methods' in *JNES* 4 (1945), 1.

O. NEUGEBAUER, *The Exact Sciences in Antiquity*. Copenhagen 1951.

G. A. WAINWRIGHT, 'Orion and the Great Star' in *JEA* 22 (1936), 45–6.

RELIGIOUS CUSTOMS OF THE POOR, PERSONAL RELIGION, AND THE USE OF ORACLES

A. M. A. AMER, 'Hori: the worried scribe of pharaoh' in *Chr.d'Ég.* 58 (1983), 60–64.

J. BAINES, 'Practical religion and piety' in *JEA* 73 (1987), 79–98.

A. M. BLACKMAN, 'Oracles in Ancient Egypt' in *JEA* 11 (1925), 249–55. Also, *JEA* 12 (1926), 176–85.

J. ČERNY, 'Le culte d'Amenophis Ier chez les ouvriers de la Nécropole thébaine' in *BIFAO* 27 (1927), 159–203.

J. ČERNY, 'L'identité des "serviteurs dans la Place de Verité" et des ouvriers de la Nécropole royal de Thebes' in *Rev.d'Ég.* 2 (1929), 200–9.

J. ČERNY, 'Questions adressées aux oracles' in *BIFAO* 35 (1935), 41–58.

J. ČERNY, 'Troisième série de questions adressées aux oracles' in *BIFAO* 72 (1972), 49–70.

J. ČERNY, 'Egyptian Oracles' in R. A. PARKER, *A Saite Oracle Papyrus from Thebes* (Providence, 1962), Ch. 4.

J. ČERNY, *A Community of Workmen at Thebes in the Ramesside Period* (Cairo, 1973).

P. CHARVAT, 'The Bes Jug. Its origin and development in Egypt' in *ZÄS* 107 (1980), 46–52.

G. DARESSY, 'Note sur des bas-reliefs du temple de Deir el-Médineh' in *BIFAO* 6 (1908), 71–4.

J. DELPECH-LABORIE, 'Le dieu Bès, nain, pygmée ou danseur?' in *Chr.d'Ég.* 16 (1941), 252–4.

F. FRIEDMAN, 'On the meaning of some anthropoid busts from Deir el-Medina' in *JEA* 71 (1985), 82–97.

H. GOEDICKE, 'A Deification of a Private Person in the Old Kingdom' in *JEA* 41 (1955), 31–3.

H. GOEDICKE, 'The Prayers of Wakh-'ankh-Antef-'Aa' in *AJSL* 50 (1991), 235–53.

G. LOUKIANOFF, 'Une statue parlante ou oracle du dieu Re-Harmakhis' in *ASAÉ* 36 (1936), 187–93.

A. PIANKOFF, 'Sur une statuette de Bes' in *BIFAO* 37 (1937–8), 29–33.

A. RADWAN, 'Six Ramesside stelae in the popular pyramidion-form' in *ASAÉ* 71 (1987), 223–28.

J. D. RAY, 'A pious soldier: Stela Aswan 1057' in *JEA* 73 (1987), 169–80.

L. K. SABBAHY, 'Observations on Bes-pots of the Late Period' in *ZÄS* 109 (1982), 147–49.

A. R. SCHULMAN, 'Ex-votos of the Poor' in *JARCE* 6 (1967), 153–6.

A. J. SPALINGER, 'Night into Day' in *ZÄS* 119 (1992), 144–56.

E. SUYS, 'La religion personelle dans l'ancienne Égypte' in *Chr.d'Ég.* 2 (1926– 7), 145.

E. S. THOMAS, 'Oracular Responses' in *Ancient Egypt* (1921), III, 76–8.

D. VALBELLE, 'Témoignages du Nouvel Empire sur les cultes de Satis et d'Anoukis à Eléphantine et a Deir el-Médineh' in *BIFAO* 75 (1975), 123–46.

H. WILLENS, 'The end of Seankhenptah's household (Letter to the Dead, Cairo JdE 25975)' in *AJSL* 50 (1991), 183–91.

VARIOUS RELIGIOUS AND FUNERARY CONCEPTS

R. ANTHES, 'The Original Meaning of *m3'hrw'* in *JNES* 13 (1954), 21.

R. ANTHES, 'Egyptian Theology in the 3rd Millenium B.C.' in *JNES* 18 (1959), 169.

A. BADAWY, 'The spiritualization of Kagemni' in *ZÄS* 108 (1981), 85–93.

J. R. BAINES, 'Restricted knowledge, hierarchy and decorum: modern perceptions and ancient institutions' in *JARCE* 27 (1990), 1–24.

J. R. BAINES, 'Egyptian myth and discourse: myth, gods and the early written and iconographic record' in *AJSL* 50 (1991), 81–105.

A. H. GARDINER, 'Notes on the Ethics of the Egyptians' in *Ancient Egypt* (1914), II, 55–8.

H. GOEDICKE, 'Early References to Fatalistic Concepts in Egypt' in *JNES* 22 (1963), 187.

J. G. GRIFFITHS, 'Remarks on the Mythology of the Eyes of Horus' in *Chr.d'Ég.* 33 (1958), 182–93.

J. G. GRIFFITHS, 'Eight funerary paintings with judgement scenes in the Swansea Wellcome Museum' in *JEA* 68 (1982), 228–52.

G. D. HORNBLOWER, 'A Further Note on the Ka' in *Ancient Egypt* (1929), IV, 104–7.

W M. F. PETRIE, 'Egyptian Beliefs in a Future Life' in *Ancient Egypt* (1914), I, 16–31.

A. ROWE, 'Newly Identified Monuments in the Egyptian Museum showing the Deification of the Dead together with Brief Details of Similar Objects Elsewhere' in *ASAÉ* 40 (1940–1), 1–67.

H. S. SMITH and H. M. STEWART, 'The Gurob Shrine Papyrus' in *JEA* 70 (1984), 54–64.

V. A. TOBIN, 'Mytho-Theology in ancient Egypt' in *JARCE* 25 (1988), 169–84.

E. F. WENTE, 'Mysticism in Pharaonic Egypt' in *AJSL* 41 (1982), 161–79.

J. A. WILSON, 'Funeral Serives of the Egyptian Old Kingdom' in *JNES* 3 (1944), 201

L. V. ŽABKAR, *A Study of the Ba Concept in Ancient Egyptian Texts* (Chicago 1968).

L. V. ŽABKAR, 'Six Hymns to Isis in the sanctuary of her temple at Philae and their theological significance, Part 1' in *JEA* 69 (1983), 115–37, and 'Part 2' in *JEA* 71 (1985), 189–90.

J. ZANDEE, *Death as an Enemy According to Ancient Egyptian Conceptions* (Leiden 1960).

SOCIAL AND EDUCATIONAL ASPECTS

S. ALLAM, 'Quelques aspects du marriage dans l'Egypte ancienne' in *JEA* 67 (1981), 116–35.

S. ALLAM, 'Egyptian law-courts in Pharaonic and Hellenistic times' in *JEA* 77 (1991), 109–28.

M. EL-AMIR, 'Monogamy, Polygamy, Endogamy and Consanguinity in Ancient Egyptian Marriage' in *BIFAO* 62 (1964), 103–8.

J. ASSMANN, 'When justice fails: jurisdiction and imprecation' in *JEA* 78 (1992), 149–62.

E. BROVARSKI, 'Two Old Kingdom writing boards from Giza' in *ASAÉ* 71 (1987), 27–52.

J. ČERNY, 'Consanguineous Marriages in Pharaonic Egypt' in *JEA* 40 (1954), 23–9.

W. F. EDGERTON, 'The Government and the Governed in the Egyptian Empire' in *JNES* 6 (1947), 152.

H. W. FISCHER-ELFERT, 'Two oracle petitions addressed to Horus-Khau with some notes on the oracular amuletic decrees (P.Berlin P.8525 and P. 8526)' in *JEA* 82 (1996), 129–44.

S. R. K. GLANVILLE, 'A New Duplicate of the Hood Papyrus' in *JEA* (1926), 171–5.

H. GOEDICKE, 'The high price of burial' in *JARCE* 25 (1988), 195–200.

L. M. LEAHY and A. LEAHY, 'The geneaology of a priestly family from Heliopolis' in *JEA* 72 (1986), 133–48.

K. RYHOLT, 'A pair of oracle petitions addressed to Horus-of-the-camp' in *JEA* 79 (1993), 189–98.

S. SAUNERON, 'La justice à la porte des temples à propos du nom égyptien des propylées' in *BIFAO* 54 (1954), 117–28.

G. P. E. VAN DEN BOORN, '*Wd'-ryt* and Justice at the Gate' in *AJSL* 44 (1985), 1–25.

H. WILLENS, 'Crime, cult and capital punishment (Mo'alla Inscription 8)' in *JEA* 76 (1990), 27–54.

J. A. WILSON, 'The Oath in Ancient Egypt' in *JEA* 7 (1948), 129.

ASPECTS OF THE AMARNA PERIOD

C. ALDRED, 'The Gayer Anderson Jubilee relief of Amenophis IV' in *JEA* 45 (1959), Brief. Comms., p. 104.

C. ALDRED, 'The Tomb of Akhenaten at Thebes' in *JEA* 47 (1961), 41–59; Appendix by A. T. SANDISON in *JEA* 47, 60–5.

A. BADAWY, 'Maru-Aten: Pleasure Resort or Temple?' in *JEA* 42 (1956), 58–64.

H. K. S. BAKHRY, 'Akhenaten at Heliopolis' in *Chr.d'Ég.* 47 (1972), 55–67.

E. F. CAMPBELL, *The Chronology of the Amarna Letters, with Special Reference to the Hypothetical Co-regency of Amenophis III and Akhenaten* (Baltimore 1964).

R. ENGELBACH, 'The So-called Coffin of Akhenaten' in *ASAÉ* 31 (1931), 98–114.

E. L. ERTMAN, 'The Cap-crown of Nefertiti: its function and probable origin' in *JARCE* 13 (1976), 63–8.

H. W. FAIRMAN, 'A Block of Amenophis IV from Athribis' in *JEA* 46 (1960) 80–2.

H. W. FAIRMAN, 'Once Again the So-called Coffin of Akhenaten' in *JEA* 47 (1961), 25–40.

H. G. FISCHER, 'An Early Example of Atenist Iconoclasm' in *JARCE* 13 (1976), 131–2.

F. FRIEDMAN, '*3ḥ* in the Amarna Period' in *JARCE* 23 (1986), 99–106.

A. H. GARDINER, 'The So-called Tomb of Queen Tiye' in *JEA* 43 (1957), 10–25.

P. GILBERT, 'La Filiation de Toutankhamon' in *Chr.d'Ég.* 37 (1962), 1922.

F. LL. GRIFFITH, 'The Jubilee of Akhenaten' in *JEA* 5 (1918), 61–3.

E. LL. GRIFFITH, 'Akhenaten and the Hittites' in *JEA* 9 (1923), 78–9.

F. LL. GRIFFITH, 'Stela in Honour of Amenophis III and Taya from Tell el-Amarnah' in *JEA* 12 (1926), 1–2.

B. GUNN, 'Notes on the Aten and his Names' in *JEA* 9 (1923), 168–76.

J. R. HARRIS, 'Kiya' in *Chr.dÉg.* 49 (1974), 25–30.

E. HORNUNG, 'The rediscovery of Akhenaten and his place in religion' in *JARCE* 29 (1992), 43–50.

S. IKRAM, 'Domestic shrines and the cult of the Royal Family at El-Amarna' in *JEA* 75 (1989), 89–102.

W. R. JOHNSON, 'Amenhotep III and Amarna: some new considerations' in *JEA* 82 (1996), 65–82.

M. JONES, 'The early Christian sites at Tell el-Amarna and Sheikh Said' in *JEA* 77 (1991), 129–44.

B. J. KEMP, '"The Window of Appearance" at el-Amarna, and the Basic Structure of this City' in *JEA* 62 (1976), 81–99.

B. J. KEMP, 'The Amarna Workmen's Village in retrospect' in *JEA* 73 (1987), 21–50.

K. A. KITCHEN, *Suppiluliuma and the Amarna Pharaohs* (Liverpool 1962).

K. A. KITCHEN, 'Review of "The Chronology of the Amarna Letters"' in *JEA* 53 (1967), 178–82.

A. LUCAS, 'Notes on Some of the Objects from the Tomb of Tutankhamun' in *ASAÉ* 41 (1942), 135–47. Also, *ASAÉ* 45 (1947), 153–4.

P. VAN DE MEER, *The Chronological Determination of the Mesopotamian Letters in the el-Amarna Archives* (Ex Oriente Lux Jaarbericht No. 15, 75 ff.)

W. L. MORAN, 'An Unexplained Passage in an Amarna Letter from Byblos' in *JNES* 8 (1949), 124.

A. PIANKOFF, 'Les grandes compositions religieuses du Nouvel Empire et la réforme d'Amarna' in *BIFAO* 62 (1964), 207–18.

M. PILLET, 'Quelques bas-reliefs inédits d'Amenhotep IV-Akhenaten à Karnak' in *Rev.d'Ég.* 2 (1929), 136–43.

A. PINHAS, 'Some Unrecognised Syrian Amarna Letters' in *JNES* 27 (1968), 163.

ABD er-RAHMAN, 'The Four-feathered Crown of Akhenaten' in *ASAÉ* 56 (1959), 247.

D. B. REDFORD, 'The Sun-disc in Akhenaten's Program: its Worship and Antecedents, I' in *JARCE* 13 (1976), 47–62.

A. ROWE, 'Inscriptions on the Model Coffin Containing the Lock of Hair of Queen Tyi' in *ASAÉ* 40 (1940–1), 623–30.

R. SAAD and L. MANNICHE, 'A Unique Offering List of Amenophis IV recently found at Karnak' in *JEA* 57 (1971), 70–2.

J. SAMSON, 'Royal Inscriptions from Amarna' in *Chr.d'Ég.* 48 (1973), 243–50.

J. SAMSON, 'Amarna Crowns and Wigs' in *JEA* 59 (1973), 47–59.

J. SAMSON, 'Nefertiti's Regality' in *JEA* 63 (1977), 88–97.

A. H. SAYCE, 'The Discovery of the Tel el Amarna Letters' in *AJSL* 33 (1916–17), 89.

A. R. SCHULMAN 'Some Remarks on the Military Background of the Amarna Period' in *JARCE* 3 (1964), 51–70.

I. SHAW, 'Balustrades, stairs and altars in the cult of the Aten at el-Amarna' in *JEA* 80 (1994), 109–28.

H. M. STEWART, 'Some Pre-Amarnah Sun Hymns' in *JEA* 46 (1960), 83–90.

E. THOMAS, 'The Plan of Tomb 55 in the Valley of the Kings' in *JEA* 47 (1961), 24

J. R. TOWERS, 'Was Akhenaten a Monotheist before his Accession?' in *Ancient Egypt* (1931), IV, 97–100.

J. R. TOWERS, 'The Syrian Problem in the el-Amarna Period' in *Ancient Egypt* (1934), I, 49–55.

E. P. UPHILL, 'The Sed-festivals of Akhenaten' in *JNES* 22 (1963), 123.

E. P. UPHILL, 'The Per Aten at Amarna' in *JNES* 29 (1970), 151.

L. V. ŽABKAR, 'The Theocracy of Amarna and the Doctrine of the Ba' in *JNES* 13 (1954), 87.

RELIGION IN THE LATE PERIOD

J. D. COONEY, 'Three Early Saite Tomb Reliefs' in *JNES* 9 (1950), 193.

J. D. COONEY, 'Persian Influence in Late Egyptian Art' in *JARCE* 4 (1965) 39–48.

G. DARESSY, 'L'art tanite' in *ASAÉ* 17 (1917), 164–76.

L. DEPUYDT, 'Murder in Memphis: the story of Cambyses's mortal wounding of the Apis bull (ca.523 BCE)' in *AJSL* 54 (1995), 119–26.

H. G. FISCHER, 'The Cult and Nome of the Goddess Bastet' in *JARCE* 1 (1962), 7–24.

A. H. GARDINER, 'Tanis and Pi-Ra'messe: A Retraction' in *JEA* 19 (1933), 122–8.

H. GAUTHIER, 'Découvertes récentes dans la nécropole saite d'Heliopolis' in *ASAÉ* 33 (1933), 27–53.

L. HABACHI, 'Sais and its Monuments' in *ASAÉ* 43 (1942), 369–416.

J. LECLANT, *Enquêtes sur les sacerdoces et les sanctuaires égyptiens à l'époque dite "ethiopienne" (XXVe dynastie)* (Cairo 1954). Reviewed in *Chr.d'Ég.* 31 (1956), 284–5.

A. LUCAS, 'Resin from a Tomb of the Saite Period' in *ASAÉ* 33 (1933), 187–9.

J. MATHIESON ET AL., 'A Stela of the Persian Period from Saqqara' in *JEA* 81 (1995), 23–42.

A. M. MOUSSA, 'A red granite door-jamb bearing the name of Nectanebo II' in *ASAÉ* 70 (1984–85), 37.

W. K. SIMPSON, 'A relief of a Divine Votaress in Boston' in *Chr.d'Ég.* 57 (1982), 231–35.

E. P. UPHILL, 'The Date of Osorkon II's Sed Festival' in *JNES* 26 (1967), 61.

RELIGION IN THE GRAECO-ROMAN PERIOD

MUSTAFA EL-AMIR, 'The Cult of *Hryw* at Thebes in the Ptolemaic Period' in *JEA* 37 (1951), 81–5.

H. I. BELL, 'Popular Religion in Graeco-Roman Egypt: I. The Pagan Period' in *JEA* 34 (1948), 82–97.

H. I. BELL, *Cults and Creeds in Graeco-Roman Egypt* (Liverpool, 1953).

M. E. BRECCIA, 'Les fouilles dans le Serapeum d'Alexandrie en 1905–6. Ist reports' in *ASAÉ* 8 (1907), 62–76.

C. DERCHAIN, 'La couronne de la justification. Essai d'analyse d'un rite ptolemaique' in *Chr.d'Ég.* 30 (1955), 225–87.

P. M FRASER, *Two Studies on the Cult of Sarapis in the Hellenistic World* (London 1960).

C. GORTEMAN, *Sollicitude et amour pour les animaux dans l'Égypte gréco-romaine.* Reviewed in *Chr.d'Ég.* 32 (1957), 101–20.

G. D. HORNBLOWER, 'Altar and Bell in later Egyptian Rites' in *Ancient Egypt* 1930, II, 40–2.

M. JUNGFLEISCH, 'Une étrange pratique funéraire d'étant de l'époque gréco-romainc en Égypte' in *ASAÉ* 55 (1958), 57.

E. KIESSLING, *La genèse du culte de Sarapis à Alexandrie.* Reviewed in *Chr.d'Ég.* 24 (1949), 317–23.

J. GRAFTON MILNE, 'Alexander and Ammon' in *Ancient Egypt* (1929), III, 74–8.

B. R. REES, 'Popular Religion in Graeco-Roman Egypt: II. The transition to Christianity' in *JEA* 36 (1950), 86–100.

E. A. E. REYMOND, 'Worship of the Ancestor Gods at Edfu' in *Chr.d'Ég.* 38 (1963), 49–70.

E. A. E. REYMOND 'A Late Edfu Theory on the Nature of the God' in *Chr.d'Ég.* 40 (1965), 61–71.

H RIAD, 'Le culte d'Amenemhet III au Fayoum à l'époque ptolemaique' in *ASAÉ* 55 (1958), 203.

S. SAUNERON, 'Les conditions d'accès à la fonction sacerdotale à l'époque gréco-romaine' in *BIFAO* 61 (1962), 55–8.

A. E. SHORTER, 'A Possible Late Representation of the God 'Ash' in *JEA* 11 (1925), 78–9.

J. TONDRIAU, *La Dynastie Ptolemaique et la religion Dionysiaque.* Reviewed in *Chr.d'Ég.* 25 (1950), 283–316.

E. ZAGHLOUL, 'An Agreement for Sale from the reign of Ptolemy I Soter II in the Museum of Mallawi (The Mallawi Papyri of Sharona I)' in *BIFAO* 91 (1991), 255–64.

SYNCRETISM BETWEEN EGYTPIAN AND GRAECO-ROMAN CULTS

T. A. BRADY, *The Reception of the Egyptian Cults by the Greeks* (University of Missouri Studies X, 1935).

P. DERCHAIN, 'Religion égyptienne et sculpture romane?' in *Chr.d'Ég.* 34 (1959), 73–5.

L. B. ELLIS, 'Isis at Cologne and Aix' in *Ancient Egypt* (1926), IV, 97–101.

J. LECLANT, 'Notes sur la propagation des cultes et monuments égyptiens en Occident, à l'époque imperiale' in *BIFAO* 55 (1955), 173–9.

G. MICHAIILIDIS, 'Eléments de synthèse religieuse gréco-égyptienne' in *BIFAO* 66 (1968), 49–88.

J. SCHWARTZ, 'Heméraclès et les syncrétisme religieux en Égypte romaine' in *ASAÉ* 47 (1947), 223–47.

V. VERHOOGEN, 'Le culte d'Isis a Pompeii' in *Chr.d'Ég.* 9 (1934), 39.

R. E. WITT, 'Isis in the Graeco-Roman world' in *Aspects of Greek and Roman Life* (Ed. H. H. Scullard), (London 1971).

The Tomb of Petosiris

E. CAVAIGNAC, 'La date du tombeau de Petosiris: Grèce ou Perse?' in *BIFAO* 30 (1931), 201–27.

F. DAUMAS, 'La scène de la resurrection au tombeau de Petosiris' in *BIFAO* 59 (1960), 63–80.

C. PICARD, 'Les Influences étrangères au tombeau de Petosiris: Grèce ou Perse?' in *BIFAO* 30 (1931), 201–7.

E. SUYS, *Vie de Petosiris* (Brussels, 1927). Reviewed in *Rev. d'Ég.* 2 (1929), 276–7.

ELEMENTS OF EGYPTIAN RELIGION TAKEN INTO (1) CHRISTIANITY, (2) ARABIC AND AFRICAN TRADITION

A. BADAWY, 'Figures de style en égyptien et en arabe' in *BIFAO* 59 (1960), 59.

A. M. BLACKMAN, 'Libations to the Dead in Modern Nubia and Ancient Egypt' in *JEA* 3 (1916), 31–4.

E. L. BUTCHER and W. M. F. PETRIE, 'Early Forms of the Cross from Egyptian Tombs' in *Ancient Egypt* (1916), III, 97–109.

P. CASANOVA, 'De quelques légendes astronomiques arabes considerées dans leurs rapports avec la mythologie égyptienne' in *BIFAO* 2 (1902), 1–39.

R. G. COQUIN, 'La christianisation des temples de Karnak' in *BIFAO* 72 (1972), 169–78.

P. GHALIOUNGUI, 'Ancient Egyptian Remedies and Mediaeval Arabic Writers' in *BIFAO* 68 (1969), 41–6.

G. D. HORNBLOWER, 'Traces of a Ka-belief in Modern Egypt and Old Arabia' in *Ancient Egypt* (1923), III, 67–70.

M. A. MURRAY, 'Nawruz, or the Coptic New Year' in *Ancient Egypt* (1921), III, 79–81.

R. RÉMONDON, 'L'Égypte et la suprême résistance au christianisme (ve–viie siècles)' in *BIFAO* 51 (1952), 63–78.

P. SAINTYRES, *Saint Christophe, successor d'Anubis, d'Hermès et d'Héraclès* (Paris 1936). Reviewed in *Chr.d'Ég.* 14 (1939), 127–30.

G. P. G. SOBHY, 'Remains of Ancient Egyptian Medicine in Modern Domestic Treatment' in *Bulletin de l'Institut d'Egypte* 20 (1937–8), 918.

N. W. THOMAS, 'The Burial Rites of West Africa in Relation to Egypt' in *Ancient Egypt* (1921), I, 7–13.

G. A. WAINWRIGHT, 'Pharaonic Survivals between lake Chad and the West Coast' in *JEA* 35 (1949), 170–5.

J. WALKER, *Folk Medicine in Modern Egypt* (London 1934). Reviewed in *Chr.d'Ég.* 10 (1935), 316.

F. M. WASSEF, 'Influence of paganism on the early Christian works in the Coptic Museum' in *ASAÉ* 67 (1988), 185–8.

Appendix D

A Chronological table of Egyptian history

Period	Date	Dynasty
Predynastic Period	c.5000–3100 BC	
Archaic Period	c.3100–2890 BC	I
	c.2890–2686 BC	II
Old Kingdom	c.2686–2613 BC	III
	c.2613–2494 BC	IV
	c.2494–2345 BC	V
	c.2345–2181 BC	VI
First Intermediate Period	c.2181–2173 BC	VII (Memphite)
	c.2173–2160 BC	VIII (Memphite)
	c.2160–2130 BC	IX (Heracleopolitan)
	c.2130–2040 BC	X (Heracleopolitan)
	c.2133–1991 BC	XI (Theban)
Middle Kingdom	1991–1786 BC	XII
Second Intermediate Period	1786–1633 BC	XIII
	1786–c.1603 BC	XIV (Xois)
	1674–1567 BC	XV (Hyksos)
	c.1684–1567 BC	XVI (Hyksos)
	c.1650–1567 BC	XVII (Theban)
New Kingdom	1567–1320 BC	XVIII
	1320–1200 BC	XIX
	1200–1085 BC	XX
Third Intermediate Period	1085–945 BC	XXI
	945–730 BC	XXII (Bubastis)

Period	Date	Dynasty
	817?–730 BC	XXIII (Tanis)
	720–715 BC	XXIV (Sais)
	715–668 BC	XXV (Ethiopian)
Late Period	664–525 BC	XXVI (Sais)
	525–404 BC	XXVII (Persian)
	404–399 BC	XXVIII (Sais)
	399–380 BC	XXIX (Mendes)
	380–343 BC	XXX (Sebennytos)
	343–332 BC	XXXI (Persian)

Alexander the Great:Conquest	332 BC	
Ptolemaic Period	332 BC – 30 BC	Graeco-Roman Period
Conquest by Romans	30 BC	
Roman Period	30 BC – 4th century AD	

Index

Note
Maps of Egypt on pp. xii and xiii:
sites indicated by number on the
maps on pp. xii and xiii are
keyed into the Index: (A1, A2
etc.) for Map 1 (p. xii) and (B1,
B2 etc.) for Map 2 (p. xiii).

Abu Gurob (A1), 50,70
Abu Roash (A2), 28, 64
Abu Simbel, 144
Abu Sir (A3), 70, 75
'Abydene Symbol', 109
Abydos, 31, 34, 35, 39, 40, 98, 108,
   109, 152;
   Temple of Sethos I, 108, 109
'Admonitions of a Prophet', 91, 92
Adonis, 107
Aegean, 148
Aeizanes, 174
Aesculapius, 139
Afghanistan, 103
Africanus, 6
Afterlife, 37, 51; Osirian, 71, 110,
   111,167;
   solar, 28, 52, 53, 57, 62, 70,71
Aiakos, 173
Akh, 77
Akhenaten (Amenophis IV), 80,
   156–71
Akhenaten Temple Project, 158
Akhetaten (el Amarna, Amarna),
   159, 160–5

Akhmim (A4), 27, 93, 155
Akhtoy, 93
Alexander the Great, 6, 7, 172
Alexandria, 15, 141, 175
Amarna (el Amarna), *see* Akhetaten
Amarna Letters, 169
Amarna, royal tomb, 163
Amaunet, 47
Amelineau, 39
Amenemmes I, 94, 95, 97, 99
Amenemmes II, 99, 100
Amenemmes III, 97, 99, 100
Amenemmes IV, 100
Amenophis I, 125, 143
Amenophis III, 144, 146, 153–7,
   163–6, 171
Amulet, 22, 23, 24, 69, 102
Amun (Amen-Re), 49, 98, 123,
   139, 142–6, 155–6, 158, 159,
   166, 167, 171, 173, 174;
   see also Karnak, Temple of
   Amun
Anat, 145
Andjeti, 109
Animal gods, 6, 24, 26
Ankhesenamun (Ankhesenpaaten),
   163, 169, 170
Ankh symbol, 102
Anthropomorphisation, 6, 26
Anubis, 27, 110, 173
Apis, 27, 173
Arabia, 28, 29
Aramaic, 175

Art, arts, 40, 41, 43, 44, 57, 164,
    165, 174;
    tomb art, 78–87, 93, 94
Artisan, 43, 60, 81–3, 88, 100, 103,
    163
'Ash, 144
Ashmunein (A5), 48, 49
Asia, 29, 103
Askelon, 146
Assiut (A6), 11, 27
Assyrians, 172, 174
Astarte, 145
Astrology, 135
Astronomy, 135
Aswan (B1), 79
Aten, 157–61, 165–8, 170
Atfih (A7), 14
Athribis (A8)
Atum, 28, 45
Avaris, 119
Awru el Nil, 176
Ay, 169, 170

Ba, 79
Ba'al, 145
Ba'alaat, 145
Badari (A9), 11, 19–22, 24,
Barbarism, 32, 33, 35, 59
Beduin, 90, 91
Benben, 46, 47, 50, 58
Beni Hasan (A10), 79
Bennu Bird, 46
Bersha (A11), 93
Bes, 142, 161
Beth shan, 146
Bible, 167, 175
Bigga (B2)
Boat, 25, 108; burial, 28, 51, 62
Book of Amduat, 148, 151
Book of the Dead, 73, 151, 168
Britain, 174
Bubastis, xi
Building Texts, 126, 128

Burial customs, 19–21, 33, 35, 36,
    68, 165
Busiris, 29, 109
Buto, *see* Pe
Byblos, 96, 146

Cairo, 15, 45
Cannibalism, 33
'Cannibalistic Hymn', 70, 71
Canopic chest, 115
Canopic jar, 115
Cenotaph, 39, 40, 60, 63, 98, 100
Ceremony of Opening the Mouth,
    67, 77, 78
Chapel, 25, 74–6, 151
Cheops, 49, 50, 62–4, 74, 88, 99
Chephren, 49, 64, 67, 74
Christianity, 7, 175–7
Cleopatra, 7
Co-regency, 95, 157, 163
Coffin, 21, 35, 36, 38, 60, 73, 128
Coffin Texts, 73
Concubine figures, 22
Corinth, 174
Coronation, 59, 106, 110, 130
Cosmic, 46
Cosmic Egg, 47
Cosmic gods, 26, 27, 45
Cosmogony, 26, 45, 46, 56;
    Heliopolitan, 45;
    Hermopolitan, 47; Memphite,
    47; Theban, 48
Cosmology, 128
Counter-revolution, 128, 169–71
Creation, 45, 175, 176; place of, 46
Crete, 28, 96, 172
Crocdilopolis (A12)
Crown Land, 88
Cult centre, 26, 27, 29, 72, 108
Cult statue, 32, 59, 109, 130–2,
    160, 161
Cult symbol, 32, 47, 59, 109
Dahshur (A13), 61, 74, 99, 100

Daily Temple Ritual, 130–2
Day of Judgment, 110, 168, 175
Decentralisation, 89
Dedun, 144
Deir el Bahri (A14), 98, 141
Deir el Gebrawi (A15), 79
Deir el Medina (A16), 144, 145, 147
Deir el Melek (A17), 79
Democratisation, 93, 105
De Morgan, 100
Denderah (A18), 98, 140
Dep, *see* Pe
Deshasheh, 79
Devil, 139
Diodorus Siculus, 66
Dionysius, 107
'Dispute with his Soul of One who is tired of Life', 92
Divine birth, 18, 41, 49, 87,
Djed pillar, 102, 109
Djedefre', 64, 71
Dynastic Race, 11, 12, 20, 26, 27

Edfu, Temple of Horus, 15, 126
Edjo, 15, 27
Education, 42, 50, 51, 133–7
Egypt Exploration Fund, 98
El Arbeiyin, 176
Elephantine, *see* Aswan
Emery, 34, 39
Enezib, 35
Ennead, 26, 45; Great, 46; Little, 46
Esna (A19)
Ethiopians, 172, 174
Euphrates, 103
Europe, 141

False door, 36, 37, 67, 75
Fayoum, 97, 99, 145
Fertility, 23, 24, 27, 102, 106
Festival, 32, 98, 101, 109, 131, 133,
143, 176; of Khoiakh, 109; of Opet, 124
Fetish, 14, 26, 46
'Fields of Reeds', 111
'First Occasion', 47, 128, 137
'First of the Westerners', 109
'Followers of Horus', 30
'Followers of Thoth', 108
Foreign influences, 12, 26, 143-6
'Four Sons of Horus', 115
Funerary customs, 4, 6, 33, 43, 52, 67, 105, 146, 168

Gaza, 146
Geb, 45
Gebel el Silsileh (A20), 15
Gem Aten, 161
Germania, 174
Gerzean, 10
Gilukhepa, 155
Gizeh, 49, 58, 62, 64, 68, 74, 75, 78, 88, 99, 145
Grave, 19, 33, 34, 36, 38, 176
Grave goods, 21, 22, 25, 35–7, 100, 102
Great Royal Daughter, 18, 155
Great Royal Wife, 18, 154, 155
Greeks, 7, 17, 42, 57, 58, 107, 138, 139, 141, 172–4

Haephaistos, 173
Hammamiya (A21)
Hapy, 4
Harem Conspiracy, 138
Hathor, 98, 103
Hatnub (A22)
Hatshepsut, 98; *see also* Deir el Bahri
Hauhet, 47
Hawara (A23), 97, 100
Hebrew, 175
Heliopolis, 28, 46–8, 50, 58, 71, 72, 89, 98, 109

Hellenistic, 175, 176
Helwan (A24), 28
Heracleopolis, 93, 98
Hermonthis (A25)
Hermopolis, *see* Ashmunein
Herneith, 35
Herodotus, 17, 66, 173, 176
Hetepheres, 62, 63
Hetep Sesostris, 104
Hieraconpolis, *see* Nekhen
Hittites, 170
Hor-aha, 32, 39
Horemheb, 169–71
Horus, 16, 18, 28–30, 47, 73, 102, 106, 132, 139, 144, 173; Sacred Eye of, 102
Household gods, 141–3, 146
House of Eternity, 125
House of the God, 128
House of the Ka, 33, 75
House of Life, 136
Huh, 47
Hurun, 145
Hymn: to Amen-Re', 143, 167; to Aten, 167, 175
Hypostyle Hall, 129, 130

Ibi, 73
Illahun, *see* Lahun
Imhotep, 42, 58, 139, 173
Inundation, 4, 72, 106, 108–10, 176
Ipuwer, 91
Irrigation, 4, 14, 44, 97
Ishtar, 146
Isis, 28, 46, 73, 139, 173–7
Islam, 7, 176, 177
Island of Creation, 56, 126, 128–30
It-towy, 95
Iwnw, *see* Heliopolis

Jewellery, Middle Kingdom, 100–4
Josephus, 6

Jubilee, 50, 59, 98, 101, 110
Judaism, 175, 177
Judge, 28, 73, 106, 110, 138, 173

Ka, 36, 75, 76, 78, 79
Kahun (A27), *see* Hetep Sesostris
Karnak (A28), Temple of Amun, 124, 133, 134, 153, 158, 171
Kauket, 47
Kawab, 64
Kenbet, 138
Kerma (B4)
Khasekhemwy, 31
Khepri, 45
Khonsu, 124, 140
King, kingship, 17, 23, 29–31, 42, 43, 48–50, 60, 72, 73, 88, 92, 106, 108, 124, 128–33, 137, 138, 148, 155, 161, 166, 172
King Lists, 171
Kom Ombo (A29), 141
Koptos (A30), 27, 98
Kuban (B5)
Kuk, 47

Labyrinth, 97
Lahun (Illahun) (A26), 99, 105
Lake Moeris, 97
Lauer, 60
Law, 43, 134, 136–9, 142, 171, 172
Libya, 9, 29, 144, 172
Lisht (A31), 95, 99
Litany of Re', 148
Luxor, 81, 153, 158

Ma'at, 41, 110, 134, 137, 171
Magic, 22, 23, 37, 50, 59, 71, 73, 76, 78, 86, 101, 107, 111, 138, 140, 141
Mahasna (A32), 13, 29
Maketaten, 163
Malkata (A33), 155–7, 166
Manetho, 6, 7, 39, 93

Mariolatry, 175
Mastabat Fara'un, 68
Mazghuna (A34), 100
Medamud (A35), 125
Medicine, 24, 134, 136, 139–41, 173
Medinet Habu (A36), 138, 153
Medinet Maadi, 125
Mediterranean, 8, 87, 155, 173
Medum (A37), 75
Meir (A38), 79
Memphis, 17, 26, 40, 43, 62, 74, 75, 79, 89, 91–3, 98, 140, 145, 173
Menes (Narmer), 7, 15–17, 27, 30, 89
Mentuhotep I, 93–5
Mentuhotep III, 94
Merenre', 73
Meritaten, 163
Meroe, 174
Mesopotamia, 12, 13, 29
Min, 23, 27, 98, 155
Mirgissa (B6)
Mitanni, 146, 155–7
Model, in tomb, 32, 57, 78, 108
Monotheism, 157, 159, 166
Montu, 97, 123
Moon god, 107
Mother goddess, 22–4
Mudnodjme, 157, 171
Mummification, 20, 38, 63, 66, 67, 72, 76, 140, 152, 153, 164, 165, 173, 176
Mummy portrait, 173
Museums: Berlin, 107; Cairo, 60, 100; Manchester, 104, 176; Metropolitan, New York, 100; Petrie, London, 104
Mut, 98, 124
Mutemweya, 155, 166
Mycerinus, 49, 68
Mystery Plays, 108

Myth of Horus and Seth, 28–31
Mythology, 26, 46–8, 126, 128, 132

Naga ed Deir (A40), 79
Nagada (A39), I: 10, 11, 20, 24, 29; II: 11–14, 20–5, 29
Napata, 174
Narmer, *see* Menes
Narmer palette, 16, 32
Natron, 67, 131
Nature gods, 45, 46
Naunet, 47
Near East, 8, 22, 52, 107, 141, 168, 171
Nebka, 71
Neferirkare, 49, 70
Nefertiti, 157–9, 163, 171
Negative Confession, 110
Neith, 28, 32, 144
Nekhbet, 15, 27
Nekhen (Hieraconpolis, el Kab), 15, 16, 31, 83
Neolithic communities, 9, 11, 12 19
Neper, 107
Nephthys, 46
New Testament, 175
Nineveh, 146
Niuserre', 50, 70
Nomarch, 43, 49, 79, 89, 90, 93, 95, 96, 106,
Nomes, 14, 25, 50
Nubia, 8, 44, 53, 87, 95, 96, 102, 144, 145, 161, 174
Nubt, *see* Ombos
Nun, 46–8, 140
Nut, 47, 48

Offerings, 31, 32, 35–7, 66, 76–8, 82, 131–3, 151–2, 161, 176
Ogdoad, 26, 47, 48
Old Testament, 175
Ombos (Nubt), (A41), 11, 29

Oracle, 143, 145, 146
Osireion, 109
Osiris, 4, 28–30, 46, 47, 73, 98, 107–11, 139, 168, 174; cult of, 71–3, 93, 105–11, 132; myth of, 106, 107, 175
Ostraca, 71, 142
Oxyrhynchus (A42)

Palace, 43, 155–9
Palaeolithic period, 19
Palermo Stone, 32
Palestine, 13, 145, 146, 175
Pantheon, 3, 25, 26, 44, 50, 93, 146, 173, 174
Papyri, 52, 138, 141
Pe (Buto, Dep) (A43), 15
Pepy I, 73, 89
Pepy II, 73, 87, 90
Persian Gulf, 11
Persians, 8, 172
Personal piety, 52, 133, 141–3, 161, 167–8
Petrie, 7, 10, 39, 97, 100, 104; *see also* Museums
Philae (B7)
Phoenicia, 96, 145, 146
Pilgrimage, 108, 133, 152
Pi-Ramesses, 145
Plutarch, 107
Priest, 25, 31, 44–50, 53, 64, 68, 73, 78, 88, 104, 108, 109, 123, 124, 129, 130–8, 142, 146, 152–9, 166, 167–71, 174; Ka-priest, 77–80, 88, 89, 139
Primaeval island, 46
Primaeval mound, 46, 47, 56
Primaeval ocean, 46, 140
Ptah, 17, 26, 27, 47, 98, 123, 144, 146, 173
Ptolemy, 172, 173
Punt, 29, 96, 102
Purification, 66, 135

Pylon, 129, 160
Pyramid, 48, 50, 52, 53, 56–68, 70, 71, 87, 88, 95, 125, 148, 174; Bent, 62; Chephren, 64–6, 68; Great, 49, 62–4; Medum, 61; Mentuhotep I, 94, 98, 99; Middle Kingdom, 95, 99, 100; Step, 35, 42, 56–60, 139; Valley Building, 62, 66, 67; workforce, 44, 53, 104, 105
Pyramidion, 58
Pyramid Texts, 19, 33, 46, 57, 58, 70–74, 106–7, 151
Pyramis, 57

Qaa, 31
Qudshu, 145
Queen, role of, 18, 42, 158, 170
Qurneh (A44)

Radiology, 165
Raising the djed-pillar, 109
Ramesses I, 171
Ramesses II, 123, 144
Ramesses III, 138, 143
Ramesses IX, 138
Re', 6, 28, 29, 45–50, 58, 68, 71–3, 98, 132, 144, 166, 167; cult of, 45, 48–51, 58, 63, 72, 73, 89, 106, 109, 132, 157
Re'-Atum, 45, 47, 98
Re'-Harakhte, 45, 46, 144, 167
Red Sea, 11, 13, 102
Resheph, 145
Resurrection, 70, 105–7, 109, 132, 175
Rifeh (A45), 113
Rituals, 29–33, 59, 64, 68, 77, 99, 100, 106–8, 123–6, 130–3, 135, 146, 151–2, 160–1, 175
Romans, 7, 172–4
Royal Ancestors, 131

Sacred Lake, 135
Sacrifice, 24, 33, 34, 59
Sahure, 49, 70
Sais (A46), 68
Sanctuary, 31, 68, 99, 130, 131, 151, 160
Saqqara, 28, 31, 35, 37, 39, 40, 42, 51, 56, 58–60, 68, 73, 74, 82, 98, 139
Sarapis, 173
Sat-Hathor-Iunut, 100, 103
Scarab, 102, 143, 155, 168
Scorpion, 14, 15, 27, 30
Scribe, 103, 136
Sebua (B3)
Sehel (B8)
Sekhmet, 134, 139
Semainian, 10
Semna (B9)
Sequence Dating, 10
Serapeum, 173
Serdab, 60, 75, 76
Serology, 165
Servants of the God, 135
Sesebi (B10)
Seshat, 28
Sesostris I, 95, 98, 99
Sesostris II, 99, 100, 104
Sesostris III, 96, 99, 100, 108, 144
Seth, 28–31, 44, 46, 102, 105, 145
Sethos I, 108, 123
Sham el Nessim, 176
Sheikh Faras, 79
Shepherd Kings, 107
Shepseskaf, 48, 68, 71
Shrine, 31, 141, 146; Hut-, 130
Shu, 46
Sinai, 9, 11, 13, 96, 102, 104
Sitamun, 156, 165
Smenkhkare, 163–5, 168
Sneferu, 62
Sobek, 97
Sobekneferu, 100

Soker, 27
Soleb (B11)
Sphinx, Great, 68
Star cult, 58, 71
State cult, 44, 46
Stela, 37, 39, 40, 108, 141, 146, 159, 171, 173, 174; of Ikhernofret, 107–8
Strikes, 143
Sudan, 9, 174
Syncretism, 25, 173, 174
Syria, 13, 29, 145–8

Tadukhipa, 155
Tammuz, 107
Tanis (A47), 171
Tarkhan (A48)
Tauert, 139, 142
Tefnut, 46
Temple, 31–3, 43, 44, 46, 103, 104, 107–9, 123–36, 139–41, 145, 146, 158, 167–71, 173; Aten, 125, 158–61, 167; consecration of, 132; cultus, 125, 131, 160; estate of, 133–5, foundation ceremony of, 130; mortuary, 32, 36, 59, 68, 88, 98–9, 125–6, 131, 148; singers and musicians, 135; solar, 49, 50, 70, 125, 160–1; wall scenes, 131, 132, 174
Teti, 73, 79
Tey, 157, 170
Thebes, 82, 93–5, 97–9, 142–3, 148, 151–3, 157–63, 168–71, 174
Theocracy, 41, 43
Theology, 29, 45, 73, 176; Heliopolitan, 45, 46; Memphite, 47, 48
Therapeutic Dream, 140
This, 17
Thoth, 27, 47, 110, 139
Thuya, 155

Tit symbol, 102

Tiye, 150, 155–7, 163–6

Tod, 125

Tomb, 21, 28, 33–40, 52–6, 74–9, 98–9, 124–6, 128, 142, 143, 146, 148, 176; archaic royal, 38–40; estate, 77, 87–8; mastaba, 32–8, 48, 53, 56, 58, 60, 63, 68, 71, 74–7, 79, 87–8, 95; menu, 78; of Mereruka, 79; of Petosiris, 174; robberies, 57, 64, 76, 138, 148, 152; rock cut, 79, 93–4, 96, 99; row, 94; of Ti, 79, 82–7; of Tutankhamun, 165, 170; of Two Brothers, 113-17; wall scenes, 79–87, 141, 148, 151, 152, 161

Toshka (B12)

Tribal gods, 14, 25, 27, 44, 124–6, 132

Trinity, 175

Tuna el Gebel (A49), 174

Tura (A50), 62, 68

Turin Papyrus, 30

Tushratta, 146

Tutankhamun (Tutankhaten), 148, 165, 169, 170; *see also* Tombs

Tuthmosis IV, 155, 158, 166

Ugarit, 146

Umm el Ka'ab (A51), 39

Unas, 73

Underworld, 24, 28, 73, 106, 107, 110, 111, 148, 152, 168

Unification, 15–17, 25, 30, 71

Uronarti (B13)

Userkaf, 50, 70

Ushabti, 111, 112

Valley of the Kings (A52), 125, 142, 143, 148, 150, 155, 164, 170

Valley of the Queens (A53), 150, 151

Vegetation gods, 6, 72, 105–7, 109, 176

Viscera, 38, 60, 63, 66, 153

Vizier, 42, 51, 52, 89, 142, 143

Wadi Hammamat, 13

W'bw, 134, 140

Wepwawet, 27

Westcar Papyrus, 49

Western Asia, 8, 28, 96, 121, 153

Wisdom Literature, 50–2, 137, 175; 'Instruction of Duauf', 52; 'Instruction of Kagemni', 51; 'Instruction of Amenemope', 175; 'Instruction of Ptah-hotep', 51

Workforce, 138, 142, 143, 155, 161; *see also* Pyramid

Writing, 12

Yuya, 155

Zer, 35

Zoser, 32, 44, 58–60